Oklahoma's Historical
Centennial Cookbook

Oklahoma's Historical
Centennial Cookbook

Foreword by
First Lady Kim Henry

author
Ronnye Perry Sharp

contributing author
Bob Burke

Tate Publishing & *Enterprises*

Published by Tate Publishing & Enterprises, LLC
127 E. Trade Center Terrace | Mustang, Oklahoma 73064 USA
1.888.361.9473 | www.tatepublishing.com

Tate Publishing is committed to excellence in the publishing industry. The company reflects the philosophy established by the founders, based on Psalm 68:11,
"The Lord gave the word and great was the company of those who published it."

Book design copyright © 2007 by Tate Publishing, LLC. All rights reserved.
Edited by Tracy Terrell
Cover design by Melanie Harr-Hughes
Interior design by Leah LeFlore and Lynly Taylor
Fruit bouquet on back cover by Ken Stafford, Droffat's Catering

Published in the United States of America

ISBN: 978-1-60462-230-0
1. Cooking: Regional: American Mid-West   2.   History: State and Local: Midwest
07.10.01

Acknowledgments

From conception to the completion of this centennial project has been nothing short of amazing, spectacular, and exhilarating. To say the least it has been an incredible journey, encountering many outstanding people along the way. Each of these people I am about to acknowledge made an essential contribution to this book.

First and foremost, the gracious consideration, support, and shared interest from Governor Brad Henry and First Lady Kim Henry, not to mention their inspirational strength. Also a special thank you goes to the enthusiastic support of the Blain family, including Johnnie and Monte Blain. Also the distinguished, multi-talented mind of Judge Robert Henry.

I am most grateful to Linda English, chief of staff to First Lady Kim Henry Kate Thompson, Lori Sutton. Also to the professionalism of Gerald Adams, chief of staff to Governor Brad Henry. The Oklahoma Centennial Committee; Oklahoma Tourism and Recreation Department; Oklahoma Today Editor in Chief, Louisa McCune-Elmore; Former First Lady Cathy Keating. Also the support and help of Jill Simpson, director of Oklahoma Film and Music.

I must acknowledge the incredible technical assistance of Gaye Etheridge, Carla Hill, Sherry Hibben, Jonathan Muller, Cody Flora, Lorrie Spears, Janet Jackson, David Musser, Wendi Wilson, Tammy Pinston, and Ron Henderson.

Special recognition goes to Ken Stafford, DROFFATS Catering, Doug Bowman, Terry West, Clif and Gloria Scott, Susan Stringer, Chuck and Karen Mills, J.R. and Jan Ross, Steve Rice, Diane Sisemore, Jay Rosser, Sally Buford, Gloria Trotter, Jennifer Smith Kiersch. Also to the culinary expertise of Chef Kurt Fleischfresser, owner of Coach House Restaurant, and the unique style of Derek Nettle, executive chef for the Governor's Mansion. Inspirational guidance was extended from Bishop Robert E. Hayes, Jr., Abbot Lawrence, and Pastor Tracy Schumpert.

I would like to express my personal gratitude to Lee Allan Smith and Hal Smith for their invaluable assistance and advice and shared love of

Oklahoma. Without the inspiration and encouragement of my family, Joan and Bill Perry and Bertie Marie Catchings, this book would not have been possible. A special tribute and heartfelt thank you is shared with Linda Praytor, Jennifer Freed, Jane Lodes, Penny Stobaugh Hague, and Linda Haneborg for their never-ending commitment and friendship. Thank you, ladies, for your faith and inspiration. Also my long-time close and personal friend, Congresswoman Mary Fallin.

I am indebted the most to the unique combination and blend of three men. These three men played a significant role in the production of this book becoming a reality. Oklahoma's most valuable historical treasure can be found in Dr. Bob Blackburn. Thank you, Bob, for your compassionate contribution and brilliant mind. I am most appreciative to the extraordinary expertise of photographer Tom Flora. His undeniable vision and creative eye made this book a work of art. Most importantly, I am truly indebted to the profound genius and wisdom of Bob Burke, not to mention his inexhaustible generosity. I am fortunate to have had the influence of his journalistic knowledge and guiding genius. Bob Burke is an example of what is best in this state/profession/industry and coupled with his love and dedication to the state of Oklahoma is an unbeatable combination. What a rare friend and mentor I found in Bob Burke!

In memory of
Lindsey Nicole Henry,
who lost her life to
muscular dystrophy,

Beloved twin daughter of
Governor Brad Henry and
First Lady Kim Henry

Table *of* Contents

Mural created by Chickasaw artist, Mike Larsen.
Can be seen in the Great Rotunda at the State Capitol

Foreword

Oklahomans know good food. For proof, look no further than the delicious recipes that Ronnye Perry Sharp has assembled *for Oklahoma's Historical Centennial Cookbook*. In this fun and entertaining volume, you will find a diverse array of recipes as offered by a number of famous Oklahomans.

But this book is about more than preparing good meals. Food is a reflection of culture, and so *Oklahoma's Historical Centennial Cookbook* is a celebration of the heritage, traditions, and attitudes that help define this amazing state.

In addition, this cookbook is a terrific way to help deserving charities, as a portion of the book's proceeds go toward cancer and muscular dystrophy research.

So enjoy—and *bon appetit!*

Sincerely,

Kim Henry
First Lady of Oklahoma

Preface

Oklahoma taste buds are versatile, ranging from French cuisine with gourmet delights to authentic Native American recipes. Hispanic flair and flavor, Creole to down-home country cooking to the fast food lane at McDonald's. Oklahoma is composed of a unique blend of flavorful recipes and people with ethnic backgrounds that reflect the heritage and diversity of this state. This book will give you the La Crème de la Crème of recipes, allowing you the opportunity to prepare and appreciate some of the finest recipes Oklahoma has to offer—special recipes from Oklahoma's finest restaurants, including celebrities, dignitaries, and everyday special people representing the flair and flavor of Oklahoma.

Throughout this book, my desire and intention was to present a lesson in Oklahoma history—an entertaining look at our heritage. This is not an attempt to recite the entire story of Oklahoma's first century, for that wonderful saga would take volumes. Instead, sprinkled among the recipes are vignettes of Oklahoma people, places, and events that make this state a great place to live, while featuring the impact and significance of 100 years in Oklahoma.

This book discusses the importance of the people, heritage, history, culture, and food and recipes of Oklahoma, thus establishing the influence, lifestyle, and quality of life that has shaped this great state. One important aspect of this book is to define the growth and leadership of Oklahoma through our industry, historical leaders, landmarks, medical leaders, state dignitaries and events, down to basic Oklahoma family roots—the essence and heart of Oklahoma—its people!

You will find this book to be three dimensional, creating the perfect blend of recipes, vignettes of Oklahoma history, and photography—what an unbeatable combination! It has been my privilege and honor to showcase the culinary delights of Oklahoma through the celebration of our centennial, while donating a portion of the proceeds from this book to cancer research and muscular dystrophy research. As the centennial passes quietly into memory, we each have our special reasons to remember the past and anticipate the challenge of the next 100 years in Oklahoma. Let this compilation of Oklahoma history, food, and fun remind you of the great importance and privilege of being an Oklahoman!

Bob Blackburn in lobby of Historical Center

Oklahoma: A Centennial Salute

by Bob L. Blackburn, Ph.D.
Director, Oklahoma Historical Society

Some people say that Oklahoma has an identity crisis. To many non-residents, the mention of Oklahoma reminds them of a great song where the "wind comes sweeping down the plains!" To others, it is the home of Indians and cowboys with an occasional oil well piercing the horizon.

Even inside the state, the image of Oklahoma takes a rough form with too many colors and too many players. To me, there is no mystery in this identity crisis. It is rooted in the history itself.

Oklahoma is like a patchwork crazy quilt, with divergent communities and overlapping themes representing a myriad of colors and patterns. Making the picture even more difficult for easy viewing is the fact that many of the pieces fit at odd angles with jagged edges. From a distance it seems to meander in all directions, but up close and personal, it provides the viewer with rich texture and vibrant visual effects. After more than thirty years studying Oklahoma history, I am still thrilled every time I uncover a new story.

It Began as Indian Territory

In the Choctaw language, Oklahoma means "red people." It is a fitting tribute, for today more than sixty tribes are represented in the population of the state. Their accomplishments, their traditions, and their leadership are important threads in the tapestry of our cultural history.

The first nomadic wanderers may have entered Oklahoma as early as 30,000 B.C. Hunters and gatherers, they lived off the land, gradually developing complex social structures, efficient hunting techniques, and eventually, cultivation of the soil. By 1541, when the first Europeans entered Oklahoma, the Indians of the region had experienced transcontinental trade, highly developed artwork, and organized religion.

From the sixteenth to the nineteenth centuries, the Indians of Oklahoma were swept forward by the winds of change. The horse, acquired from the earliest Spaniards, improved their ability to hunt buffalo. Trade, fueled by the European demand for furs and horses, provided the Indians with metal tools and firearms.

Ironically, the sources of these material advances—Europeans and Americans—destroyed the Indians' isolation. Confronted by an expanding American nation, Oklahoma became an island of Indian survival—one vast reservation known as Indian Territory.

Although bent by the forces of acculturation, the Indians were rooted in the traditions of their forefathers, creating a unique blending of two cultures. Shoulder to shoulder, appeared bark huts and frame houses, moccasins and neckties, gourd ladles and iron kettles.

By the late nineteenth century, when photographers entered the territory, the Indians of Oklahoma offered a unique cultural portrait unmatched anywhere in the world. It was a society rich in variety and contrast, laying the groundwork for the survival of traditional Indian culture in Oklahoma.

Ranch and Range

Cowboys, horses, and longhorn cattle—these are images of the Old West that linger in the hearts and minds of the public. To most people, these images come from movies and dime novels. To Oklahomans, they are part of our heritage, a chapter in the settling of this land we call home.

Even the pre-Columbian Indians of the region had their concept of cattle—the buffalo, or American bison. Roaming in vast herds across the plains and wooded hills of the Southwest, the buffalo was a "commissary on hoof," an undomesticated source of meat, clothing, and tools.

Citizens of the Five Civilized Tribes were among the first pioneers to bring cattle into the Indian Territory. By 1878, more than 55,000 citizens of the Five Tribes owned cattle. One of them, C.W. Turner, an adopted member of the Creek Nation, ran a herd exceeding 5,000 head. Even the Indians of the plains tribes developed herds. Quanah Parker, a Comanche leader, owned 500 head by the 1880s.

The most popular images of cattle in Oklahoma focus on the great cattle drives—rivers of longhorn beef pushed north by range-tough cowboys.

Four primary trails cut across Oklahoma from Texas to the railheads in Kansas: the East Shawnee Trail, the West Shawnee Trail, the Chisholm Trail, and the Western, or Dodge City Trail.

Even before this era ended, ranchers were carving spreads from the ocean of grass and running thousands of head of cattle in the territory. After 1889 and the land openings to non-Indian settlement, the range cattle industry retreated before scientific heard improvement; fenced pasturage; and smaller, mixed operations.

A common element throughout this era of ranch and range was the cowboy, a unique blend of horseman, handyman, and animal doctor. From trail driving and branding mavericks to building fences and baling hay, the cowboy cut a wide swath through Oklahoma's frontier heritage.

The images of the cowboy and his world are enduring, representing a challenging life of tending cattle, raising families, and battling the elements in a promising new land.

"Go Forth and Possess the Promised Land"

On April 22, 1889, 50,000 people gathered along the borders of the Unassigned Lands, anxious to claim a piece of the Promised Land. At high noon the signal sounded and the race began—on horseback, in buggies, in wagons, and on trains, the wall of land seekers surged forward. By nightfall virtually every part and parcel of the territory was claimed.

This dramatic scene, reproduced in countless books and movies, was only one chapter in the settlement of Oklahoma Territory. Preceding the run was the boomer movement, a ragtag army of land seekers led by David L. Payne and William Couch demanding that the federal government open unassigned Indian lands to settlement. After a series of daring boomer raids and an effective propaganda campaign in newspapers and in Congress, the land was opened.

Following the run of 1889, came a series of land openings, each providing another piece in the jigsaw puzzle that would become Oklahoma Territory. In 1890, the Panhandle, known as No Man's Land, was added to the territory by congressional action. Then in 1891, the Iowa, Sac and Fox, Shawnee, and Pottawatomie lands were opened by run. A year later, the Cheyenne-Arapaho reservation was dissolved and surplus land opened.

Oklahoma was fertile soil for professional entertainment, a quality proven by the flamboyance of the Wild West shows. Organized by frontier promoters and pioneers, such as the Miller Brothers and Gordon "Pawnee Bill" Lillie, these shows combined images of the Wild West with circus performances to create a unique form of entertainment.

That spirit of artistic expression can still be found in community theaters, school bands, and dance classes. It is a tradition of excellence, of personal expression and aesthetic appreciation that reflects the world around us. The images of that heritage, from class plays to symphony orchestras, can tell us much about ourselves.

The Image of Oklahoma

Today, we look back on this history from the perspective of the twenty-first century. We can see great cities that are still growing, rich fields that are feeding the world, and an oil and gas industry that is still creating jobs and turning the wheels of commerce. Most importantly, from our centennial hill, we can see the people who have come to Oklahoma for a better future. Together, their stories are the story of Oklahoma. And what a great history we share.

The Official Oklahoma Today
Centennial Menu

Grilled Catfish
and a Sweet Potato "Tamale"
With Chili-Peanut Sauce

Watermelon Gazpacho

Three Sisters Salad
Beans, Grilled Squash, and Corn on Mixed Greens
With White Balsamic Vinaigrette

Mixed Grill
of Buffalo, Beef, and Pork
Smoky Mustard Greens and Roasted Garlic Whipped Potatoes

Stratford Peach Strudel
Blackberry Sauce and
Southern Comfort Whipped Cream

Menu and recipes by Kurt Fleischfresser
Photography by John Jernigan

GRILLED CATFISH AND A SWEET POTATO "TAMALE" WITH CHILI-PEANUT SAUCE

Grilled Catfish with a Sweet Potato "Tamale" makes a zesty appetizer for the taste buds. The tamale, says Fleischfresser, is a salute to Oklahoma's important Hispanic population. When you taste the tamale, it looks the same, but without the masa, it is much lighter an the flavors much brighter, he says. The sauce also has a lot going on.

(Catfish and Tilapia are the only two local fresh fish. The tamale is a nod to our Hispanic populations, and sweet potatoes and peanuts are good Oklahoma-agricultural products.)

Sweet Potato "Tamale"
2 c. roasted sweet potato*
¾ c. dry breadcrumbs (like Japanese Panko)
½ tsp. cumin
½ tsp. ground black pepper
½ tsp. soy sauce
1 Tbsp. Balsamic vinegar
¼ tsp. cayenne pepper
1 tsp. kosher or sea salt*
6 oz. grated Oklahoma cheddar (Christian Farms or Watonga)
8 dried corn husks, soaked in warm water

Mix the first eight ingredients together with a fork, until thoroughly mixed but not pureed. Fold the grated cheese into the sweet potato mixture; it is not necessary to be gentle, just mix enough to incorporate the cheese. Oil a muffin tin or any heatproof cylindrical containers that will hold about 4 ounces. Lay in a corn husk so that it goes down one side and up the other, with the pointed side sticking up out of the mold. Scoop approximately 4 ounces into each mold; this should compress the corn husks against the inside of the molds. Bake at 350 for about 12 minutes, or until completely heated through.

*To make 2 cups of roasted sweet potato, place 2 washed sweet potatoes about a half pound or more each. Bake them in a 400 degree oven until soft all the way through. The higher temperature creates some caramelization under the skin for added flavor. If you're not adventurous or short on time, pure canned pumpkin can be substituted (don't tell anyone it was my idea).

*In our kitchen we only use kosher salt or sea salt. They are both coarse and act like a time-released seasoning, as opposed to super fine table salt. Also, kosher salt does not have iodine. Iodine has a bitter taste, and we really don't need the supplement.

GRILLED CATFISH

Award-winning reknown Chef Kurt Fleischfresser, owner of The Coach House Restaurant

1 4–6-oz. catfish filet*
¼ c. chopped parsley
2 Tbsp. olive oil
salt and pepper

Preheat the grill or skillet, if not grilling. Pat the filets down with paper towels to remove excess moisture. Put the parsley, salt, and pepper on the catfish then drizzle the oil over the filets. Making sure your grill is hot, place the filet on the grill with the smooth side of the filet up (this is the side where the skin was). After about 3 minutes, flip the filets. After about 3 more minutes, flip the filets again in such a way that there will be marking across the previous grill marks. Flip the fish one last time and cook until the fish is slightly opaque in the center. The filet should have great cross hatch grill marks on top with the parsley cooked and intensely green. Let the fish rest for just a couple of minutes before serving.

Tip:

The strong muddy taste that catfish can sometimes have is mainly in the fat. Taking the extra layer of fat off under the skin will make the fish taste cleaner and fresher.

CHILI-PEANUT SAUCE

¼ c. peanut oil
1 Ancho chile*
1 yellow onion, finely diced (about 2 cups)
3 cloves garlic, finely chopped
¼ c. chopped peanuts
1 tsp. chili powder
¼ tsp. cayenne pepper
1 Tbsp. brown sugar
1 tsp. kosher salt
1 tsp. smoked paprika
2 Tbsp. peanut butter
2 Tbsp. tomato puree
3 c. chicken stock (can use canned)
4 leaves fresh basil, chopped (You can also use cilantro or Italian parsley.)
1 fresh lime, juiced

Heat the oil in a one-gallon pot. When the oil is hot, add the chile, garlic, onion, and the dried spices and stir with a wooden spoon until the onions are cooked and aromatic. Then add the peanut butter and puree, sauté, and stir for about 3 minutes. Then add the rest of the ingredients and reduce by half. This sauce can be made in advance and reheated before use.

Tip:

Ancho chile is a smoked pablano. Anchos are usually not hot but more rich-flavored, like tobacco and coffee. Lightly toasting the chile over an open flame refreshes it and makes it supple and easier to cut with fuller flavor.

Watermelon Gazpacho

(I think for two weeks a year Oklahoma is the biggest supplier of watermelons in the country. And with our hot weather this makes good sense most of the year.)

1 red onion, finely diced
¼ c. raspberry vinegar
¼ c. extra virgin olive oil
¼ tsp. ground black pepper
1 tsp. kosher salt
1 tsp. finely chopped garlic
4 c. watermelon, seeded and diced
4 c. watermelon juice (watermelon pulp pushed through food mill)
1 c. peeled, seeded, and diced cucumber
1 Tbsp. fresh basil puree (pesto will work)
¾ c. dry breadcrumbs (like Japanese Panko)

Don't confuse the Watermelon Gazpacho with dessert. It's more savory than sweet because it has garlic and onions, but also has sweet components. The abundance of intense temperatures and watermelons in Oklahoma summer months make this a cool alternative to a hot soup.

Combine the first six ingredients, then prepare the watermelon. The vinegar will break down the onion and the garlic and make it more savory. Add all of the ingredients together and chill for at least 2 hours or up to 2 days. Serve in a frozen bowl with a dollop of sour cream.

Three Sisters Salad

Beans, Grilled Squash, and Corn on Mixed Greens with White Basalmic Vinaigrette (The American Indian staple crops mixed into a salad and jazzed up a bit)

1 c. white balsamic vinaigrette
1 zucchini (preferably no bigger around than ½ inch)
1 tsp. finely chopped parsley

Crisp zucchini, white beans, and roasted corn represent the three primary Native American crops in Three Sisters Salad. Paired with tangy balsamic vinaigrette, this dish proves that healthy doesn't have to be boring. Fleischfresser recommends avoiding wine with this dish. When there's a lot of acidity in the food, you don't really want to go with wine. They don't complement each other, he says.

1 c. white beans, cooked

1 c. corn (preferably grilled or roasted on the cob and then cut off)

6 c. lettuce (use your favorite cut into very thin strips)

1 red bell pepper, seeded and cut into very thin strips

kosher salt and fresh ground pepper

Wash the zucchini and cut into four strips from end to end. Brush the strips generously with some of the dressing, salt, and pepper and sprinkle with parsley and place in a bowl or Ziplock bag to marinate for at least an hour. After the zucchini has marinated, grill over a medium flame until just cooked through, about 6 minutes. Let the zucchini cool and then dice it approximately the same size as the corn and beans. Toss the lettuce with the dressing and place in the middle of eight plates. On top of each lettuce pile, sprinkle equal amounts of the corn, beans, and diced zucchini. Finish the salads with red pepper strips on top and fresh ground pepper.

CORN BREAD

1 c. flour

1 c. cornmeal

¼ c. sugar

1 ½ tsp. baking powder

1 ½ tsp. kosher salt

2 Tbsp. butter

1 egg

1 c. milk

Preheat a 10-inch iron skillet in the oven. Combine first five ingredients. Cut in butter. Cut in eggs. Incorporate milk. Put a generous coating of peanut oil in the skillet and pour in the corn bread batter. Bake at 425 until golden brown.

Corn Bread Croutons:

Using about ¼ of this corn bread, cut into bite-sized pieces and toss with 1 Tbsp. olive oil and parsley. Toast on sheet pan for 10–15 minutes at 350.

Mixed Grill of Buffalo, Beef, and Pork
Smoky Mustard Greens and Roasted Garlic Whipped Potatoes

(From the past to the present we are a meat-eating bunch of people and this covers a lot of Oklahomans' center of the plate.)

1 lb. ground buffalo (bison)
1 Tbsp. chopped fresh basil
½ tsp. crushed red pepper flakes
8 sprigs rosemary (optional)
1 lb. pork tenderloin
8 strips hickory bacon
2 10 oz N.Y. strip steaks
salt and fresh ground pepper
1 lb. large baker style potatoes
4 oz. unsalted butter
2 heads garlic
2 lbs. mustard greens, thoroughly washed (or other fresh greens of spinach)
1 c. smoked onion*
2 oz. unsalted butter

Start by cutting off the pointed end of the garlic heads, exposing the tips of all of the cloves. Soak the garlic in water for at least 10 minutes, then wrap in foil and bake at 350

The cornerstone of any Oklahoma feast gets triple play in the Oklahoma Mixed Grill, a plentiful plate that features pork tenderloin, New York strip steak, and buffalo. The latter may seem a little exotic for some tastes, but Fleischfresser compares the flavor to beef, saying, "Buffalo is gamier than beef. It's also darker and leaner. Paired with greens and fluffy potatoes, this combination is a hearty protein fix for an empty belly."

To smoke onions for seasoning, simply slice it very thin and toss with salt, pepper, and olive oil. Then place in a smoker or smoke over an iron skillet with hickory chips until cooked. They make a good vegetarian or low-fat substitution for bacon.

until the cloves are tender. Peel and the potatoes and cook them in boiling, salted water. When the potatoes are tender, drain them in a colander for at least 5 minutes then place in a bowl. Squeeze the cooked garlic out of the head into the potatoes. Add the butter and mash with a potato masher until it reaches a fairly smooth consistency, taste and adjust the salt pepper. Put the ground buffalo in a bowl and add the pepper flakes and basil. Mix these ingredients together but don't overmix (it will make it tough). Divide into 8 equal portions and roll into football shapes. Set these aside until ready to grill. Take the strips of bacon and lay them on a cookie sheet and put in a 350 degree oven until the bacon is hot but not crisp. This will blanch the bacon and make it crisper when the tenderloin is grilled. Chill the bacon. Cut the pork tenderloin into approximately 2 oz. pieces. Wrap each piece of tenderloin with a slice of the blanched bacon and hold in place with a tooth-pick. Set these aside until ready to grill. Preheat the grill to a medium high heat. Brush the grill well with a wire brush.

Season the strip steaks, pork tenderloin, and the ground buffalo footballs with salt and pepper and grill to desired temperature. Then let rest for a few minutes. To cook the greens, put the butter and the smoked onions in a large pot and cook over a medium flame until the butter begins to foam. Place all of the greens and cook until tender, stirring occasionally. On 8 plates, divide the potatoes and greens on each. Slice a steak into 4 slices and put a slice on each plate. Stick a rosemary skewer in the end of each buffalo football and put one on each plate. Remove the toothpick from each of the pork tenderloin pieces and put one on each plate. Serve immediately.

STRATFORD PEACH STRUDEL
Blackberry Sauce and Southern Comfort Whipped Cream

(Two of Oklahoma's best fruits put together in a classy dish)

6 peaches
1 c. dry breadcrumbs (like Panko)
½ c. brown sugar
¼ tsp. ground cinnamon
½ c. unsalted butter
6 sheets phylo dough
½ c. dry breadcrumbs (like Panko)
¼ c. brown sugar
½ c. unsalted butter, melted

This dessert is made in two parts. First, mix the first batch of bread crumbs, brown sugar, and cinnamon together and spread out on a 9x9 baking dish. Cut the peaches in half and remove the pits. Place the peaches, cut side down, on the breadcrumb mix as evenly spread out as possible. Put a little dollop of butter on each peach. Place this pan in a preheated 400 degree oven and bake for approximately 10 minutes, or until the skin can be easily pulled off each peach half. The breadcrumbs under the peaches will absorb all of the juices and melted butter. Pull the skins off the peaches and discard; cut the peaches into ½-inch cubes. Place the diced peaches and the baked breadcrumbs into a mixing bowl and mix together. Chill the breadcrumb and peach mixture. For part two, make 2 strudels by laying out a single sheet of phylo and brushing it with the melted butter and sprinkling some of the breadcrumbs and brown sugar over the top. Lay another sheet of phylo on top of that sheet and butter and sprinkle on it. Repeat with one more sheet of phylo. Using half of the peach mixture, put about 2 inches deep with the narrow edge of the phylo closest to you and from one edge to the other, like rolling

No meal is complete without a sugary finishing touch. Stratford Peach Strudel unites golden peaches with deep, dark blackberry sauce and Southern Comfort-infused whipped cream to create a holy trinity of flavor and texture. Fleischfresser likes to use Oklahoma Stratford peaches when they're in season, but during the off months, he heads to nearby Cresent Market for his produce needs.

a jello roll. Putting a uniform amount of pressure, roll the filling in the phylo until the strudel is complete. Repeat again with the rest of the ingredients. Refrigerate the strudels until about half an hour before serving. Before serving, bake at 400 until golden brown. Let the strudel cool for a couple of minutes, then cut with a serrated knife and serve.

Blackberry Sauce

2 c. blackberries, fresh or frozen
½ c. sugar

Place in a non-reactive pot and slowly bring to simmer. Simmer for 5 minutes, then push through a strainer. Serve immediately or chill and serve when needed.

Southern Comfort Whipped Cream:
2 c. heavy whipping cream
½ c. sugar
2 oz. Southern Comfort (or another sweet liquor)

Combine ingredients and whisk by hand or with a mixer until light and fluffy. Whipping at a medium speed for a longer time makes a more stable whipped cream than whipping it at high speed.

Trail of Tears, Cowboy Hall of Fame Museum

Native American Heritage and Culture

History of the Chickasaw Nation

Chickasaw Nation Governor Bill Anaotubby

Known as the "Unconquered and Unconquerable," Chickasaws are a proud people with a rich heritage. The Chickasaw Nation has been a sovereign nation since long before Europeans set foot on North America.

The history of the Chickasaw Nation in its present location began in 1855, when the tribe separated from the Choctaw Nation and re-formed its own government.

Before that time and until their forced removal in the late 1830s, the Chickasaw Nation occupied original homelands in what are now the states of Mississippi, Kentucky, Tennessee, and Alabama.

Living in sophisticated town sites, the Chickasaws developed a highly refined ruling system, complete with an effective legal system, time-honored traditions, and respected religious leaders.

Chickasaws have been entrepreneurs for centuries. They conducted a successful trade business with other tribes over much of what is now the southern and central United States, prior to contact with Europeans.

The earliest recorded history of the Chickasaw Nation began in 1540, when Hernando De Soto encountered the tribe in his travels throughout the southeastern portion of the continent. De Soto's historians referred to the land as the *Province of Chicaza*.

Chickasaw warriors routed De Soto's forces in that winter when he demanded slaves from among the tribe to carry his provisions throughout the remainder of his exploratory travels. Destroying most of his provisions, armor, and weapons and taking his horses and swine, De Soto's men (significantly reduced in number after the Chickasaw attack) were forced to flee with much less than with what they had entered the Chickasaw Nation.

In later history, the Chickasaw's befriended the English, becoming strong allies with them in the battles against the French and Spanish. The great friendliness with the English came about mainly because of the manner in which the English treated the Chickasaws: as equals. In trade with the Chickasaws, the English were not only fair, but they provided quality goods and stood by their word, unlike many other Europeans with whom the Chickasaws had come into contact.

The French, who had territories in the north in Canada as well as in the south at New Orleans, wanted to link both those territories by conquering the Mississippi River, thus dividing the English in two and occupying what were, at the time, considered the far western lands.

The Chickasaws, who controlled trade up and down the Mississippi for hundreds of miles, were a major obstacle to the French goal. Some historians give credit to the Chickasaws for the United States being an English-speaking rather than a French-speaking nation today. With their rigid control over all travel and trade of the lower portion of the Mississippi River, the Chickasaws prevented the French in the north from uniting with the French forces in Louisiana.

In the American Revolutionary War the Chickasaws were divided about which side to support. Some sided with the British, some with the French or Spanish, while others remained uncommitted. Many of the Chickasaw sided with the Americans against the British. They provided warriors and performed services to General Washington's Continental Army in several different battles. One Chickasaw, Miko Piomingo, was a friend of George Washington. When General Washington sent a message to Piomingo asking for his help, Piomingo led a group of twelve Chickasaw warriors, who walked more than 1,000 miles to Washington's encampment at Valley Forge. Those Chickasaw warriors attacked and routed the entire Seneca Nation in New York, because the Senecas, allied with the English, were attacking General Washington's forces in their winter camp at Valley Forge. Washington gave Piomingo an ample supply of muskets, powder, and lead balls, as well as clothing, cooking utensils, and other goods.

In the late 1830s, under President Andrew Jackson, the Chickasaw Nation was moved to its present location, but the Chickasaw were forced to move to a small portion of the Choctaw nation, called the "Chickasaw District." This was a shrewd move on the part of the Choctaws, because the Chickasaws would serve as a buffer between the Choctaws and some of Western tribes, which continually raided Choctaw farms and communities.

The Chickasaws were required to be under Choctaw rule, but were given a one-fourth vote in the Choctaw legislature. The Chickasaw people were dissatisfied with being merely a part of the Choctaw Nation; they were accustomed to operating their own system of government and, being extremely independent people, they sought an end to their arrangement with the Choctaws. By treaty with the Choctaws and the United States, the Chickasaws, in 1855, severed their relations with the Choctaw Nation and formed their own democratic republic. The boundaries of the Chickasaw Nation were established by that treaty, and continue to be recognized by the United States as the jurisdictional area of the Chickasaw Nation. The Chickasaw Nation was officially reestablished as a tribal government on March 4, 1856.

On August 30, 1856, the Chickasaw people ratified their original constitution, which established a three-branch form of government modeled on that of the United States.

Education has always been a high priority for Chickasaws. Even before the Constitution was ratified, several Chickasaw schools had been established.

The Chickasaw selected Tishomingo, named after the last great war chief who died on the Trail of Tears while leading a group of Chickasaws to the Netherlands, as the new capital city. The first council house built for the tribal government still exists and is on display at the Chickasaw nation's museum in Tishomingo. The last Chickasaw capitol building, built in Tishomingo in 1898, still stands and has been totally restored by the tribe.

Education has always been a high priority for Chickasaws. Even before the Constitution was ratified, several Chickasaw schools had been established.

Chickasaw manual labor academy was completed in 1851. By 1857, it provided an education to 140 students annually. Curriculum at the school included reading, writing, arithmetic, English, Latin, logic, biology, geometry, music, and sacred studies. Agricultural, mechanical domestic arts were also included in the curriculum. Other schools built in that era include Bloomfield Academy and Colbert Institute, which were completed in 1854. In 1857, the Chickasaw legislative body voted to erect Burney Academy near Lebanon.

One of the first steps taken by the Chickasaw government following the Civil War was to reopen the schools. Eleven neighborhood elementary schools were opened in 1867.

That number was increased to twenty-three in 1876. In the same year, the legislature also provided for the reopening of four seminaries and academies providing secondary education. Most of the teachers in those schools were Chickasaw. Douglas Johnston was appointed Chickasaw governor by President Theodore Roosevelt in 1906, just prior to statehood. Johnston served in that position until his death in 1939.

One of Johnston's proposed duties as governor was to oversee the dissolution of the Chickasaw government. However, he never accomplished that task.

Efforts by the federal government to terminate the Chickasaw Nation by way of the Dawes Act and other legislation in the 1890s and early 1900s failed, as did later efforts in the 1950s.

When Oklahoma was admitted as the forty-sixth state of the union in 1907, the Chickasaw Nation's tribal government ceased to operate because it was believed that congress had terminated the tribe (all of the Five Civilized Tribes were believed to have been terminated under federal legislation). From that time until 1971, the tribe was not allowed to elect its own leaders; instead, the president of the United States appointed a Chickasaw to serve as the tribe's governor.

In 1969, the federal government recognized that the tribal governments of the Five Civilized Tribes had not been terminated. In 1971, the Chickasaw people conducted their first election since statehood. That marked the beginning of the tribe's revitalization era.

Overton James was appointed governor of the Chickasaw Nation in 1963, and later elected to the post in 1971.

Bill Anoatubby was elected lt. governor in 1979, and served in that capacity until 1987, when he was elected to his first term as governor.

In 2003, Governor Anoatubby was elected to his fifth consecutive term as governor, with almost 80% of the vote.

A majority of the current legislators have also been elected to three or more consecutive terms of office.

In 1983, the people ratified a new constitution, establishing a new tribal government with three branches, just like the federal government. The tribe has functioned under that constitution since that time.

The Chickasaw Nation has its modern headquarters in Ada. Because of the Chickasaw Nation's commitment to self-governance, the tribe is involved in economic development through the operation of tribally-owned businesses. Those businesses include three radio stations, one community newspaper, a gourmet chocolate manufacturer (Bedré Chocolates), numerous gaming centers/casinos, smoke shops, motels and hotels, travel plazas, restaurants, a bank located in Oklahoma City, and an electric utility company. CNI contracts with the United States government to provide medical personnel and management of construction projects at military bases and other installations.

Recognizing the importance of being a good neighbor, the Chickasaw nation works closely with the city, county, and state levels of government, as well as with private enterprise. Working jointly, the tribe has provided funding to build new roads, repair and replace bridges, and help small communities with the development of their infrastructure on construction of water treatment plants, sewer lines, and other projects.

The tribe employs more than 10,400 persons in various services and industries, making it one of the largest employers in Oklahoma.

Healthy Lifestyles

Providing high quality health care for Chickasaw citizens and other Native Americans has always been a high priority. The tribe was the first in history to successfully negotiate a compact to manage a health care system.

The Chickasaw Nation assumed administrative and operational authority of the Chickasaw Nation Health System (CNHS) in October of 1994. CNHS operates the Carl Albert Indian Health Facility in Ada, as well as satellite clinics in Ardmore, Tishomingo, Purcell, and Durant as part of a plan to provide health care within thirty miles of anyone within the traditional boundaries of the Chickasaw Nation.

In April 2004, CNHS cut the ribbon on the 8,500 square foot Diabetes Care Center, which offers a full range of services, from vision care to nutrition and exercise consultation.

The Chickasaw Nation was the first tribe in Oklahoma to offer digital diagnosis of diabetic retinopathy.

This pioneering system transmits digital images over the Internet for evaluation by highly trained technicians, enabling doctors to more effectively diagnose and treat the number one cause of blindness in working-aged Americans.

In addition to the health care and educational services available at the clinic, the Chickasaw Nation offers numerous opportunities to help prevent or control diabetes.

The Chickasaw Nation operates wellness centers, health clinics, educational camps, and nutrition centers, as well as hosts healthy cooking classes.

These wellness centers are open to the public and help enhance citizens' physical health by providing state-of-the-art exercise equipment, wellness classes, walking tracks, pools, gymnasiums, cooking classes, and nutrition education.

Bedré Chocolates

Bedré Chocolates produces only the finest quality European-style gourmet chocolate in its state-of-the-art production facility near Pauls Valley.

One taste is all it takes to understand why the Norwegian word for better, Bedré, was chosen as the name. Melts in your mouth is more than just a phrase at Bedré. Their chocolate is made using higher cocoa butter content and absolutely no paraffin, which means that body heat alone transforms solid Bedré chocolate into a smooth and silky liquid taste sensation.

Since opening its Pauls Valley factory in July 2003, Bedré Chocolates has more than tripled annual sales and made changes in operations that will allow it to continue expansion far into the future.

Bedré officials made the decision to move from hand-made candies to a more automated system of production. They now utilize custom-made equipment from a variety of European manufacturers to effectively and efficiently produce the highest quality chocolates. State-of-the-art equipment not only increases production, it provides a more precisely controlled ingredient mix, producing a superior and more consistent product. Production capabilities for some products have increased from several hundred per day to thousands per hour.

Increased capacity was followed closely by increased marketing efforts. Sales to established customers, such as Neiman-Marcus, have increased and relationships with a number of new customers have been established.

In the short time the Pauls valley factory has been in operation, it has become a favorite tour destination for school and church groups who join other visitors watching highly trained professionals crafting a variety of world-class chocolate candies.

Bedré utilizes custom-made equipment from a variety of European manufacturers to produce the milk, dark, and white chocolate used to coat potato chips, nuts, cookies, and other delicious centers. That same high quality chocolate is used to form coins, cowboy boots, candy bars, and more.

WILD PLUM JELLY

7 ½ c. sugar

1 box fruit pectin

4 c. wild plum juice

1 ½ c. water

Chickasaw Women

Measure sugar and set aside. Do not reduce amount of sugar. Stir fruit pectin into juice and water, using a large pot, as the pot must not be more than a third full to allow for a full rolling boil (a boil that cannot be stirred down). Bring to a full boil over high heat, stirring constantly. At once, stir in sugar. Stir and bring to a full rolling boil, boil hard for 1 minute, stirring constantly with a wooden spoon. Remove from heat. Skim off foam with metal spoon. Immediately ladle into hot pint jars, leaving a ⅛-inch space at the top of the jars. Wipe any spills from rims and threads of jars with a damp cloth. Quickly seal the jars by covering with hot lids. Screw bands on firmly. Let jelly stand to cool. Check seals, store in cool, dry place.

BUFFALO POT ROAST

12 apricots

7 apples, ringed

4-5 lbs. buffalo roast

1 ½ c. apple cider or apple juice

1 white onion, diced

1 dash sugar

½ pinch cinnamon

¼ pinch ground ginger and cloves

1 pinch salt and black pepper

Sear roast on all sides in a small amount of oil. Put roast in a cooking pot; add apple cider, salt, pepper, onion, sugar, cinnamon, ginger, and clove. Cover and cook for 2-3 hours until meat is tender. Place fruit on top of meat and simmer for 30-40 minutes more. Make gravy in pan by using a roux of flour and butter or use cornstarch. Serve hot with fruit. Makes 6 servings.

Chickasaw Bead Workers

PASHOFA

10 lbs. dry, cracked corn
6 2-lb. pkg. of pork steak, cut into bite-sized pieces
10 gal. water (and more)
Pashofa pot and a boat oar or other large stirring device
Pashofa pot cradle

Oklahoma Historical Society of Pat Woods cooking Pashofa

Photo credit: Research Division of the Oklahoma Historical Society

Note: Traditionally prepared pashofa is normally cooked outside over an open fire. Cooks should take appropriate precautions. Prepare wood for cooking over an open fire. Position the pot cradle directly over the wood. Place the pashofa pot in the cradle. Pour 10 gallons of water into the pot and light the fire. Bring water to a boil. Add 10 lbs. cracked corn to boiling water; stir constantly and bring to a boil. Add pork steak and continue stirring. Add water as needed to keep the corn immersed. Boil for 3½- 4 hours, stirring constantly. Pashofa is done when corn is tender. Season with salt and pepper to taste. Makes 400 servings.

CATFISH

1 mess of catfish
2 eggs
1 c. milk
dash of salt and pepper
cornmeal
4 c. shortening

Catch a mess of catfish. Clean and fillet. In bowl, put 2 eggs and 1 cup of milk, a dash of salt and pepper. Place catfish fillets in the milk mixture. Pour cornmeal into another bowl. After dipping the catfish in the milk mixture roll it in the cornmeal. Melt 4 cups of shortening in a skillet. Keep the shortening hot. Carefully place prepared catfish in the oil and fry until golden brown. Serve hot and salt to taste.

PUMPKIN SOUP

3 c. pumpkin puree
1 large onion, minced
3 Tbsp. butter
6 c. hot chicken stock or broth
salt and ground pepper to
taste
⅛ tsp. nutmeg
⅛ tsp. turmeric
finely chopped cilantro or
chopped parsley
1 c. heavy cream
creme fraiche

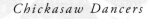
Chickasaw Dancers

Sauté the minced onions in butter until tender and transparent. Do not brown.

43

Place onions and pumpkin puree in a soup pot and add seasonings. Over a low flame, gradually add the chicken stock, stirring until the mixture is smooth. Add cream and stir. Simmer soup for 5 minutes. Sprinkle with chopped cilantro. Serve in heated bowls. Offer a bowl of creme fraiche. Makes 6-8 servings.

Chickasaw Drummers

STUFFED WILD TURKEY

1 turkey, about 12 lb. (save giblets)

6 thick bacon slices

½ lb. butter (2 sticks)

2 onions, chopped

1 c. celery, chopped fine

½ c. parsley, minced

½ c. green onions, minced

6 c. corn bread, crumbled

2 c. breadcrumbs, dry

1 ½ tsp. poultry seasoning

½ c. white wine

1 can chicken broth

salt

pepper

Rinse and dry turkey inside and out. Sprinkle cavity and skin with salt and pepper. Cover breast with slices of bacon. Set aside. Make dressing. Boil giblets until tender, and then chop very fine. Melt butter and sauté onions and celery until translucent. Add the chopped giblets, parsley, and green onions. Cook for a few minutes, add this to the cornbread and breadcrumbs. Mix well and add seasonings. Add wine and enough broth to make a moist dressing. Add salt and pepper to taste. Fill neck and cavity with stuffing and close both with skewers. Tie legs together and fold back wings. Place turkey on rack in roasting pan and roast in oven at 350 degrees for 20 minutes per pound, or until done. Baste frequently with drippings to keep bird moist. When done, transfer to heated platter and keep warm. Skim fat from pan drippings and make gravy by thickening drippings with flour.

History of the Choctaw Nation

From Past to Present

Chief Gregory Pyle

It is said the Choctaws were the largest tribe belonging to the branch of the Muskogean family, which includes the Chickasaw, Creek, and Seminole. Their name supposedly comes from a Spanish word *chato,* meaning flat, because of the Choctaw custom of flattening infants' skulls with sandbags. Originally, Choctaws occupied central and southern Mississippi and western Alabama. Choctaw people furnished the name for countries and towns in Alabama, Mississippi, Oklahoma, and Arkansas. Historians have always referred to the Choctaws as one of the most advanced, peaceful, and practical of the tribes.

The Choctaws' first encounter with civilization was not a happy one. When Hernando DeSoto appeared on the scene in the early 1500s and demanded that Chief Tuscaloosa provide the services of the tribesmen, the chief appeared agreeable, but suggested that the Spanish go with him to the principal towns of the Choctaws to carry their baggage. Tuscaloosa then sent messengers to the town warning warriors of impending battle.

Desoto was surprised when he reached Mobile to find warriors waiting and to find them such strong adversaries. The Spaniards were driven out of town and scattered. Wearing armor and firearms astride horses, Desoto's men rallied and overcame the Choctaws though the Spanish lost twenty-two men and many supplies. The Choctaws, according to Spanish reports, lost several hundred warriors. Desoto set fire to the town, and those Choctaws inside their houses were burned alive.

For the next 160 years, Choctaws were undisturbed by Europeans. In 1698, the French came from Canada and established settlements. Their principal method of livelihood was trapping the animal furs, trading with the Indians, and sending their bounty to the rich European markets.

During this peaceful time, the Choctaws were contacted by English raiders and peaceful trade was established. As they traded and intermarried, the French and English introduced the Choctaws to materials and customs that they found useful.

At the insistence of white settlers between 1801 and 1820, the United States government negotiated treaties with the Choctaws, which took more than half of their original land holdings. When Mississippi entered the Union in 1817, pressure began to mount for the Choctaws to give up all their lands and move to a territory west of the Mississippi. This territory was to be a sovereign nation for the Indians and off limits to non-Indians. The Choctaws were given two choices: take an individual land allotment and become a citizen of Mississippi or go to the new land and set up their own government. Many Indians, especially the full bloods, believed that their property in southeastern United States was a gift of the Great Spirit, so it was impossible for the Indians to leave it.

The term Trail of Tears can be applied to all the Five Civilized Tribes: Choctaw, Cherokee, Creek, Seminole, and Chickasaw. The tears when the people signed cession treaties accepted by the United States government as the will of the Indian nations. Each tribe made its own treaty, which produced intra-tribal and inter-tribal conflicts. The Treaty of the Choctaws was called the Treaty of Dancing Rabbit Creek (September 20, 1830).

Choctaw removal to Indian Territory began in the fall of 1830. With this treaty the Choctaws were given title to what is now the southeastern counties of Oklahoma in return for their 10 million acres in Mississippi. All these factors paved the way for the Choctaw's ultimate removal from Mississippi, the first tribe to traverse the Trail of Tears.

In 1830, President Jackson oversaw the intended negotiations, which led to the Treaty of Dancing Rabbit Creek. This treaty required the Choctaws, along with the other Civilized Tribes, to sell all their lands east of the Mississippi to the federal government and move to the newly designated Indian Territory. The new Choctaw lands were bound on the north by the Canadian and Arkansas rivers and on the south by the Red River in the eastern half of what was to become the state of Oklahoma. In 1907, the entire Oklahoma area became the thirty-sixth state of the Union. Oklahoma is derived from Choctaw words "Okla Homma" meaning "People Red."

Choctaw Tribal Capitol Building

Under the leadership of Chief Gregory E. Pyle, the Choctaw Nation of Oklahoma has been extremely blessed to be successful in businesses, such as gaming and travel plazas, so that services can be offered to tribal people. Federal dollars assist in many programs, but without the business revenues, there would be many people left without help.

For example, there are about $300,000 from federal funds that go toward the Higher Education Scholarships; the tribe puts in another $5 million each year to give 5,000 students a chance to go to school. The Summer Youth Program has federal funding of $340,000 and the tribe adds $1,750,000 each year so that all 1,500 eligible applicants can be employed. Jobs and job training continue to be a priority of Choctaw Nation administration, and the continued expansion of the Summer Youth Work Program is just one example of what the tribe is doing to create employment opportunities. Expanding tribal businesses creates jobs, and also creates additional revenue to put into programs.

Money from economic development projects also provides the dollars needed to build new clinics and tribal facilities, which in turn, also means additional job opportunities.

The Choctaw Nation of Oklahoma has a history of putting people first and assisting the communities around them. Funds have been given to many charities, communities, churches, fire and police departments, county sheriff offices, schools and clubs, as well as individuals. The philosophy of "What is good for Choctaw Nation is good for our communities" has proven to be true. Programs administered by the Choctaw Nation that promote heritage and culture include the Historic Preservation Program, Native American Graves Protection and Repatriation Act (NAGPRA), genealogy advocacy,

Trail of Tears walk reenactment, Wheelock Mission tours and museum, Choctaw Nation Capitol Museum, Choctaw Village activities, and Labor Day festival cultural exhibitions in stickball, dance, basketry, archery, cooking, beadwork, and tool craftsmanship.

Other services dealing with heritage and culture are pow wows, inter-tribal entertainment at casinos, Choctaw book store, tribal membership and certificate of degree of Indian blood program, cultural assimilation in Head Start classes and in the Jones Academy Residential Boarding School, and history information services through the public relations office.

The Choctaw Nation is continuously working to make sure there is *HOPE* for our future. At a time when the United States government is providing fewer and fewer services for our children, the Choctaw is securing funding and developing specific programs to ensure the next generations have *HOPE* and pride to carry on.

Choctaw Nation staff define hope this way - Helping Our People Excel.

Trail of Tears Commemorative Walk

Choctaw Code Talkers

Blue Grape Dumplings

Grape Juice:

½ gal. unsweetened Welch's grape juice

1 pkg. frozen blueberries

2 c. sugar

Bring grape juice, blueberries, and sugar to rolling boil.

Dumplings:

1 c. water

1 tsp. baking powder

2 Tbsp. shortening

flour

Mix above ingredients. Make a stiff dough, roll out thin, and cut into small pieces. Drop pieces one at a time into boiling juice. Cook 5 minutes and simmer 10 minutes, until thickened. Let stand 10 minutes with cover on before serving.

Choctaw Corn Shuck Bread

6 c. cornmeal

2 tsp. baking soda

boiling water

corn shucks

Pour enough boiling water over the meal and soda mixture to make a soft dough that can be easily handled. Prepare 4–6 handfuls of corn shucks by pouring boiling water over them to cover, then strip a few shucks to make strings. Tie 2 strips together at ends. Lay an oval-shaped ball of dough on shucks. Fold carefully and tie in the middle with strings. Place in large stew pot and boil 30–45 minutes.

Cornmeal Gravy

4 pieces side meat
2 ½ c. milk
½ c. cornmeal
bread
salt

Fry meat to have enough grease to cover cornmeal. Add cornmeal and salt to taste. Brown meat in grease. Add milk; stir and let boil until thick. Serve over any bread.

1 c. cornmeal
2 summer squash, diced
1 egg
water
¼ c. buttermilk

Cook squash in water until soft; leave ¾ cup water in pot. Combine other ingredients with squash and water; mix together. Fry in hot oil until golden brown.

Fried Squash Bread

1 c. cornmeal
2 summer squash, diced
1 egg
water
¼ c. buttermilk

Cook squash in water until soft; leave ¾ cup water in pot. Combine other ingredients with squash and water; mix together. Fry in hot oil until golden brown.

CURED VENISON (FOR PEMMICAN)

3 lb. salt
4 Tbsp. cinnamon
5 Tbsp. black pepper
4 Tbsp. allspice
Fresh venison meat

Cut meat into strips 12 inches long, 2 inches thick, and 4 inches wide. Remove all membrane so curing mixture will adhere to moist meat. Mix dried ingredients together thoroughly and rub well into every surface of strips, dusting on more. Thread each strip on string and hang in a cool, dry place out of the sun, not near artificial heat. Needs to be hung in this manner for one month, then is ready for eating without cooking as a jerked meat.

Passing on the tradition of blow guns

History of the Muscogee (Creek) Nation

Chief A.D. Ellis

The Muscogee (Creek) people are descendents of a remarkable culture that, before 1500 A.D., spanned the entire region known today as the Southeastern United States. Early ancestors of the Muscogee constructed magnificent earthen pyramids along the rivers of this region as part of their elaborate ceremonial complexes. The historic Muscogee later built expansive towns within these same broad river valleys in the present states of Alabama, Georgia, Florida, and South Carolina.

The Muscogee were not one tribe, but a union of several. This union evolved into a confederacy that, in the Euro-American described "historic period," was the most sophisticated political organization north of Mexico. Member tribes were called tribal towns. Within this political structure, each tribal town maintained political autonomy and distinct land holdings.

The confederacy was dynamic in its capacity to expand. New tribal towns were born of "mother towns" as populations increased. The confederation was also expanded by the addition of tribes conquered by towns of the confederacy, and, in time, by the incorporation of tribes and fragments of tribes devastated by the European imperial powers. Within this confederacy, the language and the culture of the founding tribal towns became dominant.

Throughout the period of contact with Europeans, most of the Muscogee population was concentrated into two geographical areas. The English called the Muscogee peoples occupying the towns on the Coosa and the Tallapoosa rivers Upper Creeks, and those to the southeast, on the Chattahoochee and Flint rivers, the Lower Creeks. The distinction was purely geographical. Due in part to their proximity to the English, the Lower towns were substantially effected by intermarriage and its consequent impact on their political and social order. The Upper towns remained less effected by European influences and continued to maintain distinctly traditional political and social institutions.

In the early nineteenth century, the United States Indian policy focused on the removal of the Muscogee and the other southeastern tribes to areas beyond the Mississippi River. In the removal treaty of 1832, Muscogee leadership exchanged the last of the cherished Muscogee ancestral homelands for new lands in Indian Territory (Oklahoma). Many of the Lower Muscogee (Creek) had settled in the new homeland after the treaty of Washington in 1827. But for the majority of Muscogee people, the process of severing ties to a land they felt so much a part of proved impossible. The U.S. Army enforced the removal of more than 20,000 Muscogee (Creeks) to Indian Territory in 1836 and 37.

In the new nation, the Lower Muscogees located their farms and plantations on the Arkansas and Verdigris rivers. The Upper Muscogees re-established their ancient towns on the Canadian River and its northern branches. The tribal towns of both groups continued to send representatives to a national council that met near High Springs. The Muscogee Nation, as a whole, began to experience a new prosperity.

The American Civil War was disastrous for the Muscogee people. The first three battles of the war in Indian Territory occurred when Confederate forces attacked a large group of neutral Muscogee (Creeks) led by Opothle Yahola. For the majority of the Muscogee people, desired neutrality proved impossible. Eventually, Muscogee citizens fought on both the Union and Confederate sides. The reconstruction treaty of 1866 required the cession of 3.2 million acres—approximately half of the Muscogee domain.

In 1867, the Muscogee people adopted a written constitution that provided for a principal chief and a second chief, a judicial branch and a bicameral legislature composed of a house of kings and a house of warriors. Representation in both houses of this Legislative assembly was determined by tribal town. This "constitutional" period lasted for the remainder of the nineteenth century. A new capital was established in 1867, on the Deep Fork of the Canadian at Okmulgee. In 1878, the Nation constructed a familiar native stone council house that remains at the center of the modern city of Okmulgee.

In the late 1800s, the Dawes Commission began negotiating with the Muscogee Nation for the allotment of the national domain. In 1898, the United States Congress passed the Curtis Act, which made the dismantling of the national governments of the Five Civilized Tribes and the allotment of collectively-held tribal domains inevitable. In 1890, the noted statesman Chitto Harjo helped lead organized opposition to the dissolution of Muscogee national government and allotment of collectively-held lands. In his efforts, he epitomized the view of all Muscogee people that they possessed an inherent right to govern themselves. For individuals like Chitto Harjo, it was unimaginable that the Nation could be dissolved by the action of a foreign government. This perception proved to be correct.

The end of the Muscogee Nation as envisioned by its architects within the United States Congress did not occur. In the early twentieth century, the process of allotment of the national domain to individual citizens was completed. However, the perceived dismantling of the Muscogee government was never fully executed. The nation maintained a principal chief throughout this stormy period.

In 1971, the Muscogee people, for the first time since the partial dismantling of their national government, freely elected a principal chief without presidential approval. In the decade of the 1970s, the leadership of the Muscogee (Creek) Nation drafted and adopted a new constitution, revitalized the National Council, and began the challenging process of Supreme Court decisions that affirmed the nation's sovereign rights to maintain a national court system and levy taxes. The federal courts have also consistently re-affirmed the Muscogee Nation's freedom from state jurisdiction.

Present day Mound building located at the Tribal headquarters, houses the national council offices and judicial offices. In the 1990s, almost 100 years after the dark days of the allotment era, the Muscogee (Creek) people are actively engaged in the process of accepting and asserting the rights and responsibilities of a sovereign nation. As a culturally distinct people, the Muscogee are also aware of the necessity for knowing and understanding their extraordinary historical and cultural inheritance.

Principal Chief A.D. Ellis belongs to the Turtle Clan, his tribal town is Locvpoka and his church is Concharty Indian Methodist Church.

The name Muscogee is an English form of the name Mvskoke, which a confederacy of Indians in Georgia and Alabama assumed after 1700. About 1,720 British agents designated a group of these Indians as Ochese Creek Indians. This designation, later shortened to Creek Indians, came to be commonly applied to the entire Muscogee tribe. The tribe's name for itself, however, remained Muscogee. The initials "I.T." on the circular border indicate "Indian Territory," the land west of the Mississippi River to which the Muscogee, or Creek, Indians removed in the early 1800s. The center signifies the advance of these Indians as agriculturalist and the influence of Christianity upon many of them. The sheaf of wheat refers to Joseph's dream (Genesis 37:7), "For behold, we were binding sheaves in the field, and lo, my sheaf arose, and also stood upright . . ." The plow depicts a prophecy (Amos 9:13), "Behold, the days come, saith the Lord, that the plowman shall overtake the reaper . . ." The Muscogee National Council adopted this seal following the War Between the States. It was used until Oklahoma statehood.[1]

Reference

1 Wright, Muriel H. "The Great Seal of the Muscogee Nation" *The Chronicles of Oklahoma,* vol. XXXIV (Spring, 1956).

Succotash

pumpkin (optional)
corn
beans

Shell some corn. Cook corn and beans separately, then together. You may add pieces of pumpkin in. Note: be sure to put the pumpkin in early enough to get done before the pot is removed from the fire. Add water (you can never tell the exact amount, just add until dough is elastic like) probably about 2 cups.

1 tsp. salt
2 Tbsp. sugar
2 c. powdered sugar
2 ½ tsp. baking powder
6 c. flour
oil for frying

Mix ingredients, knead dough (not for long). Let rise for about 10 minutes. Make pieces about ½-inch thick (if you like thick fry bread). Poke a hole in the middle of the dough before you fry it. Let cool and pour honey.

Dandelion Stir Fry

Dash salt and pepper
3 wild onions
bacon grease or fat
2 trout, salmon, or bass
6 handfuls of dandelion greens
white sage (few pinches)
1 lemon

Cut and clean fish. Cut into long strips. Chop onion. Slice lemon into thin disks. Wash and chop dandelion leaves. Grease metal fry pan slightly with bacon grease. (So you don't burn the fish). Put on a semi hot coal. Add onion, 5-6 thin slices of lemon, salt, pepper, and a few pinches of white sage (make sure sage is ground). Let cook about ¾ of the way and then add the dandelion leaves. Cook, until leaves are soft. Add salt, pepper, sage, again. When ready, drip on a little bit of lemon juice for taste. Add more grease if sticks to the pan too much. It should brown just a bit.

Corn Cakes

cinnamon
⅓ c. water
1 c. pounded corn
honey

Pound hard corn until powder like. Pour in water. Sprinkle cinnamon. Put in a small amount of honey. Make a type of patty cake. Melt butter in a small pan. Fry in oil until golden brown. Note: When bread is done, put butter on it and sprinkle with sugar.

FRY BREAD

1 pkg. dry yeast
3 c. warm water
1 Tbsp. sugar
1 Tbsp. salt
6 c. flour
2 Tbsp. oil
½ c. cornmeal

Dissolve yeast in warm water. Add the sugar and salt. Let stand 5 minutes in a bowl covered with a towel. Add flour and oil. Mix flour into liquid mixture. Turn out on a floured board and knead until dough texture is smooth. Put dough into a greased bowl, cover and let it rise until doubled in bulk (approximately 1 ½ hours). Punch down the dough and knead a few moments in ½ cup of cornmeal. Separate into two balls. Take one ball and roll the dough into a 12-inch diameter and ½ inch thick. (Make sure the other ball is covered in a bowl until you are ready to work with it.) Cut the dough into 2-inch squares. Let pieces of dough rest while oil heats in an iron skillet. Fry 5-6 pieces at a time until golden brown. When first batch is complete, work with the resting ball.

History of the Seminole Nation

Pictured Above:

Principal Chief Enoch Kelly Haney (Ocheesee Band and Sweet Potato Clan)

Assistant Chief Larry Harrison (Ocheesee Band and Deer Clan)

In 1753, a small band of Muscogee (Creek) Indians, called the Okonee, left Georgia due to frontier encroachment and moved into the Spanish territory of La Florida. Other Indians from Alabama also moved into the peninsula, and as a whole they were called *Cimarron,* a Spanish word meaning wild. The word was corrupted by the Indians who pronounced it as *Seminoli.*

The bill that was passed to remove all Indians from the Southeast to Indian Territory in the 1830s caused decades of wars and cost the government millions of dollars. Not wanting further participation in this campaign, several impoverished bands migrated to Indian Territory in 1836. These Seminoles settled for a time at Ft. Gibson, then eventually on the Canadian River near their kinsmen, the Creeks. The removal continued throughout the 1830s to the 1850s, and the wars continued on. With the last-ditch effort to remove them, the Seminoles finally agreed to relocate in May 1858.

Through the struggles and heartaches, the Seminoles continued their lifestyle while living near Ft. Gibson. Like other tribes in the area, the Seminoles were active in the fur trade and hunted deer, elk, and buffalo and also trapped beaver and other fur-bearing animals. Large community gardens stretching for miles consisted of corn, beans, pumpkins, and sweet potatoes. Seminoles fished in clear running creeks and when in season, gathered various edibles in the forests.

The matrilineal clan system was still maintained after the removal and remains important as ever today. Although dozens of clans have disappeared, many of the original ones are still present along with several off-shoots, including the wind, panther, deer, beaver, bird, bear, and alligator. In this complex society, these Clans are not allowed to intermarry within an individual clan: a person from the bear clan cannot marry another person from that clan. Severe punishment would take place if two people were discovered to be of the same clan and the punishment would be cropping of the ears, nose, and hair. Banishment was also practiced among the Seminoles.

The Seminoles began moving into the Little River region in February of 1845, and a new council house made of logs was erected near Wewoka, which became the new capitol of the Seminole Nation. Throughout this period the membership of the council consisted of a chief and assistant chief from each of the twenty-five bands. These leaders were expected to protect the interest, its members, and report on any important developments and decisions.

Gopher John, one of the black leaders, sought full independence for his group as freed slaves. These Negroes occupied a subordinate position within the Seminole society and paid an annual tribute and a degree of fealty to their Indian overlords. Other Seminoles still harbored anger over the blacks' role in the late war. Gopher John finally decided that his only hope for himself and his people was to leave Indian Territory for Mexico.

The Seminole Nation became divided during the Civil War. John Jumper was chief and served as the lieutenant colonel of the Mounted Volunteers of the Confederate Seminoles. John Chupko was also chief, leading those who favored the North, and was a sergeant in the Loyal Indian Regiment. Several factions from the Bird Creek, Eufaula, Ocheesee, and Tallahassee Bands were under Chupko. Other factions of these same bands and those from Kolomi, Tusekaya, Harjo, and others, were under Jumper's command. This division eventually caused some Seminoles to seek refuge in Kansas. Two groups of Seminole Negroes also fought for the North.

After the Civil War, the Seminole territory was reduced to boundaries of present-day Seminole County. They bought an additional 175,000 acres from the Muscogee (Creeks) for $.50 an acre.

While maintaining their native religion of the Green Corn ceremony, missionaries of the Baptist, Presbyterian and Methodist faiths became active among the Five Civilized Tribes. Although it was not widely accepted in the beginning, some Seminoles, including important leaders as John Jumper and James Factor, became active in the Baptist faith. These men recognized the importance of an education and in 1843, allowed the Oak Ridge Mission to be built. This was the first school founded among the Seminoles and was sponsored by the Presbyterian Church. Two more schools were erected in the latter part of the nineteenth century: Emahaka Mission for girls and the Mekusukey Mission for boys. Adaptation to a new way of life soon became the main focus of Seminole leaders.

The Seminoles established brave law men to protect their country, and the Light Horsemen was created. The Light Horse pursued felons and handed down punishment accordingly. The Seminoles knew only two degrees of punishment, lashing or death by execution. This form of Indian justice was infinitely more efficient and respected by all, including women. Depending upon the crime, the guilty would receive fifty lashes for the first offense and 100 for the second offense. For the third, it was 150 lashes. The hickory switch used in the punishment was thumb-sized and measured twelve feet long. For more serious offenses, such as murder, justice was quickly served at the execution tree. The Light Horsemen lined up with their rifles to bring death to the guilty. The old whipping tree still stands on the Wewoka courthouse lawn and is a harsh reminder of the punishment once given and received by the Seminoles.

The complex of the Seminole Nation of Oklahoma is still located in Wewoka and is a federally recognized tribe with a special political and legal relationship with the United States government. The General Council of the Seminole consists of fourteen individual bands with twenty-eight representatives, who meet at the Council House at the historic Mekusukey Mission grounds south of Seminole.

Seminole lands after the Civil War (Present-day Seminole County is number 5, shaded pink.)

As the Seminoles enter into the twenty-first century, they continue to pursue any available opportunities to benefit their tribal members with funding for education and the development of jobs. As a growing, multi-million dollar entity, the Seminole Nation continues to move ahead into a brighter future.

For more information on the Seminole Nation of Oklahoma go to www.seminolenation.com

INDIAN TERRITORY

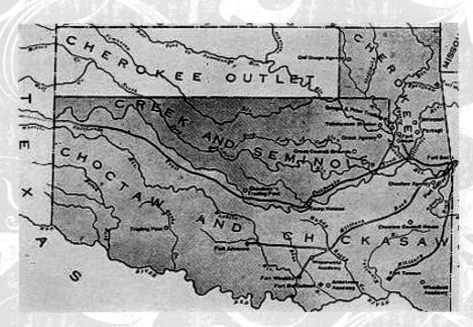

Seminole lands in Indian Territory, 1836–1856

Seminole Chiefs in Washington, D.C., 1852

Group of Seminoles and their families (Painting by American-born artist, George Catlin, 1836)

Seminole Nation Council House

Emahaka Mission, 1890s

Pictured below from left:
Chiefs John Jumper (CS),
John Chupko (US), Passukee
Yahola, the last Seminole
executed summer 1903.
Wewoka, I.T.

EGGS AND WILD ONIONS

2 dozen young, tender wild onions
water
6 eggs
bacon grease or butter for frying

Steam onions for a few minutes with a little water (cover them and cook until they are limp). Add to eggs and stir to scramble. Add butter or grease, salt and pepper to taste. Fry like scrambled eggs until they are as done as you like. Best if not overcooked. Makes 3–4 servings.

WILD RICE AND GRAPE SALAD

3 c. cooked rice
1 c. seedless green grapes, halved
1 small can water chestnuts, sliced
½ c. chopped celery
1 big bunch green onions, chopped medium to fine
½ c. slivered or sliced almonds
1 c. Hellman's mayo, do not use substitutes

Stir vegetables and mayo into rice; stir grapes in gently. If too thick, thin with a little milk. Taste for seasoning. Refrigerated, this will keep several days. Better if made the day before, so the mayo has time to blend. If you do make it in advance, don't add any more seasoning until you taste it the next day. You can also put leftover chopped up chicken or turkey in this salad. If you're going to take this somewhere, be sure to keep it chilled in a cooler until time to eat. Makes about a 1 ½ quarts.

LITTLE PORCUPINES

1 lb. ground venison or fatless round steak
⅓ c. uncooked light brown wild rice
1 small onion, minced very fine
1 seeded green pepper, minced very fine
1 tsp. salt
¼ tsp. pepper
1 can tomatoes
1 can tomato soup

Combine meat, uncooked rice, onion, green pepper, salt, pepper, mix thoroughly. Shape into 1-inch firm meat balls. Bring soup and tomatoes in their liquid to a boil in fry pan with tight cover, put in meatballs; reduce to very slow simmer. Simmer tightly until done with rice popping out of balls like porky quills, about 40–45 minutes.

FRY BREAD PUDDING

6 pieces Indian fry bread
1 c. sugar
1 c. water
½ c. raisins
1 tsp. cinnamon
1 c. grated mild cheese

Split fry bread into thin halves. Caramelize sugar, then add water to form a syrup. Layer fry bread, raisins, and cheese. Pour syrup over mixture and bake in a 300 degree oven until all syrup is absorbed.

Native American Heritage and Culture

by Congressman Tom Cole

As a member of Congress I can tell you there is no bigger issue we face as a nation than the issue of war. War affects every American. It demands sacrifices from the men and women in uniform who so bravely risk their lives to defend the freedoms we enjoy today, and it affects the families of our military who send their loved ones to fight the battle. It is to these individuals that we owe our eternal gratitude.

I have the privilege of representing the brave men and women of Fort Sill and Tinker Air Force Base in Congress, as well as members of the Reserves and National Guard and tens of thousands of veterans. My voting record reflects my firm belief in a strong national defense. I believe Congress has no greater responsibility than providing our military with the resources it needs to be the best equipped and the best trained in the world. In a post September 11 world, we are engaged in a continuous War on Terrorism—or as I call it, the War for Freedom. While we must provide funding for these most immediate needs, we must also focus on domestic security and preparation for future challenges. I am deeply committed to our military and the brave men and women who have volunteered to defend our nation.

Fort Sill is a critical part of the United States Army. Many of the soldiers who are stationed there are protecting America right now in Iraq, Afghanistan, and other places around the world. Fort Sill is the premier artillery-training site for both the Army and the U.S. Marine Corps. The U.S. Air Force also uses part of Fort Sill as a training range. Fort Sill is composed of about 94,000 acres of mountains, rolling hills, and prairie in the southwestern part of the state outside Lawton. Over 20,000 people work and train at Fort Sill, and all of us benefit from the security these military and civilian personnel provide for our country.

Tinker Air Force Base, located in Midwest City, is Oklahoma's largest employer with about 24,000 employees, including 8,000 military personnel. Tinker's 5,033 acres generates an economic impact of about $3 billion in Oklahoma. Recently, Tinker Air Force Base was awarded two prestigious environmental awards at the U.S. Air Force General Thomas D. White Environmental Awards Ceremony at the Pentagon in Washington, D.C. I am committed to helping strengthen Tinker Air Force Base, one of the most valuable depot maintenance facilities within the U.S. Air Force. Recent improvements on base in manufacturing and quality control have made Tinker a worldwide leader in innovation.

Both Fort Sill and Tinker represent the commitment of Oklahomans to the security of our nation. As we continue to fight in a war that may very well define this generation of American history, rest assured that I am committed to fighting for our military personnel, their families and the security of our nation.

Oklahoma is a state rich in Native American culture. My mother taught me that our Native American heritage was something to be cherished and celebrated. I was honored when she was inducted into the Chickasaw Hall of Fame and honored again when they added my name in 2004. As an enrolled member of the Chickasaw Nation and the only Native American currently serving in the House of Representatives, I am proud to be a part of this rich Oklahoma legacy that encompasses so much of our state's culture.

I have the great privilege of serving on the Natural Resources Committee in the House of Representatives. Through this committee I am able to work with Democrats and Republicans to produce sound policy that will benefit Native Americans in Oklahoma, as well as across the country.

Recently Congress has passed many pieces of legislation that have been signed into law that benefit Americans, in general, and Native Americans in particular. I worked to pass H.R. 3085, a bill that provided a feasibility study of the Trail of Tears National Historic Trail to include new trail segments, land components, and campgrounds associated with the trail. H.R. 3085 was signed into law in late 2006. I was also an original co-sponsor of H.R. 481, the Sand Creek Massacre National Historic Site Trust Act of 2005, which authorized the United States to take into trust certain land in Kiowa County, Colorado, owned by the Cheyenne and Arapaho Indian Tribes of Oklahoma, which became public law in 2005. The Chickasaw National Recreation Area Land Exchange Act of 2004 was also signed into law. This law provided for the conveyance of certain land from the city of Sulphur to the United States and revised the boundary of the Chickasaw National Recreation Area in Oklahoma in order to free up land for a new cultural center celebrating the history of the Chickasaw Nation.

In order to sustain and stimulate the Native American cultural and economic renaissance, tribal government must continue engaging the federal government, but ultimately remain independent. Native Americans must never be afraid to participate, negotiate, or litigate in order to defend tribal sovereignty. Fortunately, more and more people recognize and appreciate the contributions tribal government makes to all Americans.

The United States government recognizes that American Indian tribes are sovereign entities. They have their own government and rights that are guaranteed by the Constitution and numerous laws, treaties, and court decisions. Native American Indian tribes have a unique relationship with state governments, as well as the federal government. Compromising tribal sovereignty anywhere is to compromise tribal sovereignty everywhere. This is the one non-negotiable principle upon which we should always stand.

Our Native American heritage is something that must be preserved. That is why Congress should continue funding for the management and operations of three regional Native American museums across the country, including the Southern Plains Indian Museum in Anadarko, Oklahoma. Artifacts and collections from our history must be preserved and remain in their respective museums for the educational benefit of each local community and its visitors.

I am proud of my Native American heritage and proud to represent such an important symbol of American heritage in the United States Congress. I will continue to work to protect the rights of Native Americans and their sovereignty. In this country, and especially in Oklahoma, the "First Americans" should never be the last Americans.

BANANA NUT BREAD

1 c. sugar
½ c. butter, softened
2 eggs
4 very ripe (blackened) bananas
⅓ c. water
1 ⅔ c. all-purpose flour
1 tsp. baking soda
½ tsp. salt
¼ tsp. baking powder
(Optional addition: 12 oz. chocolate chips or 1 c. chopped pecans)

Preheat oven to 350. Grease bottom only of loaf pan (spray works best). Mix sugar and melted butter together in a large mixing bowl. Mix in eggs until smooth. In a blender, blend bananas and water until liquid forms. Mix into sugar, butter, and egg mixture. Add flour, baking soda, salt, and baking powder. Mix until smooth. Add optional ingredients. Pour into loaf pan. Bake for 55 minutes or until wooden toothpick inserted into center comes out clean. Cool for 5 minutes. Loosen sides of loaf pan and remove from pan onto cooling rack. Cool completely before slicing.

Note: "Old" bananas can be stored in a Ziploc bag in the fridge to gain that "blackened" condition. The older and blacker the bananas, the more moist the loaf will be.

Congressman Tom Cole

History of the Pottawatomi Nation

The Citizen Pottawatomi Nation: A Tribal Biography

The Citizen Potawatomi are among the wave of Algonquian-speaking people who occupied the Great Lakes region from prehistoric times through the early 1800s. Oral traditions indicate that the ancient Potawatomi were part of an immense group that had traveled down the eastern shores of North America along the Atlantic Ocean. This large group—the Chippewa (Ojibwa), Ottawa (Odawa), and Potawatomi—constituted a single tribe.

This larger group later split at Georgian Bay, Ontario, Canada, going their separate ways. Through early historic records, it has been confirmed that the Potawatomi were living in Michigan and had established an autonomous tribal identity at least 500 years ago. Scholars have debated the origin and translation of the word Potawatomi (Bode'-wadmink, in the Potawatomi language) for many years. Nevertheless, the Potawatomi people firmly believe that the Chippewa applied the term to them, meaning the people of the place of the fire, since they retained the original council fire once shared by all three tribes. Today, the Citizen Potawatomi Nation refers to itself as the Nishnabe or True People.

During the mid 1650s, French traders visited the tribe and found them growing corn, gathering wild rice, and harvesting an abundant supply of fish and waterfowl from the western waters of Lake Michigan in Wisconsin. The Potawatomi used mastery of the birch bark canoe for essential transportation.

They had recently relocated from southern Michigan just after eruption of the Beaver Wars in the 1640s. A French trader named Jean Nicolet established actual first contact between Europeans and the Potawatomi in 1634. This was at a place now named Red Bank. It is on the Door Peninsula on the western shore of Lake Michigan.

At the height of the Fur Trading Era, which spanned an entire century, the Potawatomi controlled a huge tribal estate that encompassed Wisconsin, Michigan, Illinois, Indiana, and a small portion of Ohio. This

Above: Chairman Rocky Barrett, middle: Vice Chairman Linda Capps

was accomplished through long-standing leadership and savvy business skills. The Potawatomi were not satisfied with just trapping furs. Instead, they entered a competition with the Ottawa for a share in the role as middlemen for trade in the Green Bay area.

Using their entrepreneurial skills, they began to hire other local tribesmen to collect and trap the furs. The Potawatomi would sell or trade the furs to the French, thus expanding their tribal control and estate over a vast area.

By 1800, tribal villages were being displaced by white settlements; they were pushed farther and farther to the outskirts of the Potawatomi tribal area. It was during the Removal Period of the 1830s that the Mission Christian converts (today known as the Citizen Potawatomi Nation) were forced to leave their homelands in the Wabash River Valley of Indiana.

From Indiana, the Mission Band was forced to march across four states (more than 660 miles) to a new reserve in Kansas. They left Indiana in September 1838, and arrived in Kansas in November. Of the 850 Potawatomi people forced to remove, more than 40 died along the way, on what is known as The Trail of Death. More died after arrival in Kansas. Most of the dead were children left in unmarked graves spanning the four-state area.

After arriving in Kansas, the tribe experienced a brief period of prosperity, returning to their entrepreneurial traditions before they were subjected to yet another ruinous government policy. In 1861, the experimental allotment act was unleashed on the Potawatomi.

Between 1838 and 1861, the Mission Potawatomi had been placed on the same small reserve with the Prairie Potawatomi. The Prairie Potawatomi had ventured west onto the Great Plains at a much earlier period than the Mission Band, had interacted with the Sioux, and had adopted different lifeways.

The two cultural groups exhibited very different ceremonial and subsistence strategies yet were forced to share the small reserve. Seeking a better opportunity for their people, Mission Potawatomi leaders chose to embrace this new policy by taking the lands in individual allotments rather than in common. The Prairie Potawatomi, on the other hand, chose to keep their lands in common in a single reserve.

Shortly thereafter and not fully understanding the Kansas tax system, most of the new individual allotment lands passed out of Mission Band ownership, into the hands of white opportunists and politicians. In 1867, Mission Potawatomi members signed a treaty through which they sold their remaining Kansas lands to purchase lands in Indian Territory with the proceeds.

Learning from their Kansas experience and hoping to protect title to their new land in what is now Oklahoma, Mission Potawatomi tribal members took U.S. citizenship as a group, hence the name Citizen Potawatomi. The Citizen Potawatomi were the first tribe to attain U.S. citizenship en masse. Native Americans did not become U.S. citizens until 1924.

By the early 1870s, most of the Citizen Potawatomi had resettled in Indian Territory, present-day Oklahoma, creating several communities near modern-day Shawnee. In 1890, the Citizen Potawatomi unwillingly participated again in the allotment process, implemented through the Dawes Act of 1887. With this Act, the Citizen Potawatomi were forced to accept individual allotments. In the Land Run of 1891, the remainder of the Potawatomi reservation in Oklahoma was opened up to white settlement. It is estimated that over half of the 900 square mile reservation was simply given away by the government.

The boundaries of the 900 square mile purchase were the north bank of the North Canadian River; the south bank of the South Canadian; the Pottawatomie-Seminole county line;, and the Indian Meridian, a north-south line across Oklahoma that cross I-40 between its 166 and 167 mile markers. That is essentially the Citizen Potawatomi Nation's present-day jurisdictional area. Today, Citizen Potawatomi Nation individual and tribal trust property totals 4,150 acres.

Over time, many tribal members followed the pattern of other Oklahomans during the Dust Bowl era, migrating to California, as well as Washington, Colorado, Idaho, and Oregon. In these states, they formed congenial, loose-knit communities. Today, these communities are well established and have expanded to Kansas, Texas, and California. In 1985, the CPN administration formally established eight CPN Regional Tribal Council centers to provide outreach to tribal members and to hold at least one regional council meeting with the tribal leadership each year.

Winter's Potawatomi Chiefs: George Winter painted this composite of leaders of the Potawatomis in the late 1830s in Indiana.

Council of Keewaunay: George Winter painted this scene of a council between Potawatomi leaders and U.S. government representatives in July 1837. Purpose of meeting was to iron out details for the impending removal of the Potawatomis from northern Indiana.

Newly constructed Citizen Potawatomi Nation Culture Heritage Center in Shawnee, Oklahoma

Loretta Barrett Oden, Native American chef, food historian, lecturer, and member of the Citizen Potawatomi Nation, is the founder of the famed Corn Dance Cafes in Santa Fe, New Mexico. Oden, along with her son, the late Chef Clay Oden of Grand Boulevard Grill, opened the first restaurants dedicated to showcasing the amazing bounty of foods indigenous to the Americas.

MOM'S 'TATER SALAD

5 lb. potatoes, preferably red but any ole 'tater will do, boiled, skin on until barely fork tender, drain, cool 1" dice
6–12 whole eggs, boiled, peeled, chopped
1 large onion, yellow or white, chopped
2 Tbsp. whole celery seeds
1 c. + mayonnaise (Hellman's, Best Foods)
¼ c. +/– French's Yellow Mustard
1 Tbsp. Durkey's Sauce*, optional

Mix potatoes, eggs, and celery seeds in large bowl. Add mayo then just enough mustard to make pale yellow, about "banana skin yellow."

Origin: Mom/Annetta Peltier Cannon
Alterations By: Chef Loretta Oden

CLAY'S BUFFALO MEATLOAF

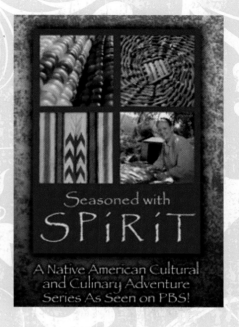

1 ½ lb. ground bison meat

¾ c. yellow onion, diced

½ c. diced celery

¾ c. diced carrots

2 eggs

4 Tbsp. canned chipotle pepper pureed with adobo sauce, very spicy, adjust to taste

⅔ c. ketchup

1 ⅔ c. panko breadcrumbs

½ tsp. minced garlic

1 tsp. ground sage

½ tsp. cumin

½ tsp. coriander

1 pinch ground thyme

salt and pepper, to taste

Host and creator of the Emmy Award-winning PBS series "Seasoned with Spirit: A Native Cook's Journey," Loretta Barrett Oden

Mix all ingredients together (by hand is best), shape into loaf or place in oiled loaf pan and bake at 350 for about 1 hour, or until done in middle and browned on outside.

Delicious as an entree with mashed potatoes or as a sandwich on bread or bun with sweet potato fries.

Origin: Grand Boulevard Grill Alterations By: Chef Clay Oden

THREE SISTERS AND FRIENDS SALAD

4 cloves garlic, minced
1 c. uncooked quinoa
½ c. Ojibwe wild rice
1 c. cooked black beans, if canned, rinse and drain well
½ c. raw, unpeeled, and diced green zucchini
½ c. raw, unpeeled, and diced yellow zucchini or yellow crookneck squash
½ c. peeled, raw, fresh and unblemished, diced jicama, (may omit if good quality not available but it really adds a nice crunch to the salad)
½ c. chopped fresh cilantro
1 jalapeno pepper, seeded and diced
1 green onion, thinly sliced
⅓ c. finely minced fresh mint
½ tsp. sea or kosher salt
¼ tsp. freshly ground cumin seeds, dry-roasted in a skillet
endive leaves, fresh, crisp and unblemished
1 ripe avocado, cubed

New Ingredient Group:
extra virgin olive oil
seasoned rice wine vinegar
fresh lime juice

If cooking black beans, no need to soak, just rinse, cover with water, and bring to boil. Simmer with 2 cloves of the minced garlic until done al dente. Drain and set aside. Rinse Quinoa thoroughly in a very fine chinoise (or use cheesecloth). Cover with cold water, bring to boil, reduce heat and simmer, stirring occasionally until quinoa becomes translucent and the little white endosperm appears. Be careful not to overcook or it will turn to mush. Drain immediately in a fine chinoise and rinse with cold water. Drain and set aside. Rinse and cook wild rice in boiling water until it just "blooms," still al dente. Drain and set aside. Dry toast cumin seeds in a skillet until aromatic. Grind seeds in a mortar with pestle or in a spice mill. Combine olive oil, rice wine vinegar, lime juice, cumin, salt and blend. Toss with cooked black beans and let sit for 15 minutes. Fluff quinoa and wild rice in a large mixing bowl; toss with all remaining ingredients ,including the dressed black beans. Spoon onto endive leaves and garnish with diced avocado.

* The Three Sisters being corn, beans, and squash are the Native American trilogy planted, grown, and eaten together, with the addition of Quinoa (keen-wah) from the Incas of South America and the Wild Rice from the Anisnabe of the Great Lakes region of North America, form an almost perfect food: protein, essential vitamins, and amino acids to keep our people healthy.

Origin: Corn Dance Cafe
Alterations By: Loretta Oden

Loretta Barrett Oden on the White Earth Reservation

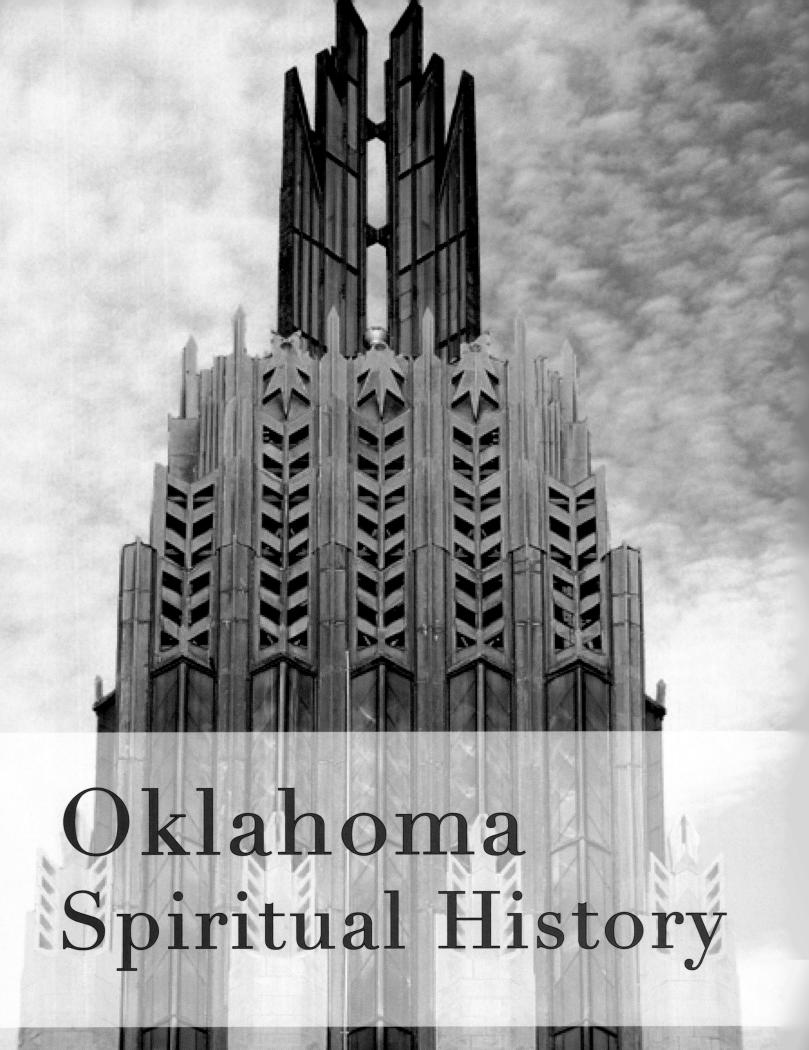

Oklahoma
Spiritual History

Oklahoma Spiritual History

Oklahoma is an overwhelmingly Protestant Christian state. The religious affiliations of the people of Oklahoma are: Christian 85%, Protestant 77%, Baptist (mostly Southern) 32%, Methodist 12%, Church of Christ 4%, Pentecostal 4%, Presbyterian 3%, Assembly of God 3%, Other Protestant 19%, Roman Catholic 7%, Other Christian 1%, Other Religions 1%, Non-Religious 14%.

Tecumseh Stained Glass Windows

IN MEMORY OF
GEO. W. HUGHBANKS

Oklahoma's religious profile varies markedly from national norms. The state's residents identify themselves as Southern Baptist almost seven times more often than other Americans, while Church of Christ, Methodist, Pentecostal, and Holiness groups are also much more common in Oklahoma than elsewhere. Correspondingly, Oklahomans are much less often associated with either mainstream Protestant churches, Roman Catholicism, or Judaism.

The resultant mix is made even richer by the continuing strength of American Indian spirituality and religious influences. Such differences stem from the state's unique history and remain a major shaper of its people and institutions.

The ten most popular religious affiliations (including "none") account for more than 90% of all Oklahomans.

Catholic History in Oklahoma

Spanish explorers under the leadership of Coronado almost certainly were the first Christians in what is today Oklahoma. Catholic priests of the Franciscan Order accompanied these explorers and would have led daily devotionals, including the Catholic Mass. One of these priests, Rev. Juan de Padilla, remained in the territory to evangelize the Wichita people. Unfortunately, members of the tribe did not appreciate fully his good will and they killed him in November 1542. According to church historian Rev. James White, Father Juan de Padilla thus became the first "martyr of the North American mainland," shedding his blood for the Gospel of Christ, possibly on the soil of the future state of Oklahoma.

By the mid nineteenth century, numerous Native American tribes were moved from their ancestral lands to the officially designated Indian Territory. Some of these tribes had accepted the Catholic faith decades earlier and now found themselves in a land with no established churches or resident Catholic clergy. In fact, the Catholic hierarchy had not established clear responsibility for the care of souls in this vast, undeveloped land. On the one hand, the bishop of Little Rock was charged with care not only for the state of Arkansas, but also for the so-called territory of "West Arkansas"–a designation for Indian Territory. On the other hand, authorities in Rome also had created the rather vague "Apostolic Vicariate of the Indian Territory East of the Rocky Mountains." This expansive swath of territory stretching from Missouri to the Rockies and from Nebraska through Kansas was entrusted to the pastoral care of the Jesuit Order, which specialized in evangelization and missionary ministry. It was in this light that the Indian Territory was occasionally visited by Jesuit priests from Kansas.

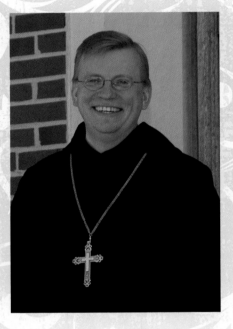

Tecumseh native Rt. Rev. Lawrence R. Stasyszen, OSB, is shown shortly after his election as the tenth abbot of St. Gregory's Abbey on January 6, 2006. The cross he is wearing was given to the first abbot of Sacred Heart Abbey (the former name of St. Gregory's Abbey), Rt. Rev. Thomas Duperou, OSB, who was elected on August 12, 1896.

Although the pastoral care for the relocated and impoverished Native Americans was insufficient, it appears that no established hierarchical authority was either willing to or capable of taking on this challenging mission. Facing this dilemma, the Catholic bishops of New Orleans and Little Rock remembered two missionary Benedictine monks who were serving temporarily as chaplains to a convent of nuns near Shreveport, LA. Originally from the Benedictine monastery of La Pierre-qui-

Vire near Dijon, France, the monks had arrived in New Orleans in 1872, with hopes of establishing a new monastery in the religiously tolerant atmosphere of the United States, preferably in the predominantly Catholic state of Louisiana. When their proposal to establish such a monastery in New Orleans was not accepted, they had moved to Shreveport. Thus the stage was set for two displaced French monks—Father Isidore Robot, OSB (Order of St. Benedict), and Brother Dominic Lambert, OSB—to be given responsibility for ministry to displaced Native Americans in a land that had yet to be appreciated fully for its beauty and wealth of natural resources.

Father Isidore Robot, OSB, and Brother Dominic Lambert, OSB, became the first resident Catholic clergymen in the future Oklahoma when they arrived by train at Atoka, Indian Territory, on October 12, 1875. There, in the Choctaw Nation, they found the only Catholic chapel in the entire Indian Territory. Named St. Patrick Church, it had been built by Irish railroad workers three years earlier during the construction of the Katy Railroad. From this base, these intrepid missionary monks explored the territory to find the best location for a permanent establishment. Two largely French-speaking and Catholic tribes provided attractive options: the Osage and the Citizen Potawatomi. The monks accepted the offer made by the Citizen Potawatomi for a square mile of land in exchange for stable pastoral care and education for their children. They established Sacred Heart Mission and School near the current town of Konawa in southern Pottawatomie County, beginning their life there on June 7, 1876. In September of that year, the hierarchy of Rome designated Father Isidore as the "Apostolic Prefect" of the Indian Territory, thus giving him the primary responsibility for pastoral care of Catholics in the region.

St. Gregory's University

From these humble beginnings, the Catholic faith quickly established a strong foothold in the Indian Territory. Additional monks soon arrived from France to staff what is considered to be the oldest institution of higher learning in the state of Oklahoma—now known as St. Gregory's University. They also established over forty Catholic churches in the territory. In this way, the Benedictines served the needs of the tribes of Indian Territory and created an infrastructure of faith to support the new settlers when the land was opened to non-Indians in the years following 1889. In fact, it was the Rev. Ignatius Jean, OSB, second Apostolic Prefect of the Indian Territory, who preached a stirring and challenging message to the crowds gathered in Purcell on April 21, 1889, the eve of the first Land Run.

In 1891, care for the Indian and Oklahoma Territories was transferred from the Benedictines to the Most Reverend Theophile Meerschaert. Originally from Belgium, Meerschaert was a priest serving in Natchez, Mississippi, at the time of his appointment as Apostolic Vicar of the Indian Territory. He was ordained as a bishop in Natchez on September 8, 1891, and arrived in Guthrie on September 19 to begin his thirty-two-year tenure of service in Oklahoma. Through his dedicated ministry and skillful recruitment of additional clergy, Bishop Meerschaert guided the rapidly growing Catholic population to the status of an independent Catholic diocese two years before Oklahoma became a state. Pope Pius X signed a decree on August 17, 1905, that created the Diocese of Oklahoma. At that time, Bishop Meerschaert moved his headquarters from the territorial capital of Guthrie to Oklahoma City and made St. Joseph Church in downtown Oklahoma City the first cathedral of Oklahoma. Since then, the Catholic community has been served by capable and visionary bishops, clergy, religious, and laity. On February 14, 1930, the Diocese of Oklahoma became the Diocese of Oklahoma City and Tulsa, a move that signaled the growth of the Catholic population in the young state.

The history of the Catholic Church in Oklahoma would be incomplete without special mention of the particular contributions made by religious sisters and nuns. Soon after the arrival of the Benedictine monks, religious sisters came to serve in various ministries, especially in education and health care. The earliest arrivals were the Sisters of Mercy, who came to Sacred Heart in 1884 to operate a school for girls alongside the school for boys operated by the monks. They then opened Mount St. Mary High School in Oklahoma City in 1904. Benedictine Sisters arrived in Guthrie from Iowa five months after the 1889 Land Run and eventually founded some fifty schools, hospitals, and orphanages throughout the state. They transferred their motherhouse to Tulsa in 1959. The Franciscan Sisters of Mary came in 1898 from Maryville,

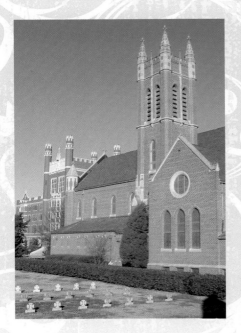

Abbey at St. Gregory's University

Facing: Mabee-Gerrer Museum of Art

Missouri, and founded St. Anthony Hospital, the first hospital in Oklahoma Territory.

Other orders of women that have served in Oklahoma include the Sisters of St. Francis of Philadelphia, the Sisters of Divine Providence, the Adorers of the Blood of Christ, the Carmelite Nuns of St. Joseph in Piedmont, the Sisters of St. Joseph of Wichita, the Sisters of Benedict in Piedmont, and the Carmelite Sisters of St. Theresa. This order of sisters was established in Atoka County in 1917, and now has its motherhouse in Oklahoma City at Villa Teresa. It would be impossible to quantify the contribution that these orders of Catholic religious sisters have made to the history of Oklahoma through prayer, education, pastoral ministry, health care, and other forms of service. In addition to the Benedictine monks, other orders of men serving in Oklahoma have included the Christian Brothers, the Augustinian Friars, the Carmelites, and the Glenmary Home Missioners, and the Apostles of Jesus.

The Catholic population has grown steadily in Oklahoma since the time of the first Land Run. This growth often came through the arrival of various ethnic groups, including African Americans, Czechs, Germans, Irish, Italians, Koreans, Latin Americans, Lebanese, Poles, and Vietnamese. Each group has enriched the culture of the state through its unique customs and faith expressions. Unfortunately, despite its many positive contributions, the growing Catholic community was not always well received. Ministers in several other Christian denominations often perpetuated unfortunate misinformation about the Catholic faith, thus fomenting resentment and even persecution of Catholics in Oklahoma. In addition to this, Catholic churches and individuals, along with other minority groups, were often the targets of harassment and even violence at the hands of extremist organizations such as the Ku Klux Klan. Fortunately, such activities and lack of understanding have, for the most part, disappeared.

The current structure of the Catholic Church in Oklahoma took form on December 19, 1972, when Church authorities in Rome announced that the state was to be divided to create the Archdiocese of Oklahoma City (covering the western forty-six counties) and the Diocese of Tulsa (covering the remaining thirty-one counties). This structure came into effect on February 6, 1973, when the Most Reverend John R. Quinn was blessed as the first Archbishop of Oklahoma City. Today, the Catholic community of Oklahoma remains organized in this way. It has over

190 parishes and maintains thirty-nine pre-Kindergarten and elementary schools, four high schools, and one university with campuses in three cities. There are twelve Catholic hospitals and clinics in the state and several parish nursing programs. Catholic Charities of Oklahoma City and Tulsa provides multi-faceted services to thousands of clients each year–including assistance with housing, food, health care, immigration, employment, family support, counseling, and adoption. The Mabee-Gerrer Museum of Art on the campus of St. Gregory's Abbey and University has one of the oldest and most extensive collections of fine art and artifacts in the state.

As the state of Oklahoma celebrates its centennial we can recognize the many contributions of the Catholic community of the state. Although a minority population, the Catholic community has provided consistent leadership in areas of education, health care, social action, charity care, cultural diversity and even political leadership. The first woman elected to statewide office (Katie Barnard), four of Oklahoma's governors (Trapp, Bartlett, Walters, and Keating), as well as numerous other civic leaders, business persons, and citizens have been proud of their Catholic heritage and faith. Other well-known Catholic Oklahomans include the ballerinas Yvonne Chouteau and Maria Tallchief; the noted artist and Oklahoma Hall of Fame Inductee Rev. Gregory Gerrer, OSB; Bishops Steven Leven, Charles Buswell, Victor Reed, and John Sullivan; and renowned athlete Jim Thorpe.

As the history of the Catholic Church in Oklahoma began with the ministry and martyrdom of Father Juan de Pedilla in 1542, it begins the twenty-first century with the official start of the process to declare Oklahoma native Father Stanley Rother of Okarche a saint in the Catholic Church as a result of his martyrdom on July 28, 1981, while he was serving as a missionary in Santiago Atitlan, Guatemala. Still rapidly growing, the Catholic community is proud to be Oklahoman and will continue to make a positive contribution to the peoples of this great land.

For further reading, consult: *Tenacious Monks,* by Rev. Joseph Murphy, OSB, and *Roman and Oklahoman, A Centennial History of the Archdiocese of Oklahoma City,* by Rev. James D. White.

Bishop Meerschaert was the first Bishop after Benedictines. This photo was his first visit to Sacred Heart in 1891.

Father John and Rev. Isidore Ricklin traveling by buggy to educate people and children.

Early 1901 procession overlooking Sacred heart.

Children's early ministry. Photo marking first day of Communion, children dressed as "Brides of Christ."

Monk's Band at St. Gregory's Abbey named "Holy Band." To the far left in this photo is Father Gregory Gerrer. Father Gerrer's father was a baker for Napoleon III in France, before the family escaped and came to America.

CRUSTY FRENCH BREAD

Prepare ahead:

¼ c. warm water*
1 pkg. yeast, dry or compressed
2 c. warm water
2 tsp. salt
2 Tbsp. sugar
6 c. flour, sifted

*105 degrees for dry yeast, 95 degrees for compressed yeast

Add yeast to ¼ cup water with a pinch of the sugar. Let rest 5 minutes. Sift and measure flour. Mix dry ingredients together in mixing bowl with yeast and additional water. Mix until dough leaves the side of the bowl and becomes a ball. Remove from mixing bowl to floured surface and knead in additional flour until dough no longer sticks to the board and is shiny and smooth. Put dough in greased bowl, turning to grease top. Cover and set in warm place to rise. Let dough rise until almost doubled, about 1 ½ hours. Punch down, squeezing out air bubbles, and divide in half. Form two elongated loaves, placing on lightly greased cookie sheets. Cover and let rise about 30 minutes. Brush top with water before baking and make diagonal slashes in top with a sharp knife. Bake in preheated 400 degree oven 45 minutes with a shallow pan of hot water in oven bottom. Makes 2 loaves. May freeze for later serving.

Methodist History in Oklahoma

The Methodist presence in Oklahoma began long before statehood. In fact, the Methodist Church in Oklahoma can trace its beginnings to October 23, 1844, when, at nine o'clock in the morning, Bishop Thomas A. Morris called to order the first Annual Conference ever held in what is now Oklahoma. The place was Riley's Chapel, located in the Cherokee Nation, about two miles from Tahlequah. The opening religious services were conducted in English and the closing in Cherokee and Choctaw.

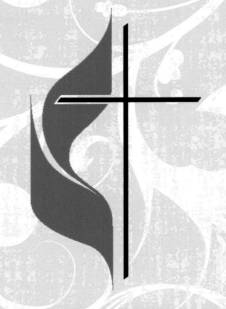

Thus began a long and colorful history of mission and ministry in Oklahoma, which has continued uninterrupted to this day. At the time of organization, all of the eastern part of what is now Oklahoma; a strip of Texas; and Kansas, as far north as Kansas City, comprised Indian Territory. There were 90,000 Indians in the territory in 1845, with 75,000 belonging to the Civilized Tribes. By orders of the Louisville Convention of the Methodist Church in 1845, it was decided that a separate body called the Methodist Episcopal Church, South, oversee the work in this new area.

Bishop Robert E. Hayes Jr.

The movement was so successful that after twelve years, from 1844–1856, the Methodist Church consisted of approximately a dozen white preachers; three Indian preachers—all former members of the Arkansas Conference; twenty-one local Indian preachers, among them Samuel Checote, a Creek; 1500 Cherokee members; 1000 Choctaw members; 600 Creek members; 150 blacks; and 100 whites, which comprised the largest number of the only denomination in Oklahoma at that time— 3,350 members! Prominent leaders, such as John Boston, W.L. and Jesse S. McAlester, and a host of others whose names are synonymous with Oklahoma history led the Methodist Church into the unknown future.

The War Years

Over the first sixteen years of the Methodist presence in Oklahoma, several schools were established, among them the Indian Labor School in the Shawnee Nation, the Robertson school in Fort Washita, the

Fort Coffee School, the Chickasaw Academy (also called the McKendree Manual Labor School), and many more. Education was greatly prized by those early pioneers, and principals and superintendents were assigned. However, because of the loss of the Kansas River District to the St. Louis area and the operations of other religious bodies—some hostile to Methodism—the church experienced a decline. This loss of members culminated in the Civil War when everything was literally lost.

The year of 1860 was one of drought and famine. In this presidential election year, the entire nation was in a state of grave apprehension, and with the election of Abraham Lincoln to the presidency, state after state in the South left the Union. On April 11, 1861, when General Beauregard opened fire on Fort Sumter, initiating the Civil War, it was a shot that was heard around the world, and especially Oklahoma.

The drain on funds and materials forced schools to close. The Union military forts at Washita, Arbuckle, and Cobb were abandoned, leaving the movement in disarray. By the time General Lee surrendered at Appomattox in April 1865, everything had been laid to waste. Crops of every description were destroyed, and those who had adhered to the Confederacy were in great distress, and those who were loyal to the Union fared little better. The social and moral conditions were at the lowest ebb. Religiously, the toil of nearly a quarter of a century had all but been destroyed. Churches were burned, members were scattered, and in the midst of such conditions, only eight ministers were present when the twentieth Annual Conference opened on September 14, 1865, at Doaksville in the Choctaw Nation.

Bishop Enoch M. Marvin, newly elected to the episcopacy, was appointed to hold the Indian Mission Conference. There was only one building left suitable to house the meeting, that of Bloomfield Academy, Chickasaw Nation. Bishop Marvin informed the conference of the desperate financial straits, and at one time considered abandoning the field. But at the close of the meeting, Bishop Marvin said, "Fear not. I will guarantee $5,000 for this mission and send it to you in regular payments as the year advances. Our work must go on!"

On that day, a new name was added to the list of immortals who planted Methodism in Oklahoma. That name was Enoch M. Marvin.

The task facing the Methodist Church following the Civil War was enormous. Its leaders had to reorganize the church societies, rebuild churches, reestablish schools, break down tribal division that had been rekindled during the war, assist in reestablishing law and order, help in ridding the country of wholesale cattle thieves, marauders and robbers, promote industry, and light again the religious fires in the homes of the people.

Over the next twenty-two years, from 1867–1889, the Methodist Conference met throughout the state in such notable places as Fort Gibson, Boggy Depot, Okmulgee, North Fork, Creek Nation, Vinita, Stringtown, Muskogee, Double Springs, Caddo, and Webber's Falls. By 1866, the Indian treaties provided that a right-of-way for railroads be granted, and new towns sprang up and white settlers moved in.

In 1889, Bishop Eugene R. Hendrix was appointed to preside over the Indian Mission Conference, and arrived in the spring of 1889 to preside over the Pauls Valley District Conference. He appointed Rev. I.L. Burrow, former president of Central Collegiate Institute, Altus, Arkansas, (later Hendrix College), presiding elder of the Oklahoma City District, a new district to be organized among the white settlers who had made the "run" on April 22, 1889. For the Methodist Church, South, which Dr. Burrow organized in Oklahoma City, Rev. A.J. Worley was named pastor. This church was later known as St. Luke's Methodist church.

At the 61st conference in Tulsa, Oklahoma, on November 17, 1906, the conference asked a committee to make a name change because the missionary character of the Indian conference had changed and the growing number of whites in the new territory was growing. The committee recommended that the name be changed to Oklahoma Annual Conference. The motion was adopted. The former Indian Conference later became the Oklahoma Indian Missionary Conference, which exists to this day. It was also during this period that the Methodists in Oklahoma created an institution of higher learning that later became known as Oklahoma City University.

At the 62nd session of the newly named Oklahoma Annual Conference, the first since statehood, convening at Durant, Oklahoma on November 13, 1907, a telegram was sent to Governor C.N. Haskell, the first governor of Oklahoma from Bishop Joseph S. Key.

The message read: "The Oklahoma Conference, Methodist Episcopal Church, South, in 62nd session assembled, congratulate you and the people of our new state upon your assuming duties of your high office as first Governor of Oklahoma. We commend you for your stand in favor of state-wide prohibition, and also for your announcement since election that same shall be faithfully enforced. In this and all other moral issues we pledge you our faithful support."

It was during these early years leading up to statehood and beyond that the Methodist movement grew dramatically. The blacks, who had been with the Methodist movement since the beginning in 1844, found themselves being placed into a racially segregated conference, which was still connected with the mother church, and later became the Oklahoma District of the Southwest Conference of the Central Jurisdiction.

In 1939, Methodism was divided into an East Oklahoma Conference and a West Oklahoma Conference, following the unification of the South Church and the North Church in Kansas City of that same year. By 1947, the East Conference reported having 208 pastoral charges, six districts, 76,796 members, eighty-six local preachers, and 278 church schools. The West conference reported having 271 pastoral charges, seven districts, 93,890 members, eighty-eight local preachers, and 335 church schools.

By 1968, the two conferences of Oklahoma and the all-black Southwest Conference of the Central Jurisdiction merged at the General Conference held in Dallas, Texas.

Conclusion

Today the Oklahoma Annual Conference and the Oklahoma Indian Missionary Conference together total 660 churches, with an estimated membership of over 265,000. With its headquarters based in Oklahoma City, the roots of Methodism in this state run long and deep.

Because of visionary leadership of those early pioneers and the sacrificial service of all those who followed, the United Methodist church stands proud and strong in a state where Methodism opened the doors for expansion and growth.

(Mitchell, Paul D. *From Teepees to Towers, A History of the Methodist Church in Oklahoma.*)

Above: Methodist Missionary Conference in 1937

Left: Historical Browning - Winfield Methodist Family

Below, left: Historical First Methodist Church of Oklahoma

Below, right: Woman's Society of Christian Service, Oklahoma Conference, Executive Committee, 1955

soaring bronze Gates of Time—marked with 9:01 on the east and 9:03 on the west—flanking a shallow reflecting pool. But most touching are the 168 bronze and glass chairs, each with the name of a victim, placed on the very spot the bomb exploded. At night, lights make the empty chairs glow hauntingly.

But the star of the memorial is the Survivor Tree, an American elm more than ninety years old that not only survived the city being constructed around it through the years, but the two-ton explosion that leveled the building just across the street. Although the blast shredded the tree's leaves, stripped it of its branches and embedded pieces of debris in the bark, the tree refused to die and a year later had new buds on its remaining branches.

The tree has become the symbol of Oklahoma's spirit and resilience. Each year, seeds are collected by the memorial staff and planted. Seedlings from the Survivor Tree are for sale and now grow all over the world.

Next to the memorial, in the remains of the building that housed the *Journal Record* newspaper, the Oklahoma City National Museum opened a year after the memorial. The museum takes visitors chronologically through the events of April 19, 1995, as well as the days, weeks, and years that followed. Multimedia exhibits follow rescue workers, survivors, and their loved ones through their emotional journey.

Eyewitness accounts and more than 800,000 artifacts and documents describe the historic event and what followed. Although the horror of that awful day is graphically depicted, visitors leave the museum with a feeling of hope and with a true appreciation of the Oklahoma Standard, that phrase rescuers and others throughout the world use to describe how Oklahomans responded to the tragedy, selflessly helping and donating and remembering.

Oklahomans will always remember April 19, and so will visitors to the memorial and museum, who will see this mission statement there: *We come here to remember those who were killed, those who survived and those changed forever. May all who leave here know the impact of violence. May this memorial offer comfort, strength, peace, hope and serenity.*

Appetizers

Honeysuckle Rose Gardens

STUFFED CHEESE MUSHROOMS

24 fresh mushrooms, stems removed

1 10-oz. pkg. frozen spinach, chopped

2 oz. cream cheese

4 oz. feta cheese

¼ c. finely chopped green onion

½ tsp. salt

½ tsp. pepper

1 c. fresh grated Parmesan cheese

Wipe the mushroom caps with a damp paper towel. Thaw spinach in a colander; squeeze out as much moisture as possible. In a mixing bowl, combine all ingredients except mushrooms and Parmesan. Mix well. Fill mushroom caps with mixture and place on a cookie sheet. Sprinkle Parmesan cheese on top. Bake for 15–20 minutes. Serve warm.

Linda Praytor

CHEESE SPREAD WITH STRAWBERRY PRESERVES

2 16-oz. pkg. sharp
cheddar cheese*
2 10-oz. pkg. mild
cheddar cheese*
1 medium white onion,
finely chopped
1 bunch green onions, finely chopped
½ tsp. cayenne pepper
1 c. mayonnaise
½ c. chopped pecans, finely buttered

Grate the cheese and place in a large bowl. Finely chop the onions and add to the cheese. Add cayenne pepper and mayonnaise. Stir together or mix together with hands until it forms a ball. It may be necessary to add more mayonnaise to hold together. Butter a large mold and sprinkle with chopped pecans. Spread the pecans around the surface to coat the mold. Press in the cheese mixture and refrigerate overnight. To unmold, dip into hot water for a few seconds and turn upside down on a platter. Fill the center with strawberry preserves and serve with buttery crackers. Apricot preserves may be used in place of the strawberry preserves.

*It is important to grate the cheese instead of buying shredded cheese. Shredded cheese has a coating of corn starch on it to keep it from clumping together, therefore, it will not adhere in a ring or ball.

Linda Praytor

115

CRAB CAKES

Combine: 1 lb. crabmeat and 1 c. fresh breadcrumbs.

Pour ⅓ c. milk over mixture.

Jennifer Freed's Crab Cakes

Add:

¼ c. mayonnaise

1 egg, beaten

2 Tbsp. butter, softened

2 Tbsp. chopped green onion

2 Tbsp. chopped jalapenos

2 Tbsp. frozen corn kernels

2 Tbsp. finely chopped parsley

½ tsp. baking powder

½ tsp. salt

¼ tsp. pepper

2 Tbsp. vegetable oil

Make patties; roll in breadcrumbs. Bake on cookie sheet at 450 for 10 minutes, turn, and then bake at 350 for approximately 14 minutes. The patties can be made large for entree or smaller for appetizers.

Tartar Sauce:

1 c. mayonnaise

1 small white onion

½ tsp. dijon mustard

1 sour kosher dill, chopped

1 Tbsp. chopped jalapenos

1Tbsp. fresh dill

1 Tbsp. parsley

pinch of tarragon

dash of hot sauce

CRAB DIP

1 lb. crabmeat from the refrigerator section (not fresh or canned)
2 cloves garlic
4 green onions
pinch of curry
mayonnaise to bind

Put crabmeat, garlic, and green onions in food processor and mix. Remove to a bowl; add the curry and enough mayonnaise to bind together. (Don't overdo the mayo.) Serve with crackers.

Jennifer Freed

GOAT CHEESE GRAPES

3 ½ oz. goat cheese
1 4-oz. pkg. cream cheese
2–3 Tbsp. finely chopped parsley
½ tsp. salt
½ tsp. pepper

Mix all of the above ingredients. Wrap around dried, washed red and green seedless grapes. Roll in finely chopped pecans or walnuts.

Amy Mainord

PRAWNS GRAND MARNIER

Jumbo prawns dipped in egg whites and lightly battered in corn starch

(Actually sprinkling corn starch on prawns)

Deep fry to a golden color

Reserve for sauce.

Sparkling Sauce:
Mayonnaise base
Add fresh lemon juice and fresh orange juice (Judge proportions on amount of sauce required and not too soupy)
Dash pineapple juice
Salt and pepper

Mix and adjust for tartness. Whip sauce. Add Grand Marnier to taste.

Heat pan with a little olive oil. Add prawns and sauce. Toss until sauce is warm.

From Amy Mainord's friend, the late Al Mass, owner of the famous Shanghai '44 restaurant in New York City

Senior Vice President of Communications and Public Relations for Express Personnel Services. As corporate spokesperson, Linda oversees corporate communications and media relations for nearly 600 Express franchises worldwide.

CAVIAR POTATOES

7 small new potatoes
1 8-oz. pkg. sour cream
1 ½ Tbsp. black caviar
1 ½ Tbsp. gold or red caviar

Cover potatoes in water and boil for 15 minutes or just until tender. Remove, drain, and chill. Slice potatoes crosswise into ¼-inch slices. Place slices on serving platter. Top each slice with 1 tsp. sour cream and ¼ tsp. caviar. Makes 3 dozen.

Amy Mainord

CRANBERRY SALSA

1 lb. cranberries, washed
½ to ¾ fresh jalapeno, washed and seeded
1 c. sugar
1 medium orange, halved and cut into slices
2 Tbsp. Grand Marnier

Freeze cranberries, orange slices, and jalapeno. In food processor, combine all of the above and pulse until mixture is like salsa. Transfer to bowl, add sugar and Grand Marnier. Cover and chill at least 24 hours.

Amy Mainord

BLEU CHEESE MEATBALLS

½ lb. lean ground meat
½ c. breadcrumbs
½ c. crumbled bleu cheese
1 egg
½ tsp. salt
1 lb. thin sliced bacon, cut in thirds

Mix above ingredients, except bacon. Roll into 1-inch round balls and wrap in bacon. Fasten with toothpick. Bake at 400 for 25–30 minutes. Recipe can easily be doubled or tripled for larger crowds.

Amy Mainord

HIDDEN VALLEY RANCH SAUSAGE STARS

1 lb. sausage, cooked and crumbled
1 ½ c. grated sharp cheddar cheese
1 ½ c. grated Monterey Jack cheese
1 c. prepared Hidden Valley Ranch Dressing
1 2¼-oz. can sliced black olives
½ c. chopped red pepper or green chilies
1 pkg. fresh or frozen wonton wrappers or egg roll wrappers, cut into fourths
cooking spray

Preheat oven to 350. Blot sausage dry with paper towels and combine with cheese, salad dressing, olives, and peppers. Lightly grease a muffin tin and press one wonton wrapper in each cup. Spray with cooking spray. Bake 5 minutes, until golden. Remove from the tins, place on cookie sheet. Fill with sausage mixture and bake 5 minutes until bubbly. Can be frozen before final baking. Makes 4–5 dozen.

Nancy Norman LeVesque

FETTEL'S FANCY

1 c. grated cheddar cheese
1 c. frozen onions
¾ -1 c. mayonnaise

Mix ingredients together and bake in greased casserole dish in 350 degree oven for 30 minutes. Serve with tortilla chips and good homemade salsa.

Nancy Norman Le Vesque

BLACK BEAN SALSA

1 bunch green onions, chopped
2 cans black beans, drained and rinsed
1 large pkg. frozen corn
3–4 tomatoes, diced
½ bunch cilantro, chopped
¼ tsp. cumin
½ tsp. pepper
juice of 2 limes
1 Tbsp. chopped jalapeno

Combine all of the above ingredients and chill before serving.

Amy Mainord

CHEESE WAFERS

4 c. grated sharp cheddar cheese
4 sticks margarine, softened
4 c. flour
4 c. rice krispies
¼ or ½ tsp. red crushed pepper (optional)

Stir ingredients together. Place in a 9x13 pan. Bake at 350 for 20 minutes. Cut and serve.

Penny Stobaugh Hague

CHEESE OLIVES

2 jars, stuffed Spanish olives
½ tsp. salt
½ tsp. paprika
1 c. sifted flour
2 c. grated sharp cheddar cheese
1 stick butter

Drain olives well on paper towels. Blend butter and cheese with paprika and salt. Add flour. Wrap about 1 tsp. dough around each olive. Place on cookie sheet. Refrigerate at least 4–5 hours before baking. Bake in 400 degree oven for 10–15 minutes. Serve warm. These are a very popular finger food at a party, but be sure to make plenty—they go fast.

Jennifer Freed

SPINACH SQUARES

4 eggs
⅔ c. milk
¼ c. melted butter
½ c. onion, minced
2 Tbsp. parley flakes
1 tsp. Worcestershire
1 ½ tsp. salt
½ tsp. thyme
½ tsp. nutmeg
2 10-oz. pkg. frozen, chopped spinach, cooked and drained*
2 c. cooked rice
2 c. shredded cheese (American, Cheddar, or other)

Beat eggs, add next eight ingredients. Combine spinach, rice, and cheese. Add to egg mixture, mixing well. Pour into greased, shallow 2-quart baking dish. Bake at 350 for 40–45 minutes. Cut into squares. Makes 8–10 servings.

*I use a 16-oz. bag of frozen, chopped spinach and cook it for just about 4 or 5 minutes. Then I drain it really well in a colander.

Jane Lodes

PESTO

2 c. fresh basil leaves, washed and sorted (dry in a tea towel or on a rack) *
4 medium-sized garlic cloves, chopped
1 c. walnuts or a mixture of walnuts and pinon (toasted)
1 c. extra virgin olive oil
1 c. freshly grated Parmesan cheese
Salt and pepper to taste

Process the basil, garlic, and nuts in a food processor fitted with a steel blade–or in 2 batches in a blender—until finely chopped. With the machine running, pour the oil in a thin, steady stream. Add the cheeses, a big pinch of salt, and a liberal grinding of pepper. Process briefly to combine. Remove to a bowl and cover until ready to use. Refrigerate any remaining pesto. Makes 2 cups.

*It's a lot of fun to grow fresh basil to make Pesto. If you grow the plants in the ground rather than in pots, be sure to harvest the tender leaves before the first frost.

I've had good success freezing the Pesto in freezer containers or bags. Omit the cheese until you're ready to serve. Probably not as good as having it fresh but it's nice to have in the winter.

CHILE ROASTED PECANS

½ c. olive oil

⅛ c. Kahlua liqueur

¼ c. Chimayo red chile powder

⅛ c. sugar

1 Tbsp. salt

3 c. whole pecans, shelled

Preheat the oven to 300. In a medium bowl place the olive oil, Kahlua, red chile powder, sugar, and salt. Mix the ingredients together. Add the pecans and toss them so that they are well coated with the mixture. Spread the pecans on a flat sheet. Bake them for 20–30 minutes, or until they are crispy (*stir frequently*). Makes approximately 3 cups.

Jane Lodes

Mexican Fudge

1 pkg. grated Colby longhorn cheese
1 can El Paso whole chilies, split lengthwise
3 eggs
1 tsp. Worcestershire
½ tsp. Tabasco
½ tsp. mustard

Grease an 8x8 pan with oleo. Place chilies on bottom of pan. In a bowl, beat eggs; add cheese, Worcestershire, Tabasco and mustard. Pour over the chilies. Sprinkle with paprika. Bake in a 350 degree oven for 35–40 minutes. Cool. Cut into bite-sized squares. Serve with toothpicks.

Sherry Claybrook

Broccoli Puffs

2 c. chopped broccoli
2 eggs, separated
1 Tbsp. flour
3 tsp. nutmeg
½ - ¾ c. mayonnaise
1 Tbsp. margarine
½ tsp. salt
2 - 2 ¾ c. grated Parmesan cheese

Cook broccoli in lightly salted water until tender. Drain well. Beat egg yolks; fold in flour and mix. Stir in nutmeg, mayonnaise, margarine, salt, and grated cheese. Add broccoli and mix lightly. Beat egg whites until stiff. Fold into broccoli mixture. Pour into lightly-greased 8x8 dish and bake for 30–45 minutes at 375. Top should be a light golden brown. This dish is great as cold or hot hors d'oeuvres, or as a warm side dish to any meal. Even if you don't like broccoli, I guarantee you'll like this dish. Broccoli is rich in vitamin C and A, which makes this nutritious.

Ronnye Sharp

BACON STUFFED MUSHROOMS

10 bacon slices
¾ c. mayonnaise
½ c. chopped onion
seasoned salt to taste
1 ½ c. grated sharp cheddar cheese
3 pt. fresh mushrooms

Fry bacon, drain and crumble. Blend with mayonnaise, onion, cheese, and seasoned salt. Fill mushroom caps with cheese mixture and place on baking dish. Cover and bake at 325 for 20 minutes or until cheese bubbles.

Karen and Chuck Mills

KAREN'S SHRIMP DIP

¼ c. chopped green onions
2 Tbsp. lemon juice
2 drops Tabasco
¼ tsp. dill weed
8 oz. fresh shrimp
1 8-oz. pkg. cream cheese
½ c. real mayonnaise
½ c. sour cream
½ c. chopped parsley
½ c. chopped celery
1 pkg. gelatin

Heat one can of cream of mushroom soup, add package of plain gelatin dissolved in 3 Tbsp. water. Cook 5 minutes. Mix other ingredients and pour into a mold. Let mold set up and serve with crackers.

Karen and Chuck Mills

HOT PRETZEL SNACK

1 large bag of pretzels
¾ c. olive oil
1 Tbsp. cayenne pepper
1 Tbsp. garlic powder
1 Tbsp. lemon pepper

Mix all of the above together and store in airtight container or Ziploc bags. This is great to take to ballgames and usually gets hotter the longer it sets.

Karen and Chuck Mills

SHRIMP MOUSSE

1 8-oz. pkg. cream cheese, softened
1 can cream of mushroom soup or ½ can tomato soup and ½ can cream of mushroom
1 pkg. Knox gelatin
¼ c. water
½ c. chopped celery
⅓ c. chopped onion
1 c. Hellmann's mayonnaise
2 4½-oz. cans shrimp, drained and rinsed
1 tsp. cayenne pepper

In a saucepan, mix soup (or soups), a little at a time, into the softened cream cheese. Heat. Soften gelatin in water and then add to cream cheese mixture until it dissolves, as you continue to heat. Remove from heat; add celery, onion, mayonnaise, and shrimp. Chill in 1 ½-quart oiled (Pam) mold. Refrigerate until ready to serve. Remove to plate. Good with wheat thins.

Mike Jones

New Orleans Bar-B-Que Shrimp

1 ½ lb. shrimp

3 slices bacon

½ lb. butter

2 Tbsp. Dijon mustard

1 ½ tsp. chili powder

¼ tsp. basil

¼ tsp. thyme

1 tsp. black pepper

½ tsp. oregano

2 cloves garlic, crushed

2 Tbsp. Old Bay Seasoning or Rex Crab boil

½ tsp. Tabasco

Dash of cayenne

Preheat oven to 375.

In small pan, fry bacon until clear; add the butter and all other ingredients, except shrimp. Simmer for 5 minutes. Place shrimp in open baking dish and pour sauce over the top. Stir to coat the shrimp. Bake, uncovered, for 20 minutes, stirring three times.

Rodney and Jennifer Freed

Honey Hot Chicken Wings

1 c. salsa or picante sauce

¼ c. honey

½ tsp. ground ginger

1 ½ lb. chicken wing pieces

Stir together the first 3 ingredients in a large bowl. Add wing pieces, tossing to coat. Place on aluminum foil-lined jelly roll pan. Spray aluminum foil with Pam. Bake at 400 for 35 minutes or until done, turning once.

Wes Mainord

Oklahoma Heroes
and Heroines

by Judge Robert Henry

Ralph Waldo Emerson, perhaps our greatest American essayist, echoes the thoughts of his British colleagues, Carlyle and Macaulay, when he notes that "all history is biography." And Oklahoma's unique history, wherein, as historian Angie Debo noted, "all the American traits have been intensified" is also essentially biography. Some might say of our interesting forebears that "it's the water," but we haven't always had that much water; 2007 is the exception rather than the rule. I have to conclude that it is more likely that it is Oklahoma cooking that nurtured as remarkable a set of pioneer leaders as one can encounter in American history. So, a book in our centennial honoring the various bills of fare that have produced the subjects of our historical biographies is timely and important.

You learn a lot about a state by looking at those great figures—the subjects of its biographies—that it chooses to honor, both in particular and as archetypes. A picture being worth at least a thousand words, perhaps the best way to get an understanding of Oklahoma history through a biography of its favorite sons and daughters is to tour our remarkable state capitol, especially the rotunda on the fourth floor. That celestial place honors some or our heroes and heroines explicitly, and others by analogy and general reference.

A great place to begin a rotunda tour is in front of perhaps the best non-professional cook of the distinguished lot. I am thinking, of course, of a portrait by the legendary Charles Banks Wilson of our state's greatest historian whom I quoted earlier, Dr. Angie Debo. Hers is the first portrait of a woman to adorn our state's capitol. Debo was the calmest and most refined firebrand in our state's heated and concentrated history. Here is the woman who was denied an academic position in any Oklahoma college or university, despite degrees from the Universities of Chicago and Oklahoma; and a woman who, without academic support, became the nation's leading scholar of things Native American, and a person who exposed the corruption of sitting political leaders with a courage that would dwarf that of most men of her time. She was above all a teacher. A prominent Methodist lay person, when the war caused the local pulpit to have vacancies, she filled the part. She constantly encouraged students to excel, often dropping off a loaf of her date nut bread to punctuate the lesson. Her baker's dozen of books are all classics, including the best single book ever written about the Sooner State, *Oklahoma: Footloose and Fancy-Free.* By the way, she made a mean date nut bread, too; see her recipe below.

After Angie, moving counterclockwise we come to the portrait of Carl Albert, the Little Giant from Little Dixie, a Rhodes Scholar from Bug Tussell, Oklahoma, who became the Speaker of the United States House of Representatives, and who provided great stability through the crisis of President Nixon's fall and resignation. The Speaker, as we all called him, used to laugh while telling the story of the young lad who came up to speak to him after a talk he gave at a small country school. The boy told him, "Mister, that speech sure was inspiring." The Speaker, wanting to remember the inspiring phraseology for the future, asked what he had said that had moved him. The boy answered, "It wasn't anything you said. It was watching you. I was thinking if a little shrimp like you can grow up to be a congressman, I can grow up to be president of the United States." The Speaker would always say, "In this country with that attitude, he can do it." Carl Albert's food preferences included the simple home-cooking of Pittsburg County, but he could often be seen in Krebs, Oklahoma, at one of the several famed Italian restaurants located there to serve the miners, many of whom came from Italy.

Continuing our cycle, the next portrait we confront—and that is a good word to describe meeting this legend—is that of Robert S. Kerr, the co-founder of our mighty Kerr McGee Corporation, the digger of the great ditch that became the Arkansas River project, a legendary intellect, an innovative cattleman, and the "uncrowned King of the United States Senate." Now I am not sure that all readers will get this bit of outhouse humor, but there are many uses for parents and especially grandparents, and explanation is one of them (ask them). Once in introducing Senator Kerr, the witty Irvin S. Cobb sought to roast him, but the opposite occurred. Cobb said, in his Kentucky accent, "I'm from Kentucky, the home of thoroughbred women, and thoroughbred horses, and thoroughbred dogs, and where I'm from we culled all the *curs,*" seeking to use the poet's word for dogs as a pun. In rising to speak and answer, Senator Kerr revealed his legendary rapier wit: "Well, I'm not from Kentucky, but from Ada, Oklahoma, and I don't know anything

7 c. unbleached, all-purpose flour (I prefer 6 c. of unbleached all
purpose flour and 1 c. of gluten flour.)
4 Tbsp. extra virgin olive oil (plus extra oil to oil bowl and pans)
2 tsp. salt

Topping:
4 Tbsp. fine olive oil
4 Tbsp. coarsely minced fresh rosemary leaves (or re-constituted dried rosemary)
2 scant tsp. coarse sea salt or 2–3 tsp. kosher salt
handful of seeded and halved black olives (optional)

Prepare a "sponge" by mixing 1 cup of very warm potato water with 1 tsp. sugar, and the yeast. Add 1 cup of the all-purpose, unbleached flour. (A food processor or commercial type mixer works well for this.) Add a little more potato water if necessary. Cover with wrap and let the yeast work for about 20–25 minutes. Boil the potato in the skin until tender (about 25 minutes). Save the water. Peel and rice or coarsely grate the potato so as to have about a generous 2 ½ cups.

After the sponge has worked for the above time, mix in the potato and other ingredients, using the paddle until the dough forms a ball, and then the dough hook to continue kneading until the dough is smooth and elastic, which usually takes about 5 minutes. (Food processor is faster.) Coat with oil, and put in oiled bowl to rise until doubled in bulk. Wet hands to avoid sticking, and press dough flat into well-oiled jelly roll pans or sheet cake pans. Cover dough with oiled baking sheet and allow to do its second rising, about 45 minutes.

Preheat oven to 425. When bread has completed its second rise, dimple the dough with tow fingers at regular intervals. Drizzle with olive oil, sprinkle with rosemary, and then Kosher salt. If you like, push the olives into the dimples. Bake 23–25 minutes until the bottom is golden brown and crisp. It holds for several hours with just reheating. It freezes well for a month or so.

Sacred Heart Bakery
Building—Oldest building in
the state

Breads *and* Brunch

CATTLEMEN'S FAMOUS ROLLS

13 oz. milk**
1 egg
2 ½ oz. sugar
3 ¾ c. flour
2 oz. salad oil
2 tsp. salt
1 ¾ oz. yeast (wet)

*Dick Stubbs, owner
Cattlemen's Steakhouse*

Put yeast in mixer and let break up on low speed with wire whip. Add oil and blend until smooth. Add eggs and sugar. Mix on speed #2 until creamy. Remove whip and attach dough hook. Add milk and mix well on low speed. Add flour, then salt. Mix on low speed until flour is wet and blended. Put on speed #2. Let mix until dough has pulled away from bowl. Remove dough from mixing bowl and place in larger bowl to rise. Place in warm (not hot!) area with light towel on top. Allow dough to rise (double in volume). Punch down air out of dough until it's flat again. Allow dough to rise a second time. Roll/cut dough into proper sizes. When dough is placed in cooking vessel**, allow to rise for third time. When dough has doubled in size, place in conventional oven at 350 for about 20 minutes on center oven rack or until light golden brown. **Dough can be placed into dinner roll pans at about 2 ½ oz. or can be rolled out and topped with sugar, cinnamon, brown sugar, and nutmeg for cinnamon rolls. Makes 2 dozen.

Rosemary Focaccia

3 c. bread flour
2 tsp. salt
1 Tbsp. sugar
1 pkg. yeast
1 ⅓ c. warm water
3 Tbsp. vegetable oil
2 Tbsp. Parmesan cheese
2 Tbsp. dried rosemary
(Italian seasoning can be used)

Mix flour, salt, sugar, yeast, water, and 2 Tbsp. oil. Mix dough until pliable. Knead dough on floured surface until smooth. Place dough in oiled bowl. Cover. Let rise until doubled for about 45 minutes. Coat baking sheet with oil and gently press the dough out to about ½-inch thickness. Brush remaining oil over the top of the dough. Make dimples in the dough. Sprinkle rosemary and cheese on top. Let rise until doubled, about 20 minutes. Bake for 25 minutes in 375 degree oven.

Amber Parsons

Georgia Welborn's Dilly Bread

1 pkg. yeast
1 egg, unbeaten
¼ c. warm water
2 ½ c. flour
2 c. cottage cheese, heated until warm
1 Tbsp. butter
2 tsp. dill seed
2 Tbsp. sugar
1 Tbsp. onion salt
2 tsp. caraway seed
¼ tsp. soda

Soften yeast in water. Combine sugar, onion salt, dill and caraway seeds, butter, soda, and egg. Add yeast and mix well. Add flour and mix well. Put in ungreased loaf pans and let rise. Bake at 350 until brown. Take out of oven and put butter and salt on top of loaf.

Georgia Welborn

POPPY SEED MUFFINS

3 c. flour

1 ½ tsp. baking powder

3 eggs

1 ½ tsp. vanilla

1 ½ tsp. butter flavoring

2–3 Tbsp. poppy seeds

1 ½ tsp. salt

2 c. sugar

1 ½ c. milk

3 tsp. almond flavoring

1 c. oil

Mix above ingredients in order. Beat 2 minutes. Fill 24 greased muffin cups, ¾ full, and bake at 350 about 30 minutes, until browned lightly and toothpick stuck in center comes out clean. These are delicious and store well.

Doris Novotny

CHEESE AND ONION BREAD

1 Tbsp. vegetable oil

¾ c. finely diced white onion

½ c. milk

1 egg

1 ½ c. biscuit mix

1 c. shredded cheddar cheese (save ½ c. for topping)
½ tsp. onion salt
2 Tbsp. butter, melted
1 Tbsp. chives
extra butter

Preheat oven to 400. Heat the oil and sauté onions. Mix egg, milk, salt, butter, and biscuit mix with sautéed onions. Add cheese and stir loosely. Spoon the mixture onto baking sheet with ice cream scoop. Sprinkle with remaining cheese and chives. Bake until brown.

Linda Praytor

PUMPKIN NUT BREAD

2 c. flour
2 tsp. baking powder
½ tsp. soda
1 tsp. salt
1 tsp. cinnamon
½ tsp. nutmeg
1 c. Libby's solid pack pumpkin
1 c. sugar
½ c. milk
2 eggs
¼ c. butter, softened
1 c. chopped pecans

Sift together first 6 ingredients. Combine pumpkin, sugar, milk, and eggs in mixing bowl. Add dry ingredients and butter and mix well until blended. Stir in nuts. Spread in well-greased loaf pan. Bake at 350 for 45–55 minutes or until toothpick inserted in center comes out clean.

Note: For 2 loaves, use 1 can (#303) Libby's pumpkin and double remaining ingredients.

Doris Novotny

NO BETTER BANANA BREAD

2 c. all-purpose flour
1 ½ tsp. baking soda
½ tsp. salt
4 overripe bananas
1 c. sugar
¾ c. butter, melted
2 large eggs
1 tsp. pure vanilla
½ c. pecans
powdered sugar for dusting

Preheat oven to 350. Grease a 9x5 loaf pan. Mix dry ingredients together. Mash 2 of the bananas with a fork. Whip the remaining 2 bananas with the dry mixture for 3 minutes until light and fluffy. Add the butter, eggs, and vanilla. Beat together. Add pecans. Bake for 1 hour and 15 minutes. Cool. Before serving, slice, toast, and dust with powdered sugar.

Linda Praytor

APRICOT PECAN PULL-APARTS

¾ c. chopped pecans
⅔ c. firmly packed brown sugar
½ c. chopped dried apricots
½ c. butter, melted
½ c. sour cream
1 tsp. maple flavoring
2 cans Hungry Jack refrigerated buttermilk biscuits

Grease Bundt pan. In large bowl, combine all ingredients except the biscuits; mix well. Separate dough into biscuits. Cut each biscuit into 4 pieces; place in bowl with pecan mixture. Toss gently to coat. Spoon biscuit mixture into greased pan. Bake at 350 for

30–40 minutes, or until deep golden brown. Immediately invert pan onto serving plate and cool for 10 minutes. Serve warm.

Amy Mainord

APRICOT MUFFINS

1 c. chopped dried apricots
1 c. boiling water
1 c. sugar
1 c. sour cream
½ c. butter or margarine
2 c. flour
1 tsp. baking soda
1 Tbsp. orange peel (zest)
½ c. chopped pecans

Soak apricots in boiling water for 5 minutes. Cream together the sugar and butter until fluffy. Add sour cream and mix well. Combine dry ingredients and stir into cream mixture until moistened. Drain apricots, discard liquid. Fold in apricots and nuts. Fill paper-lined muffin cups ¾ full. Bake in 400 degree oven for 18–20 minutes.

Glaze:
½ c. powdered sugar
½ tsp. butter or margarine
1 Tbsp. orange juice

Combine until smooth and can add a little grated orange zest. Spread on muffins.

Deborah Nickell

ANGEL BISCUITS

1 pkg. dry yeast

1 tsp. salt

2 Tbsp. lukewarm water

4 Tbsp. sugar

5–5 ½ c. sifted flour

1 c. shortening

3 tsp. baking powder

2 c. buttermilk

1 tsp. soda

Dissolve yeast in lukewarm water. Sift together dry ingredients; cut in shortening. Add yeast and buttermilk to dry mixture. Knead dough until it holds together; roll dough to ½-¾ -inch thickness. Cut with biscuit cutter and place on a baking sheet or in a baking pan. Bake in a 400 degree oven 15–20 minutes. Dough may be refrigerated or frozen for later use. Makes 2½ dozen.

Jane Lodes

CHRISTMAS SURPRISE ROLLS

1 8-oz. can Pillsbury crescent rolls
8 large marshmallows
butter or margarine
sugar
ground cinnamon
paper cupcake holders

Unroll dough; separate into eight triangles. Place one pat of butter in the center of each triangle. Then sprinkle ground cinnamon and sugar to taste. At this point, place one large marshmallow in the center of roll and begin to wrap roll around marshmallow, forming a ball, leaving no places uncovered. Place each roll in paper cupcake holder and put in muffin pans. Bake at 375 for 11–13 minutes or until golden brown. Serve warm. Happy Holidays!

Ronnye Perry Sharp

STRAWBERRY BREAD

1 c. margarine
1 ½ c. sugar
1 tsp. vanilla
¼ tsp. lemon juice
4 eggs
3 c. flour
¾ tsp. cream of tartar
½ tsp. soda
1 c. strawberry jam or preserves
½ c. sour cream

Cream margarine and sugar. Add vanilla and lemon juice. Add eggs, one at a time, beating well after each egg. Sift together dry ingredients. Add to other mixture, alternating with combined jam and sour cream. If desired, you may add ½ cup chopped nuts. Bake in 2 large or 4 small greased and floured loaf pans at 325 for about 50 minutes or until done.

Jennifer Freed

BEER BREAD

1 can Bud Light
3 c. self-rising flour
1 c. sugar

Preheat oven to 350. Mix all of the above together. Put into greased loaf pan. Bake for about 1 hour. Check with toothpick.

Amber Parsons

MOM'S MELTABLE ROLLS

2 ¼-oz. pkg. active yeast
¾ c. warm water
½ c. white sugar
1 tsp. salt
2 eggs
½ c. shortening
4 c. all-purpose flour
¼ c. butter, softened

Dissolve yeast in warm water. Stir in sugar, salt, eggs, shortening, and 2 cups of flour. Beat until smooth. Mix in remaining flour until smooth. Scrape dough from side of bowl. Knead dough, then cover it and let rise in a warm place until double (about 1½ hours). Punch down dough. Divide in half. Roll each half into a 12-inch circle. Spread with butter. Cut into 10–15 wedges. Roll up the wedges starting with the wide end. Place rolls with point under on a creased baking sheet. Cover and let rise until double (about 1 hour). Bake at 400 for 12–15 minutes or until golden brown. Brush tops with butter and enjoy!

Special Instructions: Do not serve butter with these rolls. They are incredibly buttery and will melt in your mouth at first bite. Just like Lay's, "Bet you can't each just one!!!"

From my mom, Kathleen Kelly Tenborg's, kitchen. Respectfully submitted with love and the greatest of memories,

Linda Haneborg

Mini Muffins

1 c. brown sugar
½ c. flour
2 eggs, beaten
1 c. walnuts or any nuts
⅔ c. butter

Mix together and put in mini muffin tin and cook 350 for 20 minutes.

Jody O'Rorke

Mock Danish Rolls

2 pkg. crescent rolls
2 pkg. cream cheese
1 egg
1 c. sugar
1 tsp. vanilla

Press 1 package crescent rolls in bottom of 9x13 pan. Beat together the cream cheese, egg, sugar, and vanilla. Spread cream cheese mixture over rolls. Place the second package of crescent rolls on top. Sprinkle with cinnamon and sugar mixture. Bake in 350 degree oven for 20–25 minutes.

Cora Gray

BANANA NUT BREAD

3 bananas, mashed
½ c. butter
1 c. sugar (½ white, ½ brown)
2 eggs
1 c. flour
1 c. whole-wheat flour
1 tsp. soda
½ c. chopped nuts
2 tsp. rum flavoring or dark rum

Whip bananas until light. Cream butter and sugars; gradually add eggs, one at a time, beating. Sift flour and soda together. Add to sugar/egg mixture (careful to not overmix). Add bananas, nuts, rum; mix. Pour into well-greased and floured bread pan. Bake at 350 for 50 minutes.

Jane Lodes

SUNDAY FRENCH TOAST

8 slices French bread, ¾-inch thick
4 eggs
1 c. milk
2 Tbsp. orange juice
1 Tbsp. sugar
½ tsp. vanilla
¼ tsp. salt
2 Tbsp. margarine
Powdered sugar

Arrange bread in 12x8 inch pan. In medium bowl, beat eggs with milk, orange juice, sugar, vanilla and salt, until well blended. Pour over bread; turn slices to coat evenly.

Refrigerate, covered, overnight. In hot butter in skillet, sauté bread until golden brown, about 4 minutes on each side. Sprinkle with powdered sugar.

Deborah Nickell

CARAMEL-SOAKED FRENCH TOAST

1 ½ c. firmly packed brown sugar

¾ c. butter or margarine

¼ c. plus 2 Tbls. light corn syrup

10 (1 ¾ -inch thick) slices French bread

4 eggs, beaten

2 ½ c. half-and-half

1 Tbsp. vanilla extract

¼ tsp. salt

3 Tbsp. sugar

1 ½ tsp. ground cinnamon

¼ c. butter, melted

Combine first 3 ingredients in a medium saucepan: cook over medium heat, stirring constantly, 5 minutes or until mixture is bubbly. Pour syrup evenly into a lightly greased 9x13 baking dish. Arrange bread slices over syrup. Combine eggs, milk, vanilla, and salt: stir well. Gradually pour mixture over bread slices. Cover and chill at least 8 hours. Combine 3 Tbsp. sugar and cinnamon; stir well. Sprinkle evenly over soaked bread. Drizzle ¼ cup melted butter over bread. Bake uncovered, at 350 for 45–50 minutes or until golden and bubbly. Serve immediately. Makes 10 servings.

Honey Suckle Rose Gardens

SAUSAGE ROLL

1 loaf frozen white bread (thaw and let rise)

1 lb. hot sausage

½ lb. mild sausage

sliced sandwich ham

½ c. chopped mushrooms

½ c. chopped bell pepper

½ c. chopped onion

shredded mozzarella cheese

shredded Colby Jack cheese

Brown sausage, sauté mushroom, bell pepper, and onion. Mix together and drain grease onto paper towel. Roll out bread. Pile on ingredients. Seal and brush top with butter. Bake at 350 until brown, about 20–25 minutes.

Gaye Etheridge

Cornmeal Biscuits with Sage Butter

1 ½ c. all-purpose flour

½ c. yellow cornmeal

2 tsp. baking powder

½ tsp. baking soda

¼ tsp. salt

⅓ c. cold butter, cut into pieces

⅔ c. buttermilk

⅓ c. sour cream

Stir together first 5 ingredients in a large bowl. Cut butter into flour mixture with pastry blender until crumbly; add buttermilk and sour cream, stirring just until dry ingredients are moistened. Turn dough out onto a lightly floured surface; knead 4–5 times. Roll dough to 3/4 -inch thickness; cut with biscuit cutter, or any cutter you desire, and place on a lightly greased baking sheet. Bake at 425 for 10–12 minutes. Serve with Sage Butter.

Sage Butter:

½ c. butter, softened

1 ½ Tbsp. chopped fresh sage, or ½ Tbsp. dried sage

Beat butter with a wooden spoon until creamy; stir in sage. Cover and chill.

Linda Praytor

PEAR PRESERVES

3 qt. pears, peeled and cut into small pieces
3 c. water
4 ½ c. sugar
¼ tsp. instant lemon or 3 Tbsp. lemon juice

Parboil pears with about 2 cups water until tender, stirring occasionally (approximately 20–30 minutes). Drain and use liquid as part of 3 cups water. Add the sugar to water and boil 5 minutes to make syrup. Cool about 10 minutes and add pears carefully. Bring slowly to boil and boil rapidly until clear and syrup thickens. About 2 hours all together. It depends on ripeness of pears.

Doris Novotny

CHICKEN SPINACH MUSHROOM QUICHE

1 unbaked pie shell
5 oz. frozen, chopped spinach
2 drops Tabasco sauce
2 oz. mushroom pieces, drained
½ c. diced, cooked chicken
1 c. shredded Swiss cheese
2 Tbsp. flour
½ c. milk
2 eggs, beaten
1 ½ tsp. salt

Cook spinach as package directs. Drain excess water. Beat eggs, add milk, salt, Tabasco sauce, mushrooms, and drained spinach. Toss together chicken, cheese, and flour. Stir into egg mixture. Pour into pie crust. Bake at 400, on a cookie sheet, for 20–25 minutes until center puffs up slightly. Cool 10 minutes before serving.

Doris Novotny

QUICHE

1 unbaked pie crust
8 strips bacon, fried and crumbled
½ c. Swiss cheese, diced
¼ c. ham, diced
1 ½ c. half-and-half
4 eggs
¼ tsp. white pepper
¼ tsp. nutmeg
½ tsp. salt

Scatter bacon over bottom of pie shell. Sprinkle cheese and ham over bacon. Mix spices and eggs in bowl. Add cream and mix well. Bake at 350 for 30 minutes or until firm.

Doris Novotny

BAKED OMELET

10 eggs, beaten until light
½ c. flour
2 c. cottage cheese (small curd cream style)
½ stick butter, melted
½ tsp. salt
1 tsp. baking powder
1 lb. grated Monterey Jack or Mexican Cheese
2 4-oz. cans chopped green chilies

Mix together and pour into 9x13 buttered baking dish. Bake at 350 for 30–45 minutes or until it puffs up and lightly browns. Makes 6 servings.

Gary and Mary England

DAN'S CINNAMON ROLLS

There are two steps to making these great and decadent rolls. First, you have to make the Sweet Dough that will be used for the cinnamon rolls and then create the rolls themselves. So, let's get started.

Preparing the Sweet Dough:

1 c. sugar

1 tsp. salt

3 pkg. active dry yeast

8–9 c. all-purpose flour

2 c. whole milk

1 c. butter

2 eggs

Start by using a large bowl and combining the sugar, salt, yeast and 2 cups of flour. At the same time, in a 2-quart saucepan, heat the milk and the butter until very warm (from about 120–130 degrees). The butter does not have to melt. Then, with a mixer at *low* speed, gradually beat the liquid from the saucepan into the dry ingredients. After a minute or so, increase the mixer speed to *medium* and beat an additional 2 minutes more, occasionally stopping and scraping the bowl with a spoon or spatula. After the 2 minutes, beat in the eggs and 2 cups of flour for another 2 minutes or so. Don't forget to stop occasionally to scrape the bowl. After the 2 minutes are up, stir in enough flour (with a wooden spoon) to make a soft dough. Now, turn the dough onto a large, lightly-floured, wooden cutting board. Knead the dough until it is smooth and elastic, which should take about 10 minutes. Shape the dough into a ball. Grease a large mixing bowl with Crisco and then pour dough ball into the bowl. Flip the dough over once. Now, let the dough rise in a warm and dry place for about 1 hour; it should about double in size. Finally, after the hour is up and the dough has risen, punch down the dough with your fist in the middle. Then, cover the bowl and let the dough rest for about 15 minutes. You are now ready to proceed with the preparation of the cinnamon rolls themselves.

Preparing the Cinnamon Rolls:

Sweet dough (as prepared above)

¾ c. light brown sugar

1 tsp. ground cinnamon

2 sticks butter, freshly melted

½ c. chopped pecans (optional)

½ c. dark seedless raisins (optional)

While the dough is resting, you will need to grease two 9x13 baking pans. Then, in a small bowl, combine the brown sugar and cinnamon. If you plan to use the pecans and/or the raisins, add them in also. Set aside this mixture. Now, cut the roll in half and roll out the portion into an 18x12 rectangle. If it is shorter than 18," don't panic. Once the dough has been rolled out, pour half of the melted butter onto the dough. Brush the butter to spread it equally over the dough, making sure to brush the ends. Hand-sprinkle the sugar/cinnamon mixture onto the battered dough. Use your hand to spread the mixture to the edges of the dough. Now, starting at the 1-inch (long) side of the dough rectangle, roll the dough as tight as possible into a jelly-roll fashion. Pinch the end seam to seal the roll after rolling. With the roll seam-side down, cut the rolls into 1–1 ½-inch slices. Place them in one of the 9x13 pans and cover. Let them rise for about 40 minutes. While this first batch is rising, repeat the process with the other half of the dough roll. After the first set of rolls has completed its rising, preheat your oven to 400. Place on the center rack and bake for 25 minutes or until golden brown on top. Repeat the process for the next batch. You can cover the rolls with a sugar glaze made by mixing 2 cups of confectioners' sugar, ½ tsp. of vanilla extract, and about 3 Tbsp. water, until smooth. It is better to pour the glaze after the rolls have cooled slightly. You can separate the rolls easily by pulling them apart with a fork.

Enjoy!

Dan Overland

Gary and Mary England with Bobby Mercer

SAUSAGE CASSEROLE

1 lb. sausage, crumbled, fried, and drained (hot or mild)
8 eggs, beaten
2 c. milk
1 tsp. salt
1 tsp. dried mustard
6 slices of bread with crusts, cubed
1 c. grated sharp cheddar cheese

Combine breadcrumbs and sausage in the bottom of a 9x13 dish. Mix eggs, milk, and seasonings. Pour over bread and sausage mixture. Sprinkle cheese on top. Set in refrigerator overnight, or at least 12 hours. Bake 325 for 35–45 minutes. Let sit 10 minutes before serving.

Congresswoman with children, Price and Christina

Congresswoman Mary Fallin

SOUR CREAM COFFEE CAKE

2 sticks oleo
2 c. sugar
Cream well and then add:
2 eggs, beaten until light and fluffy

1 tsp. vanilla (pure)

Add the remaining ingredients alternately:

1 c. or ½ pt. sour cream

With the combined ingredients:

2 c. sifted flour

1 tsp. baking powder

1 tsp. salt

Grease but do not flour Bundt pan (Pam).

Topping:

½ c. brown sugar

2 tsp. ground cinnamon

1 c. chopped nuts

Put a third of topping in bottom of pan. Pour in half of the cake mixture. Add a third more of topping; pour in rest of cake mixture. Add the last of the topping. Batter will be stiff. Bake at 350, 55–60 minutes on lowest shelf of oven.

Ben and Marcia Robinson

PUMPKIN CREAM CHEESE MUFFINS

1 8-oz pkg. cream cheese (cheesecake flavored works well)

3 c. flour

2 c. sugar

4 tsp. pumpkin pie spice

1 tsp. cinnamon

1 tsp. ground cloves

1 tsp. nutmeg

1 tsp. baking soda

1 tsp. salt

pinch of cardamon (optional)

2 c. canned pumpkin (not pie filling)

1¼ c. vegetable oil

4 eggs, beaten

Put the entire tub or brick of cream cheese on a piece of aluminum foil and shape it into a long log; wrap in foil. Put it in the freezer while you mix and fill the pans, up to an hour. Preheat oven to 350. Line muffin tins with paper baking cups. Stir together the dry ingredients. Mix together the pumpkin, oil, and eggs. Stir into dry ingredients just until blended. Fill cups half full. Unwrap and cut cream cheese. If disks are too big around, cut thick slices and then cut them in half. Place 1–2 tsp. cream cheese in middle of each muffin and press down. Bake at 350 for 20–25 minutes. Do not eat until cool.

Dr. Scott Stewart and Robin Stewart

POTATO PANCAKES

5 Tbsp. flour

1 small onion

1 ½ tsp. salt

1 ½ lb. potatoes, peeled

1 egg, unbeaten

⅛ tsp. pepper

To prevent darkening, plan to cook and serve pancakes as soon as batter is made. Just before serving, measure flour into medium bowl. Using fine grater, grate potatoes and onion over flour. Quickly stir in unbeaten egg, salt, and pepper. Lightly grease heavy skillet; place over medium heat. Drop heaping tablespoonfuls of pancake mix into hot skillet. Fry until crisp and golden brown, turn and brown on other side. Drain on paper towels. Serve with apple sauce or mixed stewed fruit. Makes about 16 pancakes.

Doris Novotny

APPLE AND SAUSAGE QUICHE

1 unbaked 9-inch pastry shell

1 c. cooking apple, peeled and chopped

2 Tbsp. sugar

1 Tbsp. lemon juice

Dash of salt and pepper

¾ c. chopped onion

Pott County District Attorney Richard Smothermon and wife, Connie

3 Tbsp. butter, melted
½ lb. ground pork sausage*
4 large eggs, beaten
1 8-oz. pkg. sour cream
⅛ tsp. ground nutmeg
dash of ground red pepper
½ c. (2 oz.) shredded cheddar cheese

Fit pastry in a 9-inch quiche dish. Prick bottom and sides of pastry with a fork. Bake at 350 for 8–10 minutes; cool on a wire rack. Combine apple and next 3 ingredients; toss well. Cook apple mixture and onion in butter in a large skillet over medium-high heat, stirring constantly, until onion is tender. Remove from heat, and cool 20 minutes. Brown sausage in a large skillet, stirring until it crumbles; drain well. Combine eggs and next 3 ingredients in a large bowl. Add apple mixture and sausage to egg mixture; stir well. Pour mixture into prepared pastry shell. Gently stir in cheese. Bake, uncovered, at 350 for 35 minutes or until cheese melts and a knife inserted in center comes out clean. Let stand 10 minutes before serving. Makes 1 9-inch quiche.

*Use mild pork sausage for a tamer-flavored quiche. Try hot pork sausage to pump up the flavor.

Pottawatomie County D.A. Richard Smothermon

Oklahoma:
A New State Song

A New State Song

by Bob Burke

Any keen observer of the legislative process would not have expected controversy to erupt over George Nigh's introduction of a bill in 1953 to make the popular song "Oklahoma," from the Rodgers and Hammerstein Broadway musical of the same name, the official state song. [Nigh was a twenty-six-year-old member of the Oklahoma House of Representatives from McAlester.]

Several of the tunes from *Oklahoma!* had been among George's favorites since he listened to them on the *Lucky Strike Hit Parade* on radio on Saturday nights. He remembered the pride he felt in the summer of 1943, before his junior year in high school, when he first heard the popular songs about his home state. Oklahoma had become a household word because of the success of the Broadway play that debuted on March 31, 1943, at the St. James Theater in New York City.

Before 1953, the official state song was "Oklahoma (A Toast)," written in 1905 by Harriet Parker Camden. Among the words of the song were, "Oklahoma, fairest daughter of the West, Oklahoma, 'tis the land I love the best."

When George's bill appeared on the House calendar, Representative J.W. Huff of Ada stood firmly in opposition to the move. As tears streamed down his face, he said, "I can't believe what you're doing here today. You're going to change a song written by pioneers, steeped in tradition, couched in history. You're going to change it for a song written by two New York Jews who never have even been here and they say 'taters and 'termaters.'"

Huff left the microphone and walked among fellow members on the House floor as he sang the words of the old song. Everyone in the House chamber rose to their feet as Huff completed the final verse of the old song. George thought his song was going "down the toilet," but thought quickly of a way he could diminish the effect of the emotion. He approached the only microphone at the front podium and said, "Mr. Speaker, I ask unanimous consent to lay this bill over for one legislative day."

With George laying the bill over, Huff and other opponents of the new state song thought they had won. However, George left the House chamber and went to work. He called Ridge Bond, a fellow McAlesterite and the only Oklahoman to star in the Broadway version of *Oklahoma!* Bond, who sang the lead role of Curly, lived in Tulsa at that time. George asked Bond to come to the state capitol the following day, "prepared to sing."

Next, George called Ira Humphries, the House member from Chickasha, to invite the choir from the Oklahoma College for Women (OCW) to appear at the capitol the next day, "provided they know the tunes from *Oklahoma!*" Finally, George asked Jenkins Music Company in Oklahoma City to furnish a piano.

The following day George innocently asked unanimous consent to grant privileges to the floor for a special visitor, Bond, the Broadway star, and the OCW Choir. With the House gallery packed, the college choir performed majestically. They sang "Surrey with the Fringe on Top" and "Oh, What a Beautiful Morning." As the pianist began building a dramatic introduction to "Oklahoma," Bond, in his Curly costume, strode to the microphone and brought the house down.

After the rousing rendition of the song, the crowd, including of course the 200 friends and supporters strategically placed there by George, stood and shouted. George took the microphone from Bond and shouted above the melee, "Mr. Speaker, let's do for Oklahoma what Rodgers and Hammerstein did; let's put an exclamation point there. I move we make 'Oklahoma' the state song."

And they did.

(Reprinted by permission of the Oklahoma Heritage Association from *Good Guys Wear White Hats: The Life of George Nigh* by Bob Burke, 2000)

George Nigh was elected to the Oklahoma House of Representatives while still in college. He served many years as lieutenant governor, four terms as governor of Oklahoma, a record that probably will never be broken, and was president of the University of Central Oklahoma. It was his bill that the legislature passed in 1953 to make "Oklahoma" the official state song. Courtesy Oklahoma Heritage Association.

SAUSAGE CASSEROLE

6 slices of old bread, cubed

1 tsp. dry mustard

4 eggs

½ tsp. salt

2 c. milk

1 c. grated cheddar cheese (reserve some for top of casserole)

1 lb. sausage, browned and well drained

Butter an 8x8 or 9x13 casserole dish and line with bread cubes. Spread sausage over bread. Sprinkle cheese over sausage. Mix eggs, milk, and spices and pour over cheese. Sprinkle rest of cheese on top. Bake at 325 for 40 minutes. This is best when made the night before and refrigerated. Let it reach room temperature the next morning before baking.

George and Donna Nigh

Braum's History

What does Oklahoma taste like?

Braum's, that's what.

Oklahomans have their favorite dishes and recipes, but if they have to leave the state, there's one huge favorite that often can't go with them—a Braum's ice cream cone.

For almost forty years, Braum's has been Oklahoma's favorite dairy because of a standard of excellence that's rooted in the principle that quality and freshness are top priority–a process that begins in the Sooner State. Bill and Mary Braum came from Kansas and opened the first Braum's store in Oklahoma in 1968. Twenty-three more stores followed that year.

By 1971, they built a processing plant in Oklahoma City and four years later established their dairy farm in Tuttle, Oklahoma. A bakery was opened in Oklahoma City in 1978 to produce cookies, ice cream cones, hamburger buns, and other items baked exclusively for their expanding stores. A new 260,000 square foot state-of-the-art processing plant was built on the Braum Family Farm about ten years later.

The company is unique for its vertical integration, owning everything from the cows to the delivery trucks. Braum's milks 10,000 cows several times each day on the Braum Family Farm—known as one of the largest dairy operations in the world and a showplace in the industry. And, Braum's is the only major ice cream maker in the country to milk their own cows.

Still a family-owned business run by Bill and Mary Braum, their sons, and daughters, Braum's currently has 276 stores in Oklahoma, Kansas, Texas, Missouri, and Arkansas. In addition to the dairy and bakery products for which they are known, the stores have expanded into fresh meats, fruits, and vegetables in their "Fresh Market," and each has a restaurant offering hamburgers, salads, breakfast and, of course, ice cream.

Oklahoma cows, Oklahoma employees, and an Oklahoma family that puts quality first—a favorite flavor for sure.

Bacon Garlic Bread

HOLIDAY HASH BROWN CASSEROLE

2 lb. frozen hash brown potatoes with peppers and onions
1 can cream of chicken soup
2 c. Braum's shredded cheddar cheese
potato chips (or corn flakes)
1 stick Braum's butter or margarine
16 oz. Braum's french onion dip

Pour frozen hash brown potatoes in large bowl. Melt butter (or margarine) in microwave. Combine soup, french onion dip, and melted butter. Pour over hash browns. Mix well. Add cheese and fold together. Pour into casserole dish and bake at 350 for 1 hour or until ingredients bubble throughout and top is golden brown. Sprinkle crushed potato chips or corn flakes over top and bake for approximately 5 minutes more.

BACON GARLIC BREAD

1 pkg. Braum's bacon, cooked and crumbled
1 tsp. vegetable oil
1 clove garlic, minced
¾ c. chopped green pepper
¾ c. chopped green onion
1 ½ cans Braum's jumbos buttermilk biscuits
½ c. Braum's butter or margarine, melted
½ c. Braum's shredded cheddar cheese

Cook bacon until crisp; drain, crumble, and set aside. Sauté garlic, green pepper, and green onion in vegetable oil over medium heat until tender. Cut biscuits into eighths and place in large mixing bowl. Add sautéed vegetables, bacon, butter, and cheese; toss until thoroughly mixed. Place in Bundt pan coated with cooking spray. Bake 30–35 minutes at 350. Immediately invert onto large serving plate. Serve warm.

Mary Cole's Raisin Nut Bread Pudding with Sour Cream Orange Sauce

1 loaf Braum's raisin nut bread

½ c. Braum's butter, melted

2 c. Braum's half-and-half

4 Braum's eggs

1 tsp. vanilla extract

1 c. granulated sugar

¾ c. brown sugar

1 tsp. cinnamon

½ tsp. nutmeg

Spray or butter a 9x13 cake pan. Tear bread into small pieces and place into pan. Drizzle pieces with melted butter and toss. In another bowl, mix and whisk remaining ingredients together and pour over bread mixture. Bake at 350 for 45 minutes or until center is puffy and golden brown.

Sour Cream Orange Sauce

¼ c. Braum's butter

½ c. Braum's sour cream

¾ c. granulated sugar

3 Tbsp. Braum's orange juice

1 tsp. fresh grated orange zest

Melt butter and sour cream together in 1-quart saucepan. Whisk in sugar, orange juice, and orange zest. Bring to a boil and remove from heat. Serve sauce warm over bread pudding.

(2006 Winner of the MIO "Recipe Roundup" Contest)

Eggnog Banana Cream Pie

1 9-inch graham cracker crust (ready-to-eat)
1 5.1-oz. pkg. vanilla instant pudding and pie filling
2 c. Braum's eggnog
1 envelope Dream Whip whipped topping mix*
2 tsp. rum extract
2 bananas
8 oz. frozen whipped topping, thawed
nutmeg

Combine dry pudding mix, eggnog, Dream Whip, and rum extract. Beat 5 minutes with mixer until peaks are formed. Slice bananas and arrange of bottom of crust. Pour pudding mixture over bananas. Chill several hours before serving. Spread whipped topping over pie and sprinkle with nutmeg prior to serving. (Decorate with sliced bananas if desired).

*Dream Whip is a registered trademark of Kraft Foods

Macaroon Sweet Potatoes with Apricot Preserves

6 c. Braum's sweet potatoes, cooked, peeled, and mashed (about 3 ½ lbs.)
1 stick Braum's butter, melted, divided
½ c. brown sugar, packed
¼ tsp. almond extract
1 tsp. salt
½ tsp. ground ginger
½ c. Braum's chopped pecans
¼ c. Braum's apricot preserves
6 Braum's macaroons, crumbled

In a large mixing bowl, combine sweet potatoes, 6 Tbsp. butter, brown sugar, almond extract, salt, and ginger; beat until smooth. Stir in pecans and preserves.

Place in a greased 11 x 7 baking dish. Toss macaroons with remaining butter and sprinkle over top. Bake uncovered at 325 for 30–35 minutes or until heated through.

Note: this casserole can be made the night before and chilled. Let set 30 minutes before baking. Top with buttered macaroons and bake. Sprinkle with more chopped pecans if desired.

CREAMY EGGNOG CAFÉ

½ gal. Braum's eggnog
3 c. cold Braum's coffee
16 oz. frozen whipped topping, thawed
2 pt. (half of a half gallon) Braum's cappuccino chunky chocolate frozen yogurt
1 can Braum's whipped cream
nutmeg to taste

In a large bowl add eggnog and coffee and mix well. Fold in whipped topping. Add dips of frozen yogurt to float. Prior to serving, top with whipped cream and sprinkle with nutmeg.

ICE CREAM SUNDAE DESSERT

17 3.5-oz. Braum's ice cream sandwiches
1 13-oz. jar Braum's caramel ice cream topping
1 ¼ c. Braum's pecans, chopped and divided
¼ c. chocolate chips
16 oz. frozen whipped topping, thawed and divided
¾ c. Braum's hot fudge ice cream topping, heated

Place 8 ½ ice cream sandwiches in 9x13 baking dish. Spread caramel topping evenly over ice cream sandwiches. Sprinkle with 1 cup pecans. Layer with half of the whipped topping. Top with remaining ice cream sandwiches. Spread remaining whipped cream evenly over sandwiches. Cover and freeze at least two hours. Let stand 5 minutes prior to serving then sprinkle with ¼ cup chocolate chips and remaining pecans. Drizzle with hot fudge topping.

HONEY GLAZED CRANBERRY CARROTS

½ c. Braum's orange juice
⅓ c. dried cranberries
¼ c. Braum's butter
2 Tbsp. Braum's honey
1 Tbsp. grated ginger
2 lb. Braum's baby carrots

Place carrots in a large saucepan with water to cover. Bring to a boil. Cover and cook 20 minutes or until tender. Drain well. Meanwhile, combine first 5 ingredients in a small saucepan. Bring to a boil over medium-high heat, stirring constantly. Simmer approximately 10–15 minutes or until glaze is thickened. Add honey-cranberry mixture to carrots; toss well.

Schwab's History

President Larry Schwab

Schwab & Company, the oldest meat company in Oklahoma, has been making the finest hickory smoked hams, turkeys, sausages, hot dogs, and other fine smoked meats for almost a century.

George Peter Schwab came to Oklahoma from Germany in 1912 with a handful of old-world recipes and a dream to make the highest quality, best-tasting meat products around. His philosophy was simple—don't cut corners; do things the old-fashioned way.

Now, five generations later, the company is owned and operated by Larry and Scott Schwab. The Schwab brothers still do things their great grandfather's way. Unlike most meat manufacturers who have turned to liquid smoke additives for flavor, the Schwab family still cooks their meats for hours over real hardwood hickory in old-fashioned smoke-houses. It's the "secret" to that delicious signature, back-home Schwab flavor.

Schwab's plant and smokehouses have been in the same location in downtown Oklahoma City since the company opened in 1912, and they take pride in that fact. "We're proud that our focus on high quality products has stood the test of time," said president, Larry Schwab. "We've been in the business for ninety-five years and have never lowered our quality to keep up with the competition," Schwab said.

Schwab's ships their products across the country via their mail order catalog and Web site (schwabmeat.com). And, Schwab's produces their products for a variety of companies nationally, regionally, and, locally including Eateries, Inc., Landry's, Bourbon Street, Braum's Ice Cream and Dairy Stores, Sysco Foods, Ben E. Keith, US Food Service, Sam's, Walmart, Buy For Less, Crest, and Love's Country Stores, among others.

Schwab says Oklahomans may have grown up on Schwab's products for generations and not even known it. "I'm proud to say we're pretty famous in these parts for our hot dogs and chili that are available at Coit's, Charcoal Oven, Coney Island, and Johnnie's Charcoal Broiler, just to name a few," Schwab said.

Schwab & Company has been featured in numerous publications including *Oklahoma Today Magazine,* OKCBusiness, and the *Daily Oklahoman* as one of the "100 Oklahoma Foods to Try Before You Die."

Ham Honey Apple Glaze

Jack Schwab's Beef Stroganoff

1 ½ lb. Schwab's beef tenderloin, thinly sliced

2 Tbsp. butter

1 medium onion, finely chopped

3 Tbsp. flour

4 Tbsp. butter

1 ½ cans beef consommé

2 Tbsp. tomato paste

1 4-oz. jar sliced mushrooms

½ pt. sour cream

Brown the tenderloin in 2 Tbsp. butter and season to taste. In another pan, brown the finely chopped onions until golden and add to the browned meat. Put 4 Tbsp. butter in pan and melt; then add about 3 Tbsp. flour to make thickness.

As soon as the flour is browned, add the beef consommé until of the right consistency (about medium). Add the meat and onions, tomato paste and mushrooms. Simmer about 10 minutes. When ready to serve, add the sour cream. Be sure not to let this boil or the cream will curdle. Serve over egg noodles or steamed rice. Makes 6 servings.

This recipe was featured in the *Daily Oklahoman* over forty years ago in a weekly column of "favorite recipes of Sooner State cooks." It featured the recipe, photo, and article about Jack and Lynn Schwab, Schwab Meat Company.

Schwab's Ham Honey Apple Glaze

1 Tbsp. ginger

1 Tbsp. cinnamon

1 can crushed pineapple, drained

1 c. sparkling apple cider

honey (as desired)

1 Schwab bone-in fully cooked hickory smoked ham

Combine ingredients in medium saucepan. Heat to thicken. Slowly add honey to desired consistency and taste. Baste ham every 30 minutes for the last 1 ½ hours of cooking time.

Note: All Schwab hams are fully cooked and hickory smoked. Just heat for 3 hours at 350 degrees and enjoy!

SCHWAB'S JALAPENO CHEDDAR SMOKED SAUSAGE BITES

1 pkg. Schwab's jalapeno cheddar smoked sausage
1 can crescent rolls

Unroll crescent dough and separate to form four rectangles. Press diagonal perforations to seal. Roll sausage lengthwise. Bake as directed on crescent roll package. Cut into 1-inch slices.

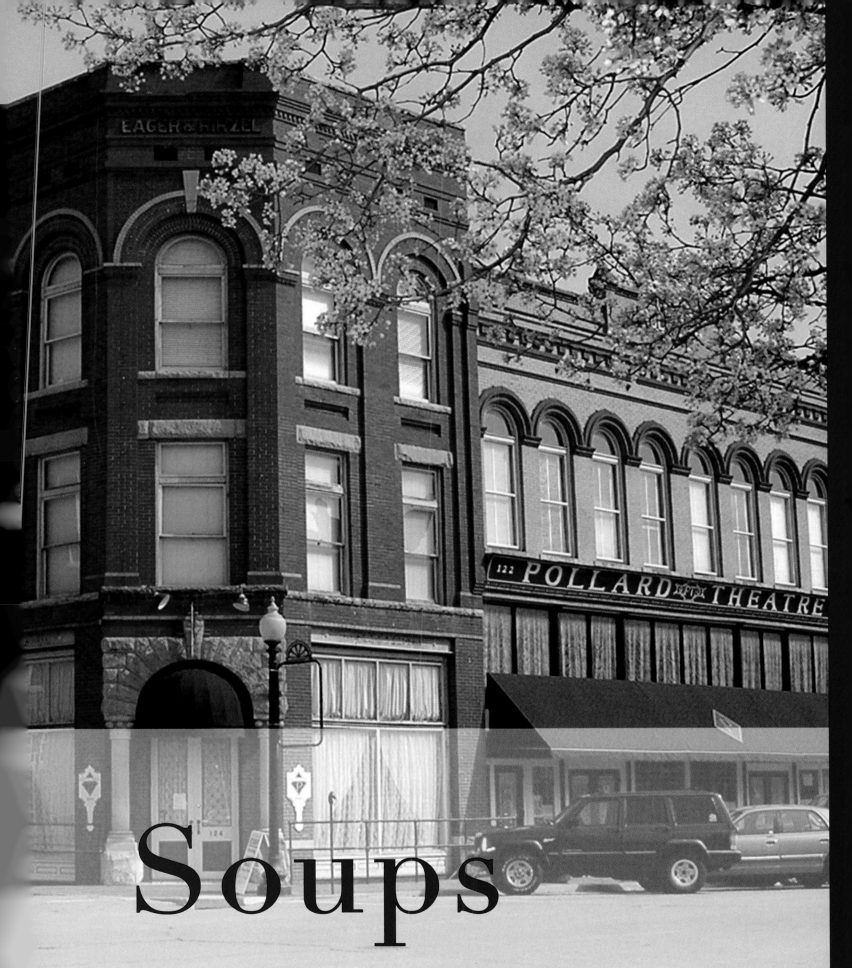

Soups

Pollard Theatre
Guthrie, Oklahoma

CREAMY CHEDDAR CHEESE SOUP

¼ c. butter
1 medium onion, chopped
¼ c. flour
3 c. chicken broth
3 c. milk
1 lb. shredded cheddar cheese (about 4 c.)

In a 3-quart saucepan over medium-high heat, cook onions in hot butter until tender (about 5 minutes). Stir in flour and cook until flour has blended with the onion mixture. Add chicken broth; cook, stirring constantly until mixture is slightly thickened. Add milk and heat to just boiling. Stirring constantly in covered blender on medium speed, blend about ¼ cup of milk mixture at a time until smooth. Return to saucepan and over medium, heat to just boiling. Remove from heat. With wire whisk or slotted spoon, stir cheese until melted—if cheese does not melt completely, cook over very low heat 1 minute. Serve soup with pumpernickel bread cubes.

Congresswoman Mary Fallin, Price and Christina Fallin

Congresswoman Mary Fallin

SPINACH MUSHROOM SOUP

1 stick butter

1 medium white onion, chopped

2 pkg. sliced mushrooms

2 pkg. frozen creamed spinach

1 qt. half-and-half

1 pt. heavy cream

Melt butter in saucepan. Sauté onions over low heat until clear. Add mushrooms and sauté for 5–6 minutes. Add spinach, either thawed or frozen. Stir until all ingredients are mixed together. Add creams. Heat until mixture almost reaches the boiling point. Add salt and white pepper. Makes 6 servings.

Nancy Norman Le Vesque

CORN CHOWDER

5 slices bacon

1 medium onion, sliced thin in rings

2 medium potatoes, pared and diced

½ c. water

1 17-oz. can cream style corn

2 c. milk

1 tsp. salt

dash of pepper

butter

Clif & Gloria Scott

In large saucepan, cook bacon till crisp. Remove bacon, crumble and set aside. Reserve 3 Tbsp. drippings in saucepan. Add onion slices to pan and cook till lightly browned. Add diced potato and water; cook over medium heat till potatoes are tender. Add corn, milk, salt, and pepper.

Cook till heated through. Pour into warm bowls, top each serving with crumbled bacon and a pat of butter.

Clif and Gloria Scott

KURSTYN'S POTATO SOUP

4–6 potatoes
2 cans chicken broth
1 medium yellow onion, chopped
2–3 ribs celery, chopped

Bring the above to a boil and add:

2 cans drained corn
1 c. heavy cream

Cook this mixture and add:

1 small block of Mexican Velveeta Cheese
Season with garlic salt and pepper if desired

Kurstyn Mills

BARRY SWITZER'S 6-GUN CHILI

In a 6-quart Crock-Pot, layer:

1 large onion, finely chopped

1 large bell pepper, finely chopped

2 stalks celery, finely chopped

3 cloves garlic, minced

¼ c. cooking sherry

2 lb. ground sirloin

1 lb. sweet Italian sausage, cut-up

1 28-oz. can chili beans, include liquid

1 15-oz. can pinto beans, include liquid

1 15-oz.can kidney beans, drained

1 15-oz. can Rotel diced tomatoes with chilies

3 Tbsp. chili powder

1 Tbsp. ground cumin

1 Tbsp. paprika

1 tsp. cayenne pepper

1 tsp. dried oregano

¼ tsp. celery salt

1 Tbsp. brown sugar

1 14½-oz. can beef broth

Stir gently and cook on low for 4–5 hours.

Barry Switzer

CHICKEN AND ANDOUILLE GUMBO

Ronnie Schultz standing by convertible at Ferguson Motors.

2 Tbsp. extra virgin olive oil

2 ½ lb. chicken breast, diced

2 Tbsp. essence (Emeril's original essence)

2 ½ lb. andouille sausage, diced

3 Tbsp. unsalted butter

5 ribs celery from the heart of the stack, chopped

2 green bell peppers, seeded and diced

1 large onion, peeled and chopped

2 bay leaves

2 Tbsp. Tabasco sauce to taste

¼ c. all-purpose flour

1 qt. chicken broth or stock

4 c. okra, chopped (fresh or if frozen, wash after you defrost)

1 28-oz. can crushed tomatoes

1 14-oz. can diced tomatoes

3 Tbsp. thyme, chopped

1 bundle green onions, thinly sliced

salt and fresh cracked black pepper

3 c. white rice, cooked to pkg. directions

Preheat a large stock pot over medium-high heat; add olive oil and rotate pan to coat. Season diced chicken with the Essence, then place in the pot. Salt and pepper to taste. Brown all sides (3–5 minutes). Add sausage to pot. Cook another 2–3 minutes. Transfer meat into a bowl.

Return pot to heat, add butter. When the butter melts, add celery, peppers, onion, Tabasco, and bay leaves. Cook 4–6 minutes to soften the mix. Add flour and cook for 2 minutes. Slowly stir in the broth and bring liquid to a boil. Stir okra, chicken, and sausage into the boiling broth; add the tomatoes and thyme. Bring back to a boil, then reduce to a simmer. Simmer for about 10 minutes to combine flavors. Taste and adjust seasonings.

Cook sausage in oil in a large Dutch oven, stirring until brown. Remove sausage, reserving drippings in pan. Add onion and next 4 ingredients; sauté over medium-high heat until vegetables are tender. Stir in sausage, peas, broth, and tomatoes; bring to a boil. Cover, reduce heat, and simmer 30–40 minutes. Stir in salsa and add salt and pepper to taste. Delicious served with cornmeal biscuits and sage butter. Makes 10–12 servings.

Honeysuckle Rose Gardens

FRENCH STEW

2 lb. stew meat, cut in bite-sized pieces
1 scant pkg. onion soup mix
1 can cream of mushroom soup
1 can mushrooms, drained
1 c. sherry wine
1 tsp. herbs of provence

Mix all of the above ingredients and put in roaster pan, cover and cook at 300 for 4 hours. Serve over rice or noodles.

Sharlene Hammons

The Victor in Guthrie

OLD-FASHIONED "BEDLAM" VEGETABLE SOUP

2 14½-oz. cans stewed tomatoes (Red)

1 red bell pepper (Red)

1 white onion, chopped (White)

1 orange bell pepper (Orange)

1 c. carrots, sliced (Orange)

1 tsp. ground pepper (Black)

1 c. mushrooms, chopped

1 c. peeled and cubed eggplant or potatoes

4 c. water

2 garlic cloves or 1 tsp. of garlic powder

2 tsp. Italian seasoning or 2 basil leaves

salt to taste

freshly grated Parmesan cheese

a little Tabasco sauce to "heat up" the competition (Optional)

Chop half of each bell pepper. Combine all ingredients except the cheese and the remaining halves of bell peppers in a large saucepan. Let simmer until the vegetables are tender, approximately 30–40 minutes. Separately, finely slice the remaining bell peppers (red and orange).

Place soup in bowls or cups with sprinkled cheese, then garnish tops with the sliced peppers. Serve with Italian bread during a Bedlam sports event or any time. Makes 4 bowls or 6 cups.

Doctor Richard Wansley and Doctor Meredith Davison

Dr. Wansley is vice president of Oklahoma State University's Center for Health Sciences in Tulsa, and Dr. Davison is a faculty member at the University of Oklahoma–Tulsa, Department of Family Medicine.

POSOLE (PORK STEW)

2 c. posole, washed and sorted (use dry or fresh)*
water
2 lb. boneless pork (shoulder or loin), cut in 1-inch cubes
flour for dredging
3 onions, peeled and coarsely chopped
4 garlic cloves, peeled and crushed
3–4 Tbsp. olive oil
2 Tbsp. butter
2 tsp. chopped oregano (more if you're using fresh)
1–2 c. chicken broth
4 dried or canned chipotle pods
2 tsp. salt (or more as needed for taste)
½ tsp. freshly ground black pepper
1 10-oz. can chopped roasted and peeled green chili peppers, drained *or* 2 fresh
roasted and chopped green chilies, remove veins and seeds
1 jalapeño, chopped, remove veins and seeds (optional)

Jane and Mike Lodes

Place posole in a large pot, cover with water, and bring to a boil. Reduce the flame and simmer until the posole begins to pop.

Dredge pork in flour and brown in a heavy skillet in 2 Tbsp. olive oil. Add onions, garlic, remaining oil, and butter. Cook until onion is translucent. Add pork and onion mixture to the pot of posole, along with the chicken broth, oregano, and chipotle pods. Let mixture simmer over a low flame for 3–4 hours. Be sure to add water if needed during the cooking time. Season with salt and pepper and add the green chilies and jalapeno. Continue cooking for 30 minutes or more. Taste and adjust seasonings. Makes 8–10 servings.

*If you're using dry posole, soak in cold water for 3–4 hours.

Jane Lodes

TORTILLA SOUP

Stock:

1 chicken, cut in pieces or 6 breasts

4 ribs of celery, chopped in large pieces, include some of the leaves

2 onions, coarsely chopped

water to cover

Cook together in a large pot. After chicken is cooked (30 minutes or so), remove the chicken. When it is cool enough to handle, remove the skin and bones and chunk the chicken. You can strain the stock or leave the onion and celery pieces in it.

Soup:

2 Tbsp. olive oil

1 onion, chopped

2 cloves garlic, crushed

1 16-oz. can tomatoes and chilies

chicken stock

salt and pepper to taste

1 tsp. chili powder

½ tsp. cumin

In small skillet, sauté onion and garlic in oil until golden brown. Add, with tomatoes and chilies and seasonings to stock. Simmer 15–20 minutes. Add chicken pieces for the last 10 minutes of cooking.

Garnishes:

Corn tortillas (1 per person or more), cut into ½-inch strips

Fry in small amount of oil in a skillet until crisp. Drain.

2 c. shredded monterey jack cheese

1–2 limes, cut into wedges

To serve, ladle soup into bowls. Top with tortilla strips, sprinkle with cheese, pass the lime.

Mike Lodes

Spinach Tortellini Soup

6 c. chicken broth
1–2 garlic cloves, minced
1 9-oz. pkg. cheese tortellini
dried basil
1 pkg. frozen, chopped spinach, thawed and squeezed
salt and pepper
1 can Italian style stewed tomatoes

In large pot, bring broth to simmer. Stir in tortellini and simmer gently for 3 minutes. Stir in spinach, garlic, basil, salt ,pepper, and tomatoes. Return to simmer and cook for 2–3 more minutes. Serve hot with Parmesan cheese.

Lisa Fulton

Nonna's Tomato Basil Bisque

4 gal. tomato base*
3 qt. water
35 oz. sugar
68 oz. tomato paste
2½ Tbsp. garlic powder
7 Tbsp. sea salt
1 c. modified food starch
2 Tbsp. white pepper
20 32-oz. jars (for processing)

Avis Scaramucci with beautifully grown tomatoes from Cedar Spring Farms owned by she and her husband. These tomatoes are used in Nonna's delicious soups.

Pass half of tomato base through fine sieve, discard pulp, and recombine with remaining base. Bring to a boil, add remaining ingredients, and season to taste. Package into sterilized jars and seal immediately. Allow to cool to room temperature and ensure button tops are down.

To serve: For each 32 oz. jar of soup mix heat gradually and add ¾ cup heavy cream. Serve topped with croutons of your choice.

*Tomato Base:

80 lb. whole tomatoes, washed

5 lb. carrots

3 lb. onions

1 lb. celery

8 oz. garlic cloves, peeled

4 oz. basil (green)

1 gal. water

Add ingredients to large, non-reactive pot and cook until carrots are soft. Purée, pass through a food mill, and chill.

Please enjoy Nonna's signature tomato bisque!

Buon Appetito...Avis
Nonna's Restaurant and Bakery

Cold Mango Soup

3–4 ripe mangoes, peeled, pitted, and chopped

1 c. plain yogurt

1 c. half-and-half

juice of 1 lime

juice of 1 lemon

juice of 1 orange

3 Tbsp. dark rum (optional)

1 tsp. red chili powder

¼ tsp. cayenne

add a little sugar if you want it sweeter

fresh mint for garnish

Purée mango in food processor or blender, adding other ingredients and processing until smooth. Taste and adjust seasoning.

Transfer soup to a container to refrigerate for at least 1 hour. Ladle into bowls, garnish and serve. Makes 4 servings.

Mary Goetz

CHILLED STRAWBERRY SOUP

6 c. sliced fresh strawberries

2 c. half-and-half

1 ½ c. sour cream

¾ c. sifted powdered sugar

¼ c. balsamic vinegar

whipped cream (optional)

strawberry slices (optional)

fresh mint sprigs (optional)

Place strawberries in a container of an electric blender or food processor; process until smooth. Transfer puree to a large bowl. Add half-and-half, sour cream, powdered sugar, and balsamic vinegar; stir with a wire whisk until smooth. Cover and chill at least 2 hours. Serve soup in chilled bowls. If desired, garnish each serving with whipped cream, strawberry slices and mint sprigs. Makes 7 cups.

Cathy Keating from Ooh La La Recipe Book

BLUEBERRY WINE SOUP

⅓ c. granulated sugar

1 Tbsp. cornstarch

1 c. chablis or zinfandel wine

juice of ½-1 whole lime

1 pt. of blueberries

In a medium saucepan, combine cornstarch and sugar. Stir in wine, juices, and blueberries. Cook over medium heat, stirring constantly, until mixture boils. Simmer on low heat for 2 minutes. Cool slightly. Purée in blender until smooth (Caution! Hot liquids create steam, which will blow the top off the blender! Be sure to securely hold blender lid down.) Serve warm or chilled.

Ken Stafford, expert chef in creating delicious cold soups for the summer months

Ken Stafford

BOY HOWDY BEEF VEGETABLE STEW

2 Tbsp. olive oil

5 slices bacon, cut into 1-inch pieces

1 ¾ lb. boneless beef tenderloin, cut into 1-inch cubes

coarse ground pepper

10–12 baby carrots

4 parsnips, peeled and cut into 3-inch lengths

8 leeks, white parts only, rinsed very well, sliced

2 Tbsp. sugar

1 ½ c. beef broth

1 ½ c. red wine or burgundy

2 Tbsp. unsalted butter

2 Tbsp. red currant jelly

2 tsp. thyme

6–8 small new red potatoes, cut in half

6–8 garlic cloves, minced

5 ripe plum tomatoes, seeded and chopped

½ c. Italian parsley, chopped

cooked egg noodles

Preheat oven to 350. Heat oil in a large pan. Add bacon and cook over medium heat for 5 minutes. Transfer bacon to large casserole dish. Brown the beef in same skillet over medium-high heat. Season with pepper. Add beef to casserole dish. In the skillet, sauté carrots, parsnips, leeks, and sugar. Cook for 7 minutes. Remove vegetables and set aside in medium bowl. Add broth, red wine, butter, jelly, and thyme to skillet and bring to boil and cook for about 2 minutes. Pour over meat in casserole dish. Add potatoes and garlic to casserole and bake for 45 minutes. Remove casserole and add vegetables and parsley, stir. Bake uncovered for another 45 minutes. Serve with egg noodles.

Jan and J.R. Ross

COLD PEACH SOUP

½ c. white Rhine Wine

1 pkg. frozen peaches or 2 c. fresh peaches

sugar, honey, or granulated sugar substitute to taste

Process peaches, wine, and sugar in a food processor using a steel blade. Add water to get desired consistency. Serve cold. Garnish with fresh mint sprigs.

Taste of the Territory Recipe Book

SANTA FE SOUP

1 lb. ground sirloin

1 large onion, diced

1 15-oz. can corn, undrained

1 15-oz. can black beans, undrained

1 16-oz. can stewed tomatoes

1 10-oz. can diced tomatoes and green chilies

1 lb. (16 oz) Mexican pasteurized process cheese food (Velveeta)

Brown meat with onion. Drain any fat. In large soup pot, combine meat mixture, corn, beans and tomatoes. Cube cheese and add to soup, stirring over low flame until melted and blended.

ONG Cookbook

BROCCOLI CHOWDER

2 lbs. (approximately) fresh broccoli

2 12-oz. cans chicken broth

3 c. milk

1 c. chopped ham, cooked

1 tsp. salt

¼ tsp. pepper

1 c. light cream (half-and-half)

½ lb. Swiss cheese, grated

¼ c. butter

Cook broccoli, covered, in 1 can chicken broth in large kettle until tender. Remove from broth; cool; chop coarsely. Return to kettle. Add second can of chicken broth, milk, ham, salt, and pepper. Bring to boil over medium heat, stirring occasionally. Stir in cream, cheese, and butter. Heat just to serving temperature. Makes 12 servings.

Margaret Forrester

Congressman Dan Boren

Congressman Dan Boren

As a member of the U.S. House of Representatives, I have worked diligently in Congress to protect these precious Oklahoma resources through my work on the House Natural Resources Committee. This committee is responsible for the management of our nation's federal parks and national forests, the development of federal lands, the supervision of plants, fish, and wildlife species, and lastly the facilitation of the relationship between the federal government and Native American tribes as well as U.S. territories and insular areas. As a representative from a state so rich in natural resources, serving on this committee has been an ideal venue for advocating for the interests of the citizens of Oklahoma. As an outdoorsman, I know how important Oklahomans find the protection of our natural resources. I have always considered some of my top priorities in Congress to be the responsible management of our wildlife populations, the wise use of our natural resources, and the promotion of outdoor conservation.

My seat on the National Parks, Forests, and Public Lands subcommittee has provided me the opportunity to oversee the management of Oklahoma's vast natural resources, like the Ouachita National Forest, and historic places like the Fort Smith National Historic Site. I am also a member of the subcommittee on Energy and Minerals, which has oversight of energy development and mineral exploration on federal lands. Over the past three decades, our nation's energy demands have increased dramatically, making us increasingly dependent on foreign energy sources. Oklahoma is an integral part of our nation's energy infrastructure. As Congress continues to debate climate change legislation and clean, alternative fuels, the Resources Committee will play a critical role in shaping that legislation, and I plan to be a strong advocate for Oklahoma's energy industry–a major segment of our state's economy.

Another important aspect of my work on this Committee has been oversight of the governments' relationship with federally recognized tribes, including the thirty-seven in Oklahoma. Similarly, I have worked to support Indian country through my work on the Financial

Services committee. We often see larger disparities for Native Americans than other minority groups, a disconcerting trend that Congress must address. For example, Native Americans have a lower home ownership rate than any other group of Americans. To respond to this need, I authored the Native American Home Ownership Opportunity Act of 2007, reauthorizing a program to provide loan guarantees to cover lenders who make mortgage loans on homes in Indian country. This act became law on June 18, 2007. I am also working closely with my colleagues to pass the Native American Housing Assistance and Self-Determination Reauthorization Act of 2007 to provide additional support to Native Americans across the country.

Native Americans have played a significant role in the evolution of America as scholars, architects, artists, and defenders of this country. Oklahoma has been home to many of these great individuals: Sequoyah, Jim Thorpe, and Willard Stone, among others. I am proud to represent the Second District of Oklahoma, which has the third highest concentration of Native Americans in the country. I will continue to work with my colleagues to ensure the protection of this great heritage and adequate provision of health care, education, and other benefits to Indian country in Oklahoma.

As an Oklahoman, I share a heritage built on the values of faith, family, hard work, and personal responsibility. Here in Oklahoma, people are our greatest asset. There is warmth in our people that you won't find anywhere else. Throughout many years of hardship, our communities endured because of our "pioneer spirit." The same strength and spirit that enabled generations before you to survive the Great Depression and two World Wars is still alive today.

Chocolate Sheet Cake

2 c. sugar
2 c. flour
1 stick butter
¼ c. Crisco
1 c. water
4 Tbsp. cocoa
2 eggs
½ c. buttermilk
1 tsp. baking soda
1 tsp. vanilla
1 tsp. cinnamon

Set aside sugar and flour in a saucepan. Cook butter, Crisco, water, and cocoa until at a rapid boil and add sugar/flour mixture. Add unbeaten eggs, buttermilk, baking soda, vanilla, and cinnamon. Beat well. Pour entire mixture into a greased cookie sheet with sides. Bake at 400 for 20 minutes.

Frosting:
1 stick butter
4 Tbsp. cocoa
1 box powdered sugar
4–6 Tbsp. milk
1 tsp. vanilla

Combine all ingredients in a bowl. Mix well. Pour entire mixture over warm cake.

Congressman Dan Boren and his wife, Andrea

An Everyday American Dream

In 1953, Troy Smith, the founder of SONIC, was living in Shawnee, Oklahoma. Troy's ultimate dream was to run a fancy steakhouse and, for a while, he did. But where his steakhouse would take him, not even Troy could imagine.

The lot where Troy's steakhouse sat also had a root beer stand, which he meant to tear down to add more parking for the restaurant. In a twist of fate, the humble Top Hat Drive-In, as the root beer stand was called, proved to be more profitable, and outlasted the steakhouse.

CEO, Chairman, and President Cliff Hudson

The Top Hat served easily-prepared hamburgers and hot dogs cooked-to-order. Customers would park on the lot, order at the walk-up window, and then eat on a picnic table or in their cars.

Sonic is Born

While traveling in Louisiana, Troy visited a hamburger stand with a homemade intercom system, allowing customers to order right from their cars. A light bulb went on in Troy's head. He contacted the innovator in Louisiana and asked him to make an intercom for the Top Hat.

Troy hired "the jukebox boys," some local electronics wizards, to install

First Sonic, originally named "Top Hat" in Shawnee, Oklahoma

the speaker system at his drive-in. He also added a canopy for cars to park under and hired carhops to deliver food directly to customers' cars. Troy Smith now had the prototype of the future SONIC.

A New Partner

Over in Woodward, Oklahoma, Charlie Pappe was managing the local Safeway supermarket. He wanted to get out of the grocery business and start his own restaurant.

While visiting friends in Shawnee, Charlie stopped by the Top Hat for dinner. He was so impressed with the whole operation that he introduced himself. Charlie opened the second Top Hat Drive-In on May 18, 1956, in Woodward, Oklahoma. Troy now had a partner.

Service With The Speed Of Sound[SM]

Troy and Charlie would have kept the Top Hat name, but they learned it was trademarked. So, they opened up the dictionary and started searching for a new name.

Top Hat's slogan had been "Service With the Speed of Sound[SM]." When Troy and Charlie ran across "sonic," meaning speed of sound, they knew they had the perfect name. The Stillwater, Oklahoma Top Hat Drive-In became the first SONIC® Drive-In and still serves customers today.

The new name sparked more requests from aspiring SONIC® operators. Troy's philosophy was that owners make better operators, so a franchise system was created.

In the early days, there was no national advertising and there were no territorial rights. If two prospects wanted the same town, Troy would talk to them and convince one to go somewhere else.

SONIC® Dons A Suit and Growing Pains

By 1973, there were 165 drive-ins in the chain. Several of the largest franchisees purchased the company from Troy, and the next round of growth began. Between 1973 and 1978, more than 800 SONICs opened.

It was not all smooth sailing. Profits fell 21% during 1978 and 1979. In 1980, sales and operating revenues decreased by more than $5 million, with an operating loss of $300,000. In response, SONIC consolidated store operations and development, and closed 28 low-volume, company-owned drive-ins.

SONIC was down, but not out.

The SONIC® Boom

In 1984, SONIC was more like a collection of independent stores than a cohesive business entity. More cooperation was needed. SONIC's new corporate counsel, Cliff Hudson, initiated several major changes in the company before eventually becoming president and CEO in 1995.

First, SONIC's management repurchased the company from its franchisee shareholders in May 1986. Second, franchisees began purchasing supplies as a group, which saved money and provided a consistent and quality menu for customers. Third, in 1991, SONIC's management took the company public once again, with a second offering in 1995, which raised enough money to pay off SONIC's debt and fund SONIC's comeback strategy.

Historical No. 3,000 Sonic built in Shawnee, Oklahoma

SONIC® 2000 and Beyond

In 1994 and 1995, customers, franchisees, suppliers, and drive-in managers came together and created SONIC® 2000, a multi-layered strategy to expand the business with a consistent menu, brand identity, products, packaging, and service. A new "retro-future" logo was introduced, and SONIC introduced new menu items, focusing on soft-serve treats and cool drinks. Once again, SONIC growth took off!

Today the chain continues to expand, delighting customers from Dover, Delaware, to Medford, Oregon, to Nacogdoches, Texas to, Rapid City, South Dakota. In 2005, Sonic opened its 3,000th drive-in in Shawnee, Oklahoma, the place where it all began!

The country and the fast food business have changed a great deal since Troy Smith installed the first intercom system at the Top Hat Drive-In. Food fads have come and gone, but SONIC has differentiated itself through its business model, unique menu items and, of course, friendly "Service With the Speed of Sound^SM."

Loyal to OKLAHOMA
Loyal to YOU

Locations in 47 Oklahoma Communities

One of the things that makes BancFirst unique is that we know the history of Oklahoma first hand. We've banked Oklahomans for more than 100 years. We have marveled at the effort required to create success from what were once modest rolling prairies or a famous winding cattle trail; and we're proud to have been a partner in those efforts. The account of how Oklahoma has grown and prospered is our own story as well.

Loyal is the best word that describes our relationship with the state we love. BancFirst's unwavering loyalty to Oklahoma, and Oklahomans, serves as a tribute to the ideas, hard work and power of everyday Oklahomans to make a difference.

As a result of our involvement, commitment and belief in this state, BancFirst is Oklahoma's largest, state-chartered bank. We owe this success to our customers. To them we say "Thank you." We're looking forward to Oklahoma's second century of success.

BancFirst®
Loyal To Oklahoma & You.℠

MEMBER FDIC EQUAL HOUSING LENDER

www.bancfirst.com

Banks: Fueling the Fires of the Economy

by Bob L. Blackburn, Ph.D.

H.E. "Gene" Rainbolt, Contributing Author

Bob Blackburn

Building a new state took courage and a lot of hard work. It also took money.

At first, on the cash-starved frontier, and later, in a new state with scarce infrastructure, much of that capital investment came from banks. Whether it was to get crops to market; manufacture mattresses for retail stores; or financing to buy houses, automobiles, and the necessities of life, banks have played a major role in the economic history of the state.

During much of Oklahoma's frontier era, there were no banks. Instead, individuals and companies extended credit specific to one type of transaction. Jesse Chisholm, the Cherokee trader and adventurer, received trade goods on credit from merchants in St. Louis, Fort Smith, or Wichita, and hopefully paid off the note after a season trading with the Comanche, Kiowa, and Cheyenne. James J. McAlester, who established his mercantile store along the MK&T tracks in 1871, provided banking services to his customers in the form of credit and safe storage of cash.

The first banks chartered under corporate law had to wait for the official organization of the Oklahoma Territory in August of 1890. In towns such as Oklahoma City, Guthrie, Norman, Edmond, Kingfisher, and Stillwater, businessmen accumulated enough money to capitalize a bank, either from their own resources or from partners, applied for a charter, and started doing business. One of those early banks was the Stillwater National Bank and Trust Company, chartered in 1894 and still in business in the twenty-first century.

Although operating with charters, these early banks were only lightly regulated, which led to frequent bank failures and a general distrust of financial institutions. In 1907, with 883 banks operating in the Twin Territories, the new state constitution included a provision for a Bank Guarantee System to deal with the problem. Funded through a 1% tax on banks, the Guarantee System acted as an insurance policy to pay depositors when a bank failed.

Early banking in Oklahoma was limited to "unit banking," which meant that a corporation could operate only one bank. A wealthy individual might have funds in several banks and he or she might be on several boards of directors, but the officers of the bank could serve only the institution with a roof over their heads. There were no branches and no chains. When coupled with the increasing difficulty in obtaining a charter for a bank, the unit banking law kept banks in one family, passed down from one generation to the next.

By law and practice, banks from 1907 to the 1930s were conservative institutions. In small towns, most loans went to farmers and ranchers, providing cash to put in a crop, buy a new piece of machinery, or build herds. In cities, bankers provided the large amounts of capital needed to undertake housing developments, construction projects, and business expansion. As oil money worked its way into the financial system, deposits grew along with skylines. Then came the hard times.

For Oklahoma bankers, the Great Depression began slowly in the late 1920s as the farming and ranching boom fizzled. From 1926 to 1930, 50% of all farm loans in Oklahoma went into foreclosure. After the Stock Market Crash and the rise in unemployment to more than a third of all workers, banks increasingly felt the strain. In 1933, to stop a series of bank failures, the federal government declared a bank holiday and passed a series of reforms and regulations, including insurance for depositors.

Typical of the family-owned local banks making this transition was the Stock Exchange Bank. It was organized in 1903 in Oleta, Oklahoma Territory, with deposits ranging from $.25 to $375. Nine years later A.M Benbrook bought the bank in Fargo, a town nearby. In 1939, after the banking crisis and increased regulations, Benbrook merged the two banks with a bank in Sharon and moved to Woodward. Under the leadership of Benbrook's son, Temple, and grandson, Bruce, the Stock Exchange Bank grew steadily into the twenty-first century.

Bank consolidation in the 1930s and 1940s accelerated even in the larger cities of Tulsa and Oklahoma City. The Bank of Oklahoma started as the Exchange National Bank of Tulsa in 1910. Founded by oilmen to serve the new oil industry, it absorbed other banks, emerged from the Great Depression as the National Bank of Tulsa, and was purchased by George Kaiser in the early 1980s. By 2007, it was the largest bank in the state.

The banking crisis of the early 1980s was a watershed era brought on by the hyper- inflation of the 1970s, compounded by the meteoric boom and bust of the energy sector. By 1982, when the federal deregulation of natural gas prices changed the economic feasibility of deep gas drilling, banks were failing in all sections of the state. The most publicized failure was Penn Square Bank, which closed in 1982, but the most harmful failure was the fall of the First National Bank of Oklahoma City. From 1982 to 1987, sixty-nine banks in Oklahoma failed.

Out of this prolonged period of change came a major reform of banking laws. The most significant was a statute allowing branch banking for the first time. One of the pioneers in that new era of expansion was H.E. "Gene" Rainbolt, who bought his first bank in 1966, created a multi-bank holding company in 1985, and formed BancFirst with multiple branches in 1989.By 2007, BancFirst offered services in more than eighty communities.

Today, Oklahoma is blessed with a wide variety of banks that encourage capital investments and consumer spending to drive the wheels of economic development.

Salads

JANE'S CAESAR SALAD

1 egg, coddled
2 large cloves garlic, mashed
juice of ½ lemon
½ tsp. salt
½ tsp. freshly ground black pepper
1 tsp. Worcestershire sauce
⅓-½ c. extra virgin olive oil
½ tsp. Dijon mustard
2 heads of romaine lettuce, washed, dried, and chilled
½ c. freshly grated Parmesan cheese
1½ c. croutons

For the dressing: Beat the coddled egg lightly, add the garlic, lemon juice, salt, pepper, Worcestershire sauce, olive oil, and Dijon mustard and mix well.

The lettuce: Remove the outer leaves of the romaine and discard. Separate the inner leaves, wash and dry and remove any discolored leaf portions. If not to be used immediately, chill.

May be made ahead of time to this point.

To make the salad: Place the lettuce in a large salad bowl. Pour the dressing over the lettuce and gently toss the lettuce with the dressing to coat thoroughly. Sprinkle on the cheese, add the croutons, and repeat the tossing process. Separate on individual salad plates and serve.

Makes 6 servings.

Jane Lodes

Jane and Mike Lodes with Sterling

Spring Mix Baby Spinach Fiji Apple Salad

Fuji apples, thinly sliced
toasted walnuts
dried cranberries or mixed berries
spring mix greens
baby spinach
Feta cheese
Dressing:
¼ c. maple syrup
¼ c. mayonnaise
3 Tbsp. sugar
3 Tbsp. white wine vinegar

Whisk in ½ c. vegetable or olive oil. Mix the greens with apples, walnuts, and cranberries. Pour dressing over and sprinkle with Feta cheese.

Honeysuckle Rose Gardens

ARTICHOKE BLUE CHEESE SALAD

⅓ c. olive oil or salad oil

2 Tbsp. red wine vinegar

4 tsp. lemon juice

1½ tsp. salt

1 tsp. sugar

¼ tsp. pepper

1 large head of lettuce

1 large romaine or bibb lettuce

1 14-oz. can artichoke hearts

¼ c. crumbled blue cheese

Mix oil, vinegar, lemon juice, salt, sugar, and pepper in large bowl until well mixed. Remove about 6 outer leaves from lettuce and set aside. Tear remaining lettuce into bite-sized pieces in oil mixture. Drain artichokes and cut each in half. Add artichokes and blue cheese to lettuce mixture. Toss well. Line a large salad bowl with reserve lettuce pieces and spoon mixture into bowl. Makes 8 servings.

Cathy Keating from Ooh La La Recipe Book

WALT'S CHAMPAGNE CHICKEN SALAD

Mixed greens with chunks of fresh pineapple, dates, sliced smoked chicken breast, croutons, spiced pecans tossed in a citrus champagne vinaigrette, and topped with feta cheese, sliced strawberries, and toasted sunflower seeds.

9 oz. salad mix

8 pc. sliced strawberries

8 pc. pineapple chunks

6 pc. dates, chopped length wise

4½ oz. sliced, smoked chicken

¼ c. croutons

1 Tbsp. spiced pecans

3 oz. Champagne Vinaigrette (1 oz. on plate, 2 oz. in salad)

1 Tbsp. toasted sunflower seeds (on top)

1 Tbsp. Feta cheese crumbles (on top)

Walt's Champagne Vinaigrette

¾ c. lemon juice (fresh squeezed)

½ c. champagne vinegar (Roland Brand)

½ c. sugar

¼ c. fresh garlic, minced by hand

2 Tbsp. mustard (French's)

1 Tbsp. + 1 tsp. kosher salt

1 Tbsp. fresh ground pepper

1 egg yolk

5 c. olive oil (Tutino blended oil)

2 Tbsp. fresh tarragon, chopped medium

2 Tbsp. fresh chives, minced

Put the first 4 ingredients in a blender. Transfer to a mixing bowl and complete recipe using hand whip. Mix in the next 4 ingredients; then add the oil at a slow steady stream emulsifying the dressing. When thoroughly blended, add the herbs and incorporate them. Place in an ice bath to bring dressing to serving temperature of 35–38 degrees.

Charleston's

Walt's Champagne
Chicken Salad

Splendid Raspberry Spinach Salad

2 Tbsp. raspberry vinegar

2 Tbsp. raspberry jam

⅓ c. vegetable oil

8 c. fresh spinach leaves, torn

¾ c. Macadamia nuts, chopped

1 c. fresh raspberries

3 kiwis, peeled and sliced

Combine vinegar and jam in blender or small bowl. Add oil in thin stream, blending well. Toss spinach with half of the nuts, half of the raspberries, half of the kiwi, and the dressing. Put on serving plate and top with remaining nuts, raspberries, and kiwi. Dressing is good on everything. Equally good using strawberry vinegar, strawberry jam, and fresh strawberries.

Oklahoma Women: Nancy, Penny, Ronnye

Zucchini and Hominy Salad

6 small zucchini

2 avocados, peeled, diced

2 medium tomatoes, seeded, diced

1 14½-oz. can white hominy, rinsed and drained

2 Tbsp. fresh cilantro leaves, rinsed and dried

½ c. fresh Parmesan, shaved

3 Tbsp. fresh lime juice

1 tsp. salt

1 tsp. sugar

6 Tbsp. extra-virgin olive oil

black pepper, for garnish

shaved Parmesan, for garnish

Blanch the whole zucchini in salted, boiling water until crisp-tender; refresh in ice-cold water and pat dry. Cut into large dice and place in a medium bowl. Add the avocados, tomatoes, hominy, cilantro, and Parmesan and lightly mix together.

In a small bowl, whisk together the lime juice, salt, sugar, and olive oil. Add to the zucchini mixture, toss lightly and chill for 30 minutes.

To serve, place salad on a serving platter, top with a few grinds of black pepper, and garnish with shaved Parmesan. Serve cold or at room temperature. Makes 8 servings.

Jane Lodes

SPINACH SALAD WITH CREAMY MUSTARD DRESSING

1 lb. spinach, rinsed, stemmed, and torn into pieces
½ lb. bacon, fried crisp, drained, and crumbled
¼ lb. mushrooms, sliced
1 c. sliced water chestnuts
½ c. sliced black olives

Creamy Mustard Dressing:
2 hard-boiled eggs, mashed with fork while still warm
½ tsp. salt
1½ tsp. sugar
1 Tbsp. coarsely ground black pepper
1 clove garlic, crushed
½ c. virgin olive oil
1 Tbsp. Dijon mustard
5 Tbsp. heavy cream
¼ c. red wine vinegar

In a large bowl, combine all ingredients and toss well with creamy mustard dressing.

Dressing: One at a time and in order, thoroughly blend all other ingredients into mashed eggs. Do not substitute. When blended, whisk until smooth.

Nancy Norman Le Vesque

Party Layered Salad

½ head iceberg lettuce
1 10-oz. bag fresh spinach
4 hard-boiled eggs, chopped
1 bunch green onions, chopped
1 lb. bacon, crisply fried and crumbled
1 10-oz. pkg. frozen tiny peas, thawed
1 can water chestnuts
2 tsp. sugar
salt and pepper
1 c. Swiss cheese

Dressing:
1½ c. sour cream
1½ c. mayonnaise (not miracle whip)

Wash, drain, tear lettuce and spinach into pieces. In a 9x13 dish, using only half of the ingredients, layer the lettuce, spinach, egg, onion, bacon, peas, water chestnuts, and cheese. Sprinkle 1 tsp. sugar, salt, pepper. Spread half of the dressing mixture. Repeat the layers using the remaining ingredients. Spread the remaining dressing and cover with Swiss cheese. Cover and refrigerate overnight.

Penny S. Hague

Southwest Cornbread Salad

¾ c. purchased ranch salad dressing
15 slices purchased pre-cooked bacon
8 c. cornbread, cut in ¾-inch cubes
1 medium tomato, diced

¼ c. red onion, chopped

¼ c. chopped fresh cilantro

1 11-oz. can Mexicorn

Combine and refrigerate for 2 hours and serve.

Linda Praytor

Pear Salad

1 avocado

1–2 cans well-drained Sun Pears (S&W)

½ red onion, sliced thin

1 c. toasted broken walnuts or pecans (Toast 350 degrees for about 5–7 minutes.)

lettuce (I use Romaine and mixed lettuce or spinach.)

Dressing:

⅓ c. red wine vinegar

⅓ c. salad oil

½ c. sugar

Lawry's seasoning

pepper

Place all salad ingredients in bowl in order listed. Mix salad dressing ingredients and set aside. Just before serving, shake dressing and pour over salad. Toss.

Note: The dressing will toss 2x the recipe. (I eyeball the amounts - like half of the ⅓ c.) You can make the salad and place in a cool place and toss later. Be sure to add ingredients in the order listed. I do not put nuts in until last.

Lloyd and Alma Baum

White Shoe Peg Corn Salad

1 16-oz. can white shoe peg corn, drained
1 16-oz. can French style green beans, drained
1 c. celery, chopped fine
1 c. green bell pepper, chopped
2 bunches green onions, chopped
½ c. green olives, chopped
1 tsp. salt
1 tsp. pepper

Dressing:
1 c. sugar
½ c. salad oil
½ c. vinegar

Boil sugar, salad oil, and vinegar until sugar melts. Let cool. Pour in mixture over vegetables. Refrigerate overnight before serving.

Winnie Fiddler

Granny Blain's Bean Salad

1 head lettuce
½ onion
1 stalk celery
3 sweet pickles
3 hard-boiled eggs
1 can pinto beans, drained
Miracle Whip

Chop all ingredients. Add Miracle Whip to taste.

Johnnie and Monte Blain

ORIENTAL SALAD

1 pkg. cole slaw mix
4 carrots, grated
6 green onions, cut up
1 pkg. seasoning in noodles
1 pkg. Ramen noodles (oriental)
Break noodles in to small pieces. Mix all together.

Dressing:
½ c. oil
1 Tbsp. vinegar
2 Tbsp. sugar
1 pkg. seasoning from noodles

Mix and pour over salad.

Jody O'Rorke

PEA SALAD

1 can French-sliced green beans
1 can green peas
2 cans shoe peg corn
1 can water chestnuts, sliced
1 can bean sprouts
2 small cans sliced mushrooms
1–2 jars sliced pimientos
1 large green pepper, diced
1 red onion, sliced in thin rings

Amy Mainord

STRAWBERRY DELIGHT JELL-O SALAD

1 6-oz. pkg. strawberry gelatin

1 c. boiling water

2 12-oz. pkg. frozen sliced strawberries, thawed

1 20-oz. can crushed pineapple, drained

3 medium bananas, mashed

1 c. chopped nuts

1 8-oz. pkg. cream cheese

1 c. sour cream

In a large bowl, stir gelatin into boiling water until dissolved. Add strawberries with juice, pineapple, bananas, and nuts. Pour half the mixture into 12x8 container and refrigerate until firm. Soften cream cheese and combine with sour cream. Beat the mixture until very smooth. Spread evenly over chilled layer. Then spoon remaining half of strawberry mixture over the cream cheese. Chill until firm and cut into squares and serve.

Linda Praytor

STRAWBERRY SALAD

2 c. crushed pretzels

1 c. + 2 Tbsp. sugar

¾ c. oleo, melted

1 8-oz. pkg. cream cheese

1 8-oz.pkg. whipped topping

1 large box strawberry Jell-o

2 c. boiling water

2 10-oz. pkg. frozen strawberries, with juice

1 8-oz. can crushed pineapple with juice

Mix pretzels and 2 Tbsp. sugar. Add melted oleo. Press into a 9 x12 pan. Bake at 400 for 7 minutes. Remove from oven and cool. Have cream cheese and whipped topping at room temperature, then cream together. Add 1 cup sugar. Pour over cooled pretzel crust, making sure that all is covered. Cool. Dissolve Jell-o in boiling water. Add strawberries and pineapple. Chill until thick. Pour over cream cheese mixture. Place in refrigerator.

Jennifer Freed

CHERRY MOLD WITH LEMON CREAM

1 large pkg. cherry gelatin
2 20-oz. cans cherry pie filling
1 c. boiling water
1 8-oz. container whipping cream or nondairy whipped topping
1½ c. sour cream
1 small pkg. lemon gelatin
¼ c. chopped nuts (sliced almonds, slightly toasted)
1 c. cold water

Dissolve cherry gelatin in boiling water. Add cherry pie filling and cold water. Pour cherry mixture into large gelatin mold or into glass dish. Chill until firm. Mix whipping cream, sour cream, and lemon gelatin powder. Spread cream mixture over molded cherry gelatin. Garnish with sliced almonds.

Nancy Norman Le Vesque

CORNBREAD SALAD

1 8½-oz. box corn muffin mix
½ c. chopped white onion
½ c. sugar
1 bell pepper, chopped
9 slices bacon, cooked and crumbled
2 small tomatoes, seeded and chopped
1 c. real mayonnaise

Make 9 x 9 pan of cornbread according to package directions, adding sugar to batter.

Cool cornbread, crumble into bowl and add remaining ingredients. Mix well and refrigerate overnight. Makes 8–10 servings.

Note: This is a great recipe to double for a large group. Real bacon bits can be substituted in a pinch. Very unusual, but very good!

Diane Sisemore from Cafe Oklahoma Cookbook

BLACK-EYED PEA SALAD

Salad:
3 10-oz. packages frozen black-eyed peas
1 medium red bell pepper, chopped
⅓ c. fresh chopped parsley, divided
1 small red onion, thinly sliced, divided

Vinaigrette Dressing:
1 c. red wine vinegar
1 c. sugar
¼ c. vegetable oil
1 ¾ tsp. salt
¾ tsp. coarsely ground black pepper
⅛ tsp. minced garlic

Cook frozen black-eyed peas according to package directions and drain. In large bowl, combine black-eyed peas with remaining salad ingredients, holding out 1 Tbsp. parsley and some red onion slices for garnish. For vinaigrette dressing, whisk vinegar and sugar until sugar is dissolved. Gradually whisk in oil and remaining ingredients until thoroughly combined. Pour dressing over salad and allow to marinate 2 hours in refrigerator before serving. Salad can be placed on large platter lined with lettuce leaves and garnished with remaining parsley and red onion slices. Makes 12–14 servings.

Diane Sisemore from Cafe Oklahoma Cookbook

ALMOST HERMAN'S RESTAURANT OF OKC SALAD

2 medium heads cabbage, shredded

2 medium onions, thinly sliced

⅞ c. sugar

In a bowl, combine cabbage and onions. Sprinkle sugar over cabbage and onions. Pour dressing over cabbage and onions. Mix well and cover. Refrigerate at least 4 hours.

Dressing:

2 Tbsp. sugar

2 tsp. mustard

2 tsp. celery seed

1 Tbsp. salt

¾ c. oil

1 c. vinegar

Mix sugar, mustard, celery seed, salt, oil, and vinegar and bring to boil.

Note: Keeps indefinitely. I like grated carrots added to slaw and it's prettier too!

Thelma (Roberts) Cooper

CRANBERRY SALAD

3 pkg. whole cranberries

3 c. sugar

3 small cans mandarin oranges

3 c. miniature marshmallows

3 c. chopped pecans

Wash and grind cranberries, add sugar, and mix well. Refrigerate overnight. The next morning, drain excess liquid, stir in oranges, marshmallows and nuts. Return to refrigerator until served. Stir well before serving. Best made 2 or 3 days in advance.

Clif and Gloria Scott

CLARA MILLS FROZEN CRANBERRY SALAD

1 can Eagle brand milk
¼ c. lemon juice
1 21-oz. can crushed pineapple, drained
¼ c. walnuts, chopped
1 can whole berry cranberry sauce
1 8-oz. tub cool whip

Mix Eagle brand milk and lemon juice together. Add pineapples, walnuts, and cranberry sauce; mix well and fold in cool whip. Pour into a 9x13 dish and freeze. This makes a great dessert to serve with Thanksgiving Dinner.

Clara Mills

HOLIDAY SALAD

1 large pkg. raspberry Jell-o
1 can applesauce
2 pkg. frozen raspberries, drained
1 c. boiling water

Mix all ingredients and refrigerate until Jell-o is set.

Joan Perry

GRAPE SALAD

2 c. seedless grapes
2 c. chopped broccoli
1 c. raisins
1 lb. bacon, fried and crumbled
3 oz. sunflower seeds
1 Tbsp. finely chopped onion

Mix and cover with dressing.

Dressing:
1 c. mayonnaise
¼ c. milk
¼ c. sugar
1Tbsp. lemon juice

Note: Can use red or green grapes or combination and add more if desired. Best to mix and refrigerate over night.

Dot Fry

CHICKEN SALAD

4 chicken breasts, cooked and diced
½ c. sliced water chestnuts
½ c. chopped pecans
½ c. seedless grapes, red or green
¼ c. finely chopped celery
1 tsp. finely minced candied ginger
¾ c. mayonnaise
2 Tbsp. wine vinegar
1 Tbsp. soy sauce
2 tsp. minced onion

½ tsp. curry powder

Mix chicken, water chestnuts, pecans, grapes, celery, and ginger. In a separate bowl, blend mayonnaise, vinegar, soy sauce, onion, and curry powder. Toss dressing with the chicken mixture. Chill. To serve, either spoon onto pineapple slices arranged on lettuce leaves, or as a sandwich on croissants.

Jennifer Freed

SHRIMP AND PASTA SALAD

1 lb. cooked shrimp, peeled, de-veined, and chilled
12 oz. mini seashell pasta, cooked, drained, and peeled
3 oz. capers, drained
1 c. Hellman's mayonnaise
3 Tbsp. fresh dill, minced
¼ c. whole grain mustard
2 julienne sweet red peppers
⅓ c. champagne vinegar
¼ c. canola oil
2 Tbsp. white sugar to taste
salt and pepper to taste

Combine all ingredients, reserving shrimp and pasta. Mix well, season to taste. Drain and pat dry shrimp. Add shrimp and pasta to mix; adjust seasoning. Remember the dressing for this salad will be slightly strong, but the addition of the shrimp and pasta will tone it down. Garnish with few reserved shrimp and fresh watercress or sweet pea shoots. Makes 6–7 servings.

Cathy Keating from Ooh La La Recipe Book

AMARETTO CHICKEN SALAD

Salad:

4 c. cooked chicken, diced

1 15-oz. can crushed pineapple

¾ c. chopped celery

½ c. toasted slivered almonds

½ c. mayonnaise

pineapple rings

Dressing:

1 c. mayonnaise

¼ c. amaretto

Stir dressing ingredients together. Combine chicken, crushed pineapple, celery, half of the almonds (save half for garnish), and mayonnaise. Chill for several hours. Serve on lettuce leaves with pineapple rings. Top with dressing and sprinkle with almonds.

Taste of Territory Recipe Book

BLUE CHEESE POTATO SALAD

8 medium potatoes

2 Tbsp. chopped parsley

3 green onions with tops, chopped

1½ tsp. salt

1 c. sour cream

½ c. slivered almonds, toasted

¼ tsp. white pepper

8 oz. bleu cheese (or to taste)

¼ c. wine vinegar

3 eggs, hard-boiled

bacon, crumbled for garnish

Boil and peel potatoes. Cool and dice. Combine remaining ingredients. Garnish with crumbled bacon and refrigerate. For the bleu cheese lover! Unique and delicious!

Jr. Service League of Bartlesville

Hearts of Palm and Shrimp Salad

Salad:
1 14-oz. can hearts of palm, drained
romaine lettuce leaves

Dressing:
2 Tbsp. white wine vinegar
4 Tbsp. olive oil or salad oil
3 Tbsp. green onion, minced
⅓ lb. small shrimp, cooked
salt

Prepare dressing by combining vinegar, oil, green onion, shrimp, and salt to taste. Cut each heart of palm stalk crosswise into ½-inch thick slices; place in deep bowl. Mix dressing gently with hearts of palm; cover and chill for 2–6 hours. Arrange several romaine leaves on each of 6 salad plates. Spoon equal portions of hearts of palm mixture onto lettuce.

Ronnye Sharp

Margarita Caesar Salad

Salad:
1 large head romaine lettuce, torn
1 c. (4 oz.) shredded Monterey jack cheese
¼ c. fresh cilantro, chopped
1 sweet red pepper, cut in thin strips

Dressing:

⅓ c. canola oil

¼ c. lime juice

1½ Tbsp. tequila

1¼ tsp. Triple Sec

1 clove garlic, minced

½ -1 Serrano chile, finely chopped

¼ tsp. salt

¼ tsp. ground cumin

2 Tbsp. egg substitute

Prepare dressing by mixing ingredients with a wire whisk. Cover and chill. Combine lettuce, cheese, cilantro, and red pepper in a large bowl. Toss dressing and salad gently. Salt the rims of salad plates by rubbing with lime wedges and rolling rim of plate in Kosher salt. Garnish with lime wedges and tortilla chips.

Jr. Service League of Bartlesville

Avocado Shrimp Salad

Salad:

2 lbs. medium-sized shrimp

1 large avocado, cubed

leaf, romaine, or Boston lettuce, shredded

Dressing:

½ c. olive oil

¼ c. white wine vinegar

2 Tbsp. lemon juice

½ tsp. garlic salt

⅛ tsp. seasoned pepper

½ c. minced green onion

Place shrimp in a pan, cover with boiling water, and simmer 5–8 minutes or until shrimp turn pink. Shell and de-vein shrimp. Place shrimp and avocado in bowl. Mix dressing ingredients and pour over shrimp and avocado to coat well. Cover and chill 1–2 hours. Lift shrimp and avocado from dressing and serve on platter with shredded lettuce. Use remaining dressing as needed.

Jr. Service League of Bartlesville

FRUITY CHICKEN SALAD

1 15¼-oz. can pineapple tidbits

4 c. chopped, cooked chicken (9 chicken breasts)

1 11-oz. can mandarin oranges, drained

1 2½- oz. pkg. sliced almonds, toasted

1 c. chopped celery

1 c. seedless green grapes, cut in half

1½ c. mayonnaise

1 Tbsp. soy sauce

1 tsp. curry powder

1 3-oz. can chow mien noodles

Drain pineapple, reserving 2 Tbsp. juice. Combine pineapple tidbits and next 6 ingredients; mix well. Combine 2 Tbsp. pineapple juice, mayonnaise, soy sauce, and curry powder; stir well, add to chicken mixture. Chill. Sprinkle noodles on top before serving.

Dr. Scott Stewart and Robin Stewart

Hot Ma Ma

¾ -1 c. of raw rice
2 cartons sour cream
1 can green chilies
longhorn cheese, grated and divided

Cook rice. Add sour cream and salt, to taste. Pour half of mixture into 8 x 9 casserole. Spread layer of green chilies and top with grated cheese. Top with remaining rice. Dot with butter and ½ cup grated cheese. Bake at 375 for 30 minutes.

Mainord Family

Phil Tower in Tulsa

*Capitol Dome
painting*

Oklahoma:
The Energy State

Oklahoma: The Energy State

by Bob Burke

Each year, the majority of Oklahoma's top ten fastest growing companies are from the energy sector. Also, for most of the twentieth century, Oklahoma's largest companies were energy-related corporations. Those facts are a reflection of the large role energy has played in the state's history.

The naturally occurring pools of oil and pockets of gas deep beneath the Oklahoma landscape are legendary, as are the many lakes that produce hydroelectric power and the Oklahoma wind that provides energy through windmill farms.

In the nineteenth century, oil seeping into streams caught the attention of Native Americans. Shallow wells were drilled before the Civil War, but the first commercial oil well, the Nellie Johnston No. 1, was not completed at Bartlesville until 1897. From that time, well into the 1920s, Oklahoma led the world in oil production. Wildcatters made millions by sinking holes into the rich, petroleum-soaked sands underneath Oklahoma.

The names of Oklahoma oil barons are among the most famous in American energy history. George Getty, and his son, J. Paul Getty, made their first millions in Oklahoma. So did Harry F. Sinclair, William G. Skelly, Erle P. Halliburton, the Phillips brothers, and E.W. Marland. John Nichols, the founder of Devon Energy Corporation, created the first plan to finance oil and gas production that was approved by the Securities and Exchange Commission, a move that changed the way that petroleum production was financed worldwide.

Because of the discovery of oil in Red Fork in 1901, Tulsey Town, a sleepy Creek village across the Arkansas River, became a thriving center of oil and gas activity and was later dubbed as the "oil capital of the world." At one time, many of America's largest oil companies headquartered in Tulsa.

Marland founded what became Conoco. Later, as governor of Oklahoma, he was largely responsible for creation of the Interstate Oil and Gas Compact Commission, an organization of the governors of oil and natural gas producing states that helps regulate the industry.

Kerr-McGee Corporation, Conoco, and Phillips outlasted competitors to take their place among the nation's largest petroleum companies. In the current generation, Devon Energy and Chesapeake Energy are among the energy leaders in the United States. Kerr-McGee drilled the world's first commercial offshore oil well in the Gulf of Mexico. Phillips' scientists invented plastic and the aerosol spray can in Bartlesville. Devon is the largest independent producer of natural gas in the United States. The Williams Companies began as a design and construction business in the oil and gas pipeline business and built the nation's first coal-slurry pipeline in 1956.

By 2002, more than 500,000 oil and gas wells had been drilled in Oklahoma. Oil and gas production, through booms and busts, has been a steady part of the growth of Oklahoma. Oklahoma ranks second, behind Texas, in natural gas production in the nation.

Oklahoma has been blessed with community-friendly suppliers of electricity and natural gas. Oklahoma Gas and Electric Company is the state's largest supplier of electricity. AEP Public Service Company is also a major player in supplying electricity. Many electric cooperatives provide electric power in rural areas of the state. Natural gas is supplied to much of the state by the giant utility, Oklahoma Natural Gas Company. Reliant Energy Arkla also serves many customers in the state with natural gas.

Since before statehood, coal has been mined in eastern Oklahoma. In 1975, Kerr-McGee Corporation drilled the deepest coal mine shaft in the Western Hemisphere in that part of the state.

Alternative fuel is part of the story of Oklahoma energy. In the future, Oklahoma is expected to lead the way with research and development of new fuels.

It is hard to imagine Oklahoma's first century as a state without the positive influence of the energy industry.

CEO Tom Ward

SandRidge
ENERGY

Discovering Beneath | Exploring Beyond™

Headquartered in Oklahoma City, Oklahoma, SandRidge Energy, Inc. is a rapidly growing independent natural gas and oil company concentrating on exploration, development, and production activities. The company is comprised of employees who value integrity and community and are dedicated to harvesting and supplying this country's natural resources to the U.S. market in a safe, quick, and cost-effective manner. In the process, SandRidge protects the environment, recognizes and rewards the individual efforts of those who work for it, and enriches the communities where its employees live and work.

SandRidge focuses its exploration and production activities in West Texas, the Cotton Valley Trend in East Texas, and the Gulf Coast. SandRidge also owns oil and gas properties in the Piceance Basin of Colorado, the Gulf of Mexico, and the Anadarko and Arkoma Basins. In addition, the company owns and operates drilling rigs and a related oil field services business operating under the Lariat Services, Inc. brand name; gas gathering, marketing, and processing facilities; and, through its subsidiary, PetroSource Energy Company, CO_2 treating and transportation facilities and tertiary oil recovery operations.

SandRidge strives to be an asset to every community where it operates by developing partnerships that help enhance the quality of life for every resident in the area. Specifically, the company seeks to form partnerships with non-profit programs that reflect a true dedication to the populations they serve.

The company places its primary community focus on child advocacy efforts by supporting a variety of initiatives and organizations that further the health/wellness, education, and well-being of children. For example, SandRidge actively supports White Fields, a community-style home for boys in Piedmont, Oklahoma.

In addition to providing direct financial support, SandRidge encourages its employees to participate in community enrichment efforts and to share their personal knowledge, expertise, time, income, and talent through volunteerism, fundraising activities, and financial support. SandRidge employees are active participants in local efforts to improve health and human services, education, and rural revitalization. As a result, SandRidge Energy, Inc. plays an integral role in every community where our employees live or work.

The company's Internet address is www.sandridgeenergy.com.

OLETA'S CAKE

1 c. ripe bananas, mashed (a little more will not hurt)
1 tsp. lemon juice
1½ c. sugar
1 tsp. vanilla extract
1 tsp. baking soda
½ c. buttermilk or sour milk
⅔ c. Crisco
2 eggs
2 c. flour
½ tsp. salt
½ c. chopped pecans or walnuts

Preheat oven to 350 (325 if using a glass pan). Mash bananas and mix lemon juice. Set aside. Cream Crisco and sugar. Add eggs and vanilla. Mix well. In a separate bowl, mix flour, soda, and salt. Add this alternately to creamed mixture with buttermilk. Blend in the bananas. Stir in the nuts. Bake in a greased and floured 9x13 pan for 35–40 minutes. Cool completely then frost with cream cheese icing.

Cream Cheese Icing:
1 8-oz. pkg. cream cheese
4 c. powdered sugar
½ c. butter
1 tsp. black walnut or vanilla extract
coconut (optional)

Cream together cream cheese and butter. Add flavoring and powdered sugar. Spread on cooled cake. Sprinkle with coconut and enjoy.

Tom and Sch'ree Ward

Entrees

Roast Tenderloin of Beef with Whiskey Peppercorn Jus

1 3–4 lb. beef tenderloin, well-trimmed

salt and freshly ground black pepper

2 Tbsp. oil

½ c. sour Mash Whiskey

1 shallot, peeled and minced

3 tsp. assorted color peppercorn

¼ c. beef stock

4 Tbsp. butter, cut in pieces

Linda Praytor, owner of
Honeysuckle Rose Gardens

Preheat oven to 400. Generously season beef with salt and pepper (Kosher and fresh ground pepper). Heat oil in a large oven-proof skillet over high heat and add the meat and brown on all sides. Transfer to oven and roast (30 minutes - rare, 45 minutes - medium). Transfer to cutting board, cover with foil, and wait 15 minutes before slicing. Warm the whiskey in a small pan over low heat. Return the oven-proof skillet to medium heat. Add the shallots to the drippings, 1–2 minutes. Add the peppercorns, then the whiskey, and carefully ignite with a kitchen match. When the flame has died out, continue cooking 1 minute. Add the stock and cook. Reduce to half (1–2 minutes). Add butter and continue to cook for 2–3 minutes. Serve over meat.

Honeysuckle Rose Gardens

Grillades and Baked Cheese Grits

4 ½ lb. round steak (½ -inch thick)

2 tsp. salt

2 tsp. pepper

⅔ c. vegetable oil, divided

⅔ c. all-purpose flour

1½ c. chopped onion

1½ c. chopped green bell pepper

½ c. chopped green onions

½ c. chopped celery

½ c. chopped fresh parsley

3 garlic cloves, minced

2 c. water

1 tsp dried thyme

2 14½ -oz. cans stewed tomatoes, undrained

2 bay leaves

Garnish: fresh parsley sprigs

Pound steak to ½-inch thickness, using a meat mallet or rolling pin. Cut steak into 12 serving-size pieces. Combine salt and pepper; sprinkle evenly over both sides of beef. Cook beef, a few pieces at a time, in ⅓ cup hot oil in a large Dutch oven over medium-high heat until browned on both sides. Remove beef from Dutch oven, and set aside. Add remaining ⅓ cup oil to drippings in Dutch oven; gradually stir in flour. Cook over medium heat 5 minutes, stirring constantly. Stir in 2 cups onion and next 5 ingredients; cook over medium-high heat, stirring constantly, 7 minutes or until vegetables are tender. Stir in water and next 3 ingredients. Add beef; bring to a boil. Cover, reduce heat, and simmer 1½ hours or until beef is tender, stirring and scraping bottom of Dutch oven often. Discard bay leaves. Transfer beef mixture to a serving platter, garnish, if desired. Serve with Baked Cheese Grits. Makes 12 servings.

BAKED CHEESE GRITS

5 c. water

1 tsp. salt

⅔ c. uncooked quick-cooking yellow grits

⅔ c. uncooked quick-cooking white grits

2 c. (8 oz.) shredded sharp cheddar cheese

½ c. butter

1 15½-oz. can yellow hominy, drained (optional)

¾ c. grated Parmesan cheese

Bring water and salt to a boil in a large saucepan; gradually stir in grits. Cover, reduce heat, and simmer 5 minutes, stirring occasionally. Add cheddar cheese, butter, and hominy, stirring until cheese and butter melt. Pour mixture into a lightly greased 9x13 baking dish; sprinkle evenly with Parmesan cheese. Bake, uncovered, at 350 for 45 minutes or until set. Makes 12 servings.

SIRLOIN TIPS OVER ALMOND RICE

1 lb. mushrooms, sliced
¼ c. butter
2 Tbsp. vegetable oil
3 lbs. sirloin steak, cut in 1-inch cubes
¾ c. beef bouillon
¾ c. red wine
2 Tbsp. soy sauce
2 cloves garlic, crushed
½ onion, grated
2 Tbsp. cornstarch
½ c. beef bouillon
½ can cream of mushroom soup

Almond Rice:
½ c. slivered almonds
3 Tbsp. butter
1½ c. rice
3½ c. water

Saute mushrooms in 2 Tbsp. butter in a skillet until brown. Spoon into 3-quart casserole. Add remaining butter and oil to skillet. Brown meat. Spoon over mushrooms. Combine ¾ cup bouillon, wine, soy sauce, garlic, and onion in skillet. Blend cornstarch with ½ cup bouillon. Stir into skillet. Cook, stirring, until thick. Spoon over meat. Bake covered at 275 for at least 1 hour. Add mushroom soup and a dash of salt. Bake 15 minutes longer. Prepare almond rice by sautéing almonds in butter. Add rice and water. Stir briefly, cover and cook for 20 minutes. Serve sirloin tips over almond rice.

Foster Ranch

Boeuf Bourguignon (Burgundy Beef)

2 lb. lean beef
2 Tbsp. bacon drippings
10 small or 5 medium-sized onions
1½ Tbsp. flour
marjoram
thyme
salt
pepper and Tabasco sauce
½ c. beef bouillon
1 c. dry red wine
½ lb. fresh mushrooms

Fry sliced onions in bacon drippings in heavy skillet until brown. Remove to separate dish. Cut lean beef to 1-inch cubes and sauce in the same drippings, adding more fat if necessary. When the beef is browned, sprinkle over them the flour, salt, pepper, Tabasco sauce, marjoram, and thyme. Then add ½ cup beef bouillon to contents of skillet, and 1 c. of good red wine. Stir well and then let simmer slowly for 3 ¼ hours. The liquid may cook away some, so add a little more bouillon and wine (one part stock to two parts wine) as necessary to keep beef barely covered. After 3 ¼ hours, return the browned onions to skillet, add the mushrooms, and stir well. Allow to cook for 45 minutes-1 hour longer. Add more stock and wine if necessary. The sauce should be thick and dark brown.

Mrs. William W. Coulter, Jr.

Filet De Boeuf

Roast whole 5 lb. filet in 425 degree oven 30–34 minutes. Should be served rare and with Sauce Marchand du Vin. Allow to repose 15 minutes before serving.

½ c. thinly sliced mushrooms
4 Tbsp. butter, divided
1 ½ c. hot beef broth, divided
½ c. thinly sliced onions

½ c. Madeira wine

2 Tbsp. flour

salt and paprika

Sauté mushrooms in 2 Tbsp. butter until tender. Add ½ cup beef broth and simmer, covered, 10 minutes. In separate pan, sauté onions and 2 Tbsp. butter. Add remaining 1 cup beef broth and wine. Cover and simmer 20 minutes. Sprinkle flour over onion mixture and cook until smoothly thickened. Add mushroom mixture, heat well. Season with salt and paprika.

Mrs. Walter B. Comeaux, Jr.

BETSY'S ROUND STEAK

1 ½ lb. round steak, thick

1 egg, beaten

½ c. grated Parmesan cheese

⅓ c. fine, dry breadcrumbs

1 onion, minced

⅓ c. Wesson oil

1 6-oz. can tomato paste

2 c. hot water

½ tsp. pepper

1 tsp. sugar

½ tsp. oregano

Pound flour into round steak. Trim off fat and cut into pieces. Dip meat into beaten egg. Roll meat in bread crumbs and half of cheese. Brown in oil. Put browned meat in shallow baking dish. Put onions in pan meat was browned in and sauté. Combine tomato paste, hot water, and spices. Boil mixture for 5 minutes. Pour most of sauce over meat, add half cheese and rest of sauce. Bake at 350 for 1 hour.

Betsy Brady Wild

COKE ROAST

4 lb. roast (chuck, round, or sirloin tip)
salt, pepper, garlic salt
3 Tbsp. oil
small bottle Coca-Cola
14 oz. chili sauce
Worcestershire sauce
Tabasco sauce

Score roast in several places. Fill each slit with salt, pepper, and garlic salt. Sear roast on all sides in oil. Remove, drain or blot fat from roast. Place roast in foil-lined pan. Pour Coke, chili sauce over roast, then Worcestershire and Tabasco sauce. Cover loosely with foil and bake 3 hours in a 325 degree oven. It will have a barbecued flavor and tastes good the next day, too.

Mrs. Richard P. Sevier

OKLAHOMA DAD'S SWISS STEAK

5 lb. round steak or rump roast

3 large onions

½ bunch of celery

Wesson Oil

1 Tbsp. flour

1 small can tomato sauce

1 can cream of mushroom soup

1 pt. tomato juice

Chop onions and celery; boil and drain. Save to cover steak. Trim fat from steak or roast, slice and cut in pieces. Flour and brown (season) in oil. Put all pieces in Dutch oven or roaster. In oil, brown flour, stir. Add tomato sauce, juice, and cream of mushroom soup. Sitr well over heat. Then cover steak and onions. Bake in oven 2 hours at 300.

Jane Jayroe Gamble

Jane Jayroe, Miss America 1967, has long been an ambassador of goodwill for Oklahoma. Following her reign as Miss America she was an award-winning news anchor and Secretary of Tourism in the administration of Oklahoma Governor Frank Keating.

The recipe is from Jane's grandfather, Homer Lyle Smith, called "Oklahoma Dad." He continued to farm his land in the Oklahoma Panhandle until his death, but he loved to cook beef dishes and make pickles.

Mullendore Cross Bell Sandwich

1 New York strip steak
seasoned salt to taste
1 pear

Cook inside in skillet sprayed with non-stick vegetable spray or outside on grill. Serve on Texas toast accompanied by tomato wedges, kosher dill pickles, and green onions on a large lettuce leaf. Garnish each plate with its own brand. Make the bell by using the top half of a pear and make the cross by using two slices from the bottom half. No steak sauce of any kind is offered. The true flavor of a good steak should never be covered.

Oklahoma Classic

Beef Parmigiana

1 lb. round steak
½ c. Parmesan cheese
½ c. breadcrumbs
oil
garlic (optional)
1 onion, chopped
1 tsp. salt
¼ tsp pepper
½ tsp. sugar
½ tsp. marjoram
1 tsp. oregano
1 16-oz. can tomato sauce
½ c. water
6–8 oz. Mozzarella cheese

Preheat oven to 350. Pound meat and cut into serving pieces. Dip meat in mixture of Parmesan cheese and crumbs, coating well. Brown in oil. Add garlic, if desired. Remove to baking dish. Brown onion and put on top of meat with seasonings. Pour over tomato sauce and ½ cup water. Bake 1 hour. Top with Mozzarella cheese just before done, to melt. Makes 4–6 servings.

Mrs. Mark Dunn

FAMILY FAVORITE MEATLOAF

salad oil to sauté
1 carrot, diced
2 stalks celery, diced
1 medium onion, diced
1 lb. ground chuck
1 lb. ground beef
2 eggs
salt and pepper
2 tsp. prepared yellow mustard
¼ c. brown sugar
dash of Tabasco
2 Tbsp. Worcestershire sauce
1 sleeve of saltine crackers, crumbled
½ c. seasoned Italian breadcrumbs
¼ c. ketchup

Topping:
⅓ c. ketchup
2 Tbsp. brown sugar
1 Tbsp. prepared mustard

Preheat oven to 375. Sauté the carrots, celery, and onions in the salad oil until tender. Mix in a large bowl the ground chuck and ground beef. Add the sautéed carrots, celery, onions. Mix and add the eggs, salt and pepper, mustard, brown sugar, ketchup, Tabasco, crackers, and bread crumbs. Form into a loaf and place in pan. Spread topping over the top. Cook 45–55 minutes. Let set 10 minutes before serving.

Linda Praytor

EASY BRISKET

5–6 lb. brisket
2 pkg. Lipton dry soup mix
½ c. water

Put one package soup mix on the bottom of the pan. Put brisket in pan and cover with other package of soup mix. Pour water over all. Cover pan with foil and don't open till done. Bake at 225 for 8 hours.

Cynthia Ferguson

DRIP BEEF

3–4 lb. rump roast
1 Tbsp. garlic salt
½ tsp. oregano
¼ tsp. rosemary
¾ tsp. savory
2 bouillon cubes

Half cover roast with water, add garlic salt, oregano, rosemary, savory, and bouillon cubes. Cook on top of stove 8–9 hours, adding water during cooking if necessary. Chop and serve on rye bread with hot mustard. Salt and pepper to taste.

Jim Cooper

PEPPER STEAK

1½ lb. sirloin, cut in strips
¼ c. oil
1 c. water
1 onion, cut in slices

½ tsp. garlic salt

¼ tsp. ginger

2 bell peppers, cut in strips

2 Tbsp. flour

3 Tbsp. sugar

1 ½ tsp. soy sauce

2 tomatoes

Trim fat from sirloin and cut into strips; brown in hot oil. Stir in water, onion, garlic salt and ginger. Heat until it boils. Cover and simmer 5–8 minutes. Add peppers during the last 5 minutes of simmering. In small bowl, blend flour, sugar and soy sauce. Stir into meat mixture until thickens. Boil one minute. Add tomatoes. Cook over low heat until heated. Serve over rice.

Deborah Nickell

BAKED STEAK WITH MUSHROOMS

3 ½ lb. round steak, cut 1½ -2 inches thick

meat tenderizer

1 Tbsp. olive oil

2 Tbsp. butter

½ tsp. salt

¾ tsp. thyme

2 cloves garlic, peeled

sliced mushrooms

½ c. burgundy wine

2 Tbsp. parsley

Wipe steak with damp paper towel and sprinkle with tenderizer. Heat oil in large skillet until very hot. Brown steak well, about 5 minutes on each side. Remove steak when browned; drain off all fat; replace steak. Spread with 1 Tbsp. butter; sprinkle with salt and thyme. Place garlic beside steak. Bake, uncovered, 25 minutes. Remove steak to serving platter and keep warm. Add mushrooms to skillet; sauté for 3 minutes until brown. Add wine and bring to a boil, stirring constantly. Boil uncovered to reduce slightly. Remove from heat. Stir in 1 Tbsp. butter, pour over meat, and sprinkle with parsley.

Amy Mainord

BARBEQUED BRISKET

Sprinkle 6 lb. brisket with 3 Tbsp. liquid smoke, garlic powder, onion, salt, and celery salt. Allow to stand overnight covered with foil. Next morning, sprinkle with pepper and Worcestershire sauce. Cover and bake at 275 for 5 hours. Drain grease off. Uncover and bake 1 hour with barbeque sauce.

Barbeque Sauce
1 c. catsup
1 tsp. salt
1 tsp. celery seed
1 onion, chopped
¼ c. brown sugar
¼ c. Worcestershire sauce
2 c. water
¼ c. vinegar

Boil 15 minutes.

Janice Cooper

OKLAHOMA JALAPENO MEAT LOAF
One of Hal Smith's favorites

1 ½ lb. ground sirloin

½ c. Manero's steak sauce

½ c. Peter Luger steak sauce

1 Tbsp. Worcestershire sauce

1 c. plain breadcrumbs

2 eggs, beaten

sea salt and pepper (coarse ground) to taste

½ c. J.R.'s BBQ and Grilling Sauce

1 Tbsp. garlic powder

1 tsp. seasoned salt

1 Tbsp. dried onions

¼ c. Heinz ketchup

Hal Smith of HSRG

Preheat oven to 350. Mix all ingredients, except the ketchup, well. Bake in a 8–9 inch loaf pan for 45 minutes at 350. Remove from oven and drain off meat. Top with the ketchup then bake for 15 minutes more. Serve hot.

GREEN CHILE CASSEROLE

2 lb. hamburger meat
1 onion
1 can green chilies
1 c. grated cheese
1 can mushroom soup
1 can chicken soup
1 can enchilada sauce
1 c. milk
salt and pepper to taste
Doritos

Brown hamburger meat and add onion, green chilies, cheese, soups, enchilada sauce, milk, salt, and pepper. Place a layer of Doritos and meat mixture in 2 layers. Repeat layers. Bake at 350 until bubbly. Makes 10 servings.

Note: Extra cheese may be sprinkled over top when almost done. Meat mixture may be frozen in 2 containers or use 1 and freeze 1 for smaller casserole.

J. Cooper

HAMBURGER-NOODLE CASSEROLE

1 c. sour cream
3 oz. cream cheese, softened
3 green onions, chopped
1 lb. ground beef
2 8-oz. cans tomato sauce
1 tsp. sugar
1 garlic clove
1 pkg. thin noodles
2 c. grated cheddar cheese

Put sour cream, cream cheese, and green onions in large bowl and mix together. Cook noodles. Brown meat with garlic. Add tomato sauce and sugar. Simmer. Pour meat mixture over sour cream mixture and mix. Add drained noodles. Put in a 9x12 casserole dish, cover with cheese, and bake at 325–350 for 30 minutes.

Jennifer Freed

Enchilada Casserole

2 lb. ground chuck
1 medium onion, chopped
2 8-oz. cans tomato sauce
1 11-oz. can Mexicorn, drained
1 10-oz. can red enchilada sauce
1 tsp. chili powder
½ tsp. dried Oregano
½ tsp. pepper
¼ tsp. salt
1 6½-oz. package corn tortillas, divided
2 c. (8 oz.) shredded cheddar cheese, divided
Garnish: green chili peppers

Brown the beef and onion in a large skillet, stirring until it crumbles; drain. Stir in tomato sauce and the next 6 ingredients into the mixture; bring to a boil. Reduce the heat to medium, and cook, uncovered, 5 minutes, stirring occasionally. Place half of the tortillas in the bottom of a greased 9x13 baking dish. Spoon half of the beef mixture over tortillas; sprinkle with 1 cup cheese. Repeat the layers with the remaining tortillas and beef mixture. Bake at 275 for 20 minutes. Sprinkle with remaining cheese; bake 5 additional minutes or until cheese melts. Garnish, if desired. Makes 8 servings.

Cody Smith

Hamburger Casserole

1 ½ lb. Hamburger
2 Tbsp. onions
1 can whole kernel corn, drained
1 can cream of mushroom soup
1 can cream of chicken soup
1 c. sour cream
salt and pepper to taste
2–3 c. cooked noodles

Brown the meat and onions, drain. Add rest of ingredients. Pour into baking dish. Add buttered breadcrumbs on top. Bake at 350 for about 30 minutes.

Monte and Janiece Blain

Mama Mia's Lasagna
(This recipe takes time but is so worth it!)

14 dried lasagna noodles
2 Tbsp. olive oil
1 ½ c. (3 medium) finely chopped carrots
2 c. (1 medium) finely chopped zucchini
4 cloves garlic, minced
3 c. (8 oz.) sliced fresh button mushrooms
2 6-oz. pkg. pre-washed baby spinach
1 lb. Italian sausage
12 slices of small pepperoni
2 Tbsp. snipped fresh basil
1 egg, beaten
1 15-oz. container ricotta cheese
⅓ c. finely shredded Parmesan cheese
½ tsp. salt
¼ tsp. ground black pepper

1 26-oz. (2 ½ c.) jar tomato and basil pasta sauce
2 c. (8 oz.) shredded Italian fontina or mozzarella cheese

Cook noodles according to the package directions. Rinse with cold water. Drain well; set noodles aside. In a large skillet, heat 1 tsp. of the olive oil over medium-high heat. Add carrots, zucchini, and half of the garlic. Cook and stir about 5 minutes or until crispy and tender. Transfer vegetables to a bowl. Add the remaining oil to the same skillet; heat over medium heat. Add mushrooms and remaining garlic. Cook and stir about 5 minutes or until tender. Gradually add spinach. Cook and stir until spinach is wilted. Remove with a spoon to another bowl; stir in basil. Set aside. Combine the egg, ricotta, and Parmesan cheeses, salt, and pepper. Set aside. Preheat oven to 375. To assemble in a 9x13 pan, spread ½ cup pasta sauce. Arrange 3–4 cooked noodles over sauce. Top with half of the spinach-mushroom mixture. Spoon half of ricotta cheese mixture over the spinach mixture. Top with another layer of noodles. Spread with half of remaining pasta sauce. Top with all of the zucchini-carrot mixture. Sprinkle with half of fontina cheese. Top with another layer of noodles. Brown the Italian sausage and drain. Place on noodles. Also layer pepperoni slices on the sausage. Layer with noodles and the remaining spinach-mushroom mixture and the ricotta cheese mixture. Top with another layer of noodles and remaining sauce. Gently press down with the back of a spatula. Bake in preheated oven about 60 minutes. Top with remaining fontina cheese and bake for 15 more minutes. Let stand for 15 minutes before serving to set. Makes 10–12 servings.

Cary Smith

San Remos Restaurant

SALMON POMADORO

1 onion, diced

8 oz. salmon

6 medium mushrooms, sliced

4 Tbsp. olive oil

2 oz. Marsala Wine

2 ⅓ c. of water

1 Tbsp. flour

1 pinch fresh basil

½ pt. cherry tomatoes

6 Tbsp. tomato sauce

In a hot pan add olive oil, chopped onions, basil, and mushrooms; sauté for 2 minutes. Add flour immediately, Marsala wine, water, and tomato sauce. Let boil for 4 minutes once the sauce is lightly thick.

Season salmon with salt and pepper. Lightly oil, put on medium flame grill for 6 minutes: 3 minutes on each side. Once done, add the prepared sauce on top, also add the cherry tomatoes on top.

Laziee Mustani
Tony Veliu

MARGARITA CHICKEN

½ c. frozen nonalcoholic margarita mix, thawed
3 Tbsp. lime juice, freshly squeezed
1 clove garlic, crushed
1 ½ lb. skinless boneless chicken breast halves
coarse salt

Mix margarita mix, lime juice, and garlic in a large re-sealable freezer plastic bag. Add chicken to bag. Seal and turn a few times to coat chicken. Refrigerate, turning bag occasionally. Marinate at least 1 hour, but no longer than 24 hours. Remove chicken from bag and reserve the marinade. On your grill place chicken, skin side up. Brush with marinade and sprinkle with salt. Cover grill with lid and grill, 5–6 inches from medium heat, for 15 minutes. Turn chicken, brush with remaining marinade, and sprinkle with more salt. Cover and grill for 20–40 minutes or until meat is done.

Rhonda Watkins

SOUTHWEST CHICKEN QUESADILLAS

1 10-oz. pkg. Perdue ready cooked chicken
½ c. sliced onions
½ tsp. seasoned salt and pepper to taste
4 10-inch flour tortillas
8 oz. shredded lite Monterey Jack cheese
4 Tbsp. Santa Fe Salsa
2 Tbsp. diced jalapenos (or to taste)
chopped cilantro to taste
low-fat sour cream
Pam nonstick spray
coarse ground pepper to taste

Spray Pam in a medium pan over medium heat, and add chicken and onion until lightly sautéed or onions are translucent, adding seasoned salt and pepper. Set aside. Spray another nonstick pan with Pam, and place over medium-high heat. Place a tortilla in the pan and sprinkle with ¼ of the cheese and ¼ of the jalapenos and top with ¼ of the chicken mixture and 1 Tbsp. of the salsa. Fold the tortilla in half and press with spatula. Cook for about 2 minutes, turn, and cook the second side about 1 minute. Repeat with remaining tortillas. Cut into triangles and serve hot. Garnish with Cilantro and serve with extra salsa and sour cream. Make 4 servings.

Hal Smith's Charleston's Restaurant

Hal Smith

CHICKEN WITH PEACH SALSA

½ c. chopped onion

1 14½-oz. can whole tomatoes, drained and chopped

⅔ c. diced peaches

½ c. peach preserves

1 cinnamon stick

1 Tbsp. chopped fresh cilantro

1 tsp. chopped fresh ginger root or ¼ tsp. dried ginger

¼ tsp. salt

⅛ tsp. pepper

3 whole chicken breasts, skinned, boned, and halved

3 c. cooked rice

Spray a medium non-stick saucepan with cooking spray. Heat over medium heat until hot. Add onion; cook and stir 3 minutes. Add next 8 ingredients. Bring to a boil, reduce heat. Simmer, uncovered, 20–30 minutes or until sauce thickens, stirring occasionally. Keep salsa warm. When ready to serve, remove and discard cinnamon stick. Broil chicken

4–6 inches from heat for 18–20 minutes or until chicken is fork-tender, turning half-way through broiling. Or, charcoal the chicken on a grill for approximately 20 minutes. Serve chicken breast on top of rice; spoon salsa over chicken.

Penny Hague

PARMESAN CRUSTED CHICKEN

2 boneless, skinless chicken breast halves
2 egg whites
2 tsp. cornstarch
juice of ½ lemon
Whisk together the egg whites, cornstarch, and the lemon juice.
Crusting mixture:
½ c. Parmesan cheese
1 c. course dry breadcrumbs
1 Tbsp. chopped fresh parsley
1 tsp. kosher salt
¼ tsp. ground black pepper
zest of one lemon, minced

Honeysuckle Rose Gardens and Linda Praytor at the piano

Preheat oven to 450. Prepare chicken breasts by halving and pounding. Whisk egg whites, cornstarch, and lemon juice in small shallow dish for dipping mixture. Add Parmesan to the crusting mixture. Crust and prepare chicken; let rest, sauté, and roast. Serve with sage butter sauce.

Sage Butter Sauce:
Sauté 1 Tbsp. unsalted butter, 3 Tbsp. shallot, minced.

Add and reduce:

½ c. dry white wine
½ c. heavy cream
½ c. chicken broth

1 tsp. fresh lemon juice

1–2 tsp. minced fresh sage

salt

white pepper

cayenne

Whisk in 4 Tbsp. (½ stick) cold unsalted butter, cubed. Keep in a warm water bath until serving time.

Linda Praytor

RITZY CHICKEN

6 chicken breast halves, with bone, skinned

1 pt. sour cream

⅓ c. milk

4 rolls Ritz crackers, crushed

½ c. butter, melted

paprika

Wash chicken and pat dry. Mix the sour cream with the milk until smooth. Place in a shallow bowl. Put the crackers in a separate shallow bowl. Dip the chicken breasts in the sour cream mixture, then in the crackers. Place on a foil-lined jelly roll pan (the pan must have sides). Repeat with remaining chicken breasts. Drizzle breasts with butter and sprinkle with paprika. Bake in a 350 degree oven for 1 hour.

Nancy Norman Le Vesque

Anna's Brazilian Chicken Stroganoff

3 whole boneless, skinless chicken breasts

1 can mushroom

1 c. whole corn

1 Tbsp. olive oil

2 Tbsp. minced garlic

1 c. diced onions

1 Tbsp. garlic salt (Add garlic salt or salt to taste)

1 c. hot water

1 jar (1lb. 10oz.) of *Prego* pasta sauce - fresh mushrooms

1 pt. heavy whipping cream

Steam or boil the chicken; add salt to taste. Shred the chicken into small pieces

Rep. Shane Jett with wife, Anna and daughter, Rachael

Heat the olive oil in a pot and stir-fry the garlic and onions until golden brown, then add the garlic salt and stir. Add the Prego sauce and hot water, and then bring to a boil and let it boil for 5 minutes. Add the corn, mushrooms, and shredded chicken, and then let it boil for 5 minutes. Add the heavy whipping cream, stir briefly, turn off burner, and then let it sit for a few minutes. Serve with rice and crispy potatoes sticks. Makes 6–8 servings.

CHICKEN MARSALA

4 skinless, boneless, chicken breasts
all-purpose flour
kosher salt and fresh ground pepper
¼ c. extra-virgin olive oil
4–6 cloves garlic, minced
4 oz. proscuitto, sliced thin
8 oz. Crimini or Porcini Mushrooms, stemmed and quartered
1 c. Marsala wine
¾ c. chicken stock
4 Tbsp. unsalted butter
½ c. finely chopped parsley

Place the chicken breasts on a cutting board. Cover with plastic wrap. Pound with flat meat mallet until the breasts are about ¼-inch thick. Put a light coat of flour on the breasts. Heat the oil in a large skillet over medium-high heat. When the oil is hot, shake off any excess flour and place the breasts into the hot oil. Fry for about 5 minutes on each side (until golden brown). Remove the breasts and place into a large platter in a single layer to keep warm. Lower the heat to medium. Place the prosciutto into the remains in the skillet (scrape loose the goodies). Sauté for about 1½ minutes to render out some of the fat. Now add the mushrooms and sauté until nicely browned. The moisture should evaporate in about 5 minutes.

Salt and pepper to taste. Add the garlic. Pour the wine into the pan (remove the pan from the flame to add any spirits). Bring to a boil for a few seconds to cook out the alcohol. Add the chicken stock and simmer for a few minutes to reduce the sauce slightly. Stir in the butter once incorporated. Return the chicken to the pan. Simmer gently for 3–4 minutes. Re-season with salt and pepper (to taste).

Serve on a plate and garnish with parsley. Makes 4 servings.

Ronnie E. Schulz

CHICKEN ASPARAGUS CASSEROLE

6 chicken breasts
1 medium onion, chopped
½ c. butter
1 8-oz. can mushrooms
1 can cream of mushroom soup
1 can cream of chicken soup
2 cans asparagus
1 5-oz. can of pet milk
½ lb. grated cheddar cheese
¼ tsp. Tabasco sauce
2 tsp. soy sauce
1 tsp. salt and pepper
1 tsp. accent
2 Tbsp. pimentos
½ c. slivered almonds

Boil chicken breasts in seasoned water. Cool and then cut into bite-sized pieces. Sauté onion in butter; add remaining ingredients, except the asparagus and almonds. Simmer sauce until cheese melts.

In a 9x13 pan, layer chicken, asparagus, sauce, and then repeat. Top with almonds. Bake in 350 degree oven to heat.

Amy Mainord

CHEDDAR CHICKEN LASAGNA

1 8-oz. pkg. lasagna noodles
1 can cream of chicken soup
1 can cream of mushroom soup
1 c. grated Parmesan cheese
1 c. sour cream
1 c. sliced, black olives
¼ c. chopped pimentos
½ tsp. garlic salt
3 c. cubed, cooked chicken
1 c. finely chopped onion
1 small can sliced mushrooms
2 c. shredded cheddar cheese

Cook and drain noodles. Combine the soups, Parmesan cheese, sour cream, onions (I sauté onions with mushrooms), mushrooms, olives, pimentos, and garlic salt. Add the chicken. Layer in 9x13 pan: half of the noodles, half of the chicken mixture, half of the cheddar cheese and then repeat. Cover and bake for 20 minutes in 350 degree oven. Uncover and bake for 10 minutes more.

Wes Mainord

CHICKEN HUNTINGTON

1 lg. hen or chicken
1 lg. pkg. egg noodles
1 medium-sized jar sliced mushrooms
1 jar chopped pimentos
1 can English peas, drained
2-lb. box Velveeta cheese

Cook and debone chicken or hen. Put egg noodles in the chicken water and then add rest of ingredients. Cook until the cheese is melted. Add chicken.

Wanda Hackney

Fried Pecan Crusted Chicken with Plum Sauce

4 boneless chicken breast halves (1 ½ lb.)
1 Tbsp. sherry
1 Tbsp. dijon-style mustard
1 tsp. salt
¼ tsp. black pepper
2 egg whites, at room temperature
½ c. cornstarch
2 to 2 ½ c. finely chopped pecans
vegetable oil

Prepare plum sauce, set aside. Cut chicken into finger-sized strips. Mix together sherry and mustard; coat chicken with mixture. Sprinkle pieces with salt and pepper; set aside. Using an electric beater set at high speed, beat egg whites until foamy. Gradually add cornstarch; continue beating until stiff peaks form. Gently fold in chicken. Roll each piece of chicken in chopped pecans. Fry in at least 2 inches of hot oil (350 degrees) until golden brown. Remove from heat and drain on paper towels. Serve chicken pieces with gingered plum sauce for dipping. Makes 4 servings.

Gingered Plum Sauce:

Heat 1 c. plum jam in a small saucepan over medium heat until melted. Stir in 1 Tbsp. ketchup; 2 tsp. grated lemon rind; 1 Tbsp. lemon juice; 2 tsp. vinegar; ½ tsp. ground ginger; ½ tsp. anise seeds, crushed (may omit); ¼ tsp. dry mustard; ½ tsp. ground cinnamon; ⅛ tsp. ground cloves; and ⅛ tsp. hot pepper sauce. Bring to a boil and cook 1 minute, stirring constantly. Remove mixture from heat and let cool. Makes 1 ½ c.

Ronnye Perry Sharp

Smoked Chicken and Shrimp with Pasta Alfredo

1 lb. shaped pasta, cooked and drained
½ lb. julienne smoked chicken breast
½ lb. grilled shrimp
½ c. julienne zucchini
⅓ c. chopped sun-dried tomatoes in olive oil

Alfredo Sauce:
3 Tbsp. butter
3 Tbsp. flour
1 clove garlic, crushed
2 c. milk
2 c. heavy cream
½ c. white wine
salt and coarse black pepper
½ c. grated fresh Parmesan cheese

Melt butter in medium saucepan with a clove of crushed garlic. Remove garlic and stir in flour. Cook over medium heat 1 minute. Scald milk and cream. Stir into roux and continue stirring until slightly thickened. Stir in wine, salt, pepper, and Parmesan cheese. Stir until cheese is melted and sauce is smooth. Toss hot pasta with chicken, shrimp, zucchini, tomatoes, and cream sauce. Serve immediately.

Ronnie Schultz

Aye's Cuisine DBA Thai Kitchen Restaurant

Issara Attamakuisri, Mar Mar Aye Attamakuisre, Natthapume and Anant Attanmakuisri (sons)

PHAT THAI

3½ oz. thin medium-sized, dried rice noodles
6 shrimp
2 eggs
2 c. bean sprouts
¼ c. Chinese chives
2 tsp. chili flakes
2 Tbsp. palm sugar
2 Tbsp. vinegar juice
2 Tbsp. fish sauce
4 Tbsp. vegetable oil

Vegetables:
bean sprouts
Chinese chive
lime wedge

Soak rice noodles in warm water for 2–3 minutes, or until soft. Clean the shrimp. Fry oil over medium heat; add palm sugar, vinegar

juice, and fish sauce; stir together. Remove and set aside. Heat 2 Tbsp. of oil in a pan, add beaten eggs and stir until the eggs are almost set. Add shrimp and sauté until done. Add rice noodles, stir for 2–3 minutes and pour the sauce over and stir again. Follow with bean sprouts and Chinese chives and continue stirring for 2 more minutes. Place onto a serving dish, sprinkle with roasted peanuts and chili flakes. Serve with fresh bean sprouts, Chinese chives, and lime wedge.

Panaeng Curry

7 oz. chicken breast, cut into bite-sized pieces

1 c. coconut milk

1 ½ Tbsp. Panaeng curry paste

2 red spur chilies, sliced

6 Kaffir lime leaves

⅛ tsp. salt

2 tsp. sugar

1 Tbsp. fish sauce

Vegetables:

green and red bell peppers

carrots

pea pods

basil leaves

Garnish the Kaffir lime leaves and red spur chilies. Heat ½ cup of coconut milk until the oil surfaces, then add the Panaeng curry paste. Add the chicken and fry for 3 minutes, then add the rest of the coconut milk. Season with salt, fish sauce, sugar, and add vegetables and simmer for 5 minutes, until chicken is tender. Add Kaffir lime leaves and chilies. Turn off the heat. Spoon into a serving bowl, garnish with Kaffir lime leaves, basil leaves, and chilies, and serve hot with cooked jasmine rice.

Roast Turkey

1 12-lb. fresh or frozen white turkey, thawed
1 medium Granny Smith apple, quartered
1 medium onion, quartered
1 1-oz. bunch parsley sprigs
⅔ c. apple butter
2 Tbsp. brown sugar
2 Tbsp. dijon mustard
¼ tsp. ground nutmeg
1 ¼ tsp. salt, divided
1 ¼ tsp. black pepper, divided
⅛ tsp. ground red pepper
2 10½ -oz. cans low-salt chicken broth
cooking spray
2 Tbsp. all-purpose flour
¾ c. apple cider
¼ c. 1% low-fat milk

Entertainers Amy Grant and Vince Gill

Preheat oven to 325. Remove giblets and neck from turkey; discard, if desired. Rinse turkey thoroughly with cold water; pat dry. Tie ends of legs to tail with cord, or tuck flap of skin around tail. Lift wing tips up and over back, and tuck under bird. Stuff cavities of turkey with quartered apple, onion, and parsley sprigs. Starting at neck cavity, loosen skin from breast and drumsticks by inserting fingers, gently pushing between skin and meat. Combine apple butter, sugar, mustard, and nutmeg in a small bowl; stir well. Spread apple butter mixture under loosened skin and rub into the body cavity. Sprinkle bird with 1 tsp. salt, 1 tsp. black pepper, and ground red pepper. Pour broth and enough water to equal 3 cups liquid into the bottom of the pan. Place turkey on a rack coated with cooking spray; place rack in a shallow roasting pan. Insert meat thermometer into meaty part of thigh, making sure not to touch bone. Bake at 325 for 3 hours or until thermometer reaches 160 degrees. Cover turkey loosely with foil; let stand 10 minutes. Discard skin. Remove turkey from pan, reserving 1 ½ cups cooking liquid; reserve remaining cooking liquid for another use. Place turkey on a platter. Set aside; keep warm. Pour reserved 1 ½ c. cooking liquid into a Ziploc plastic bag. Snip off 1 corner of bag; drain liquid into measuring cup, reserving 1 cup of broth, and stopping before the fat layer reaches the opening. Drain fat layer into another bowl, reserving 2 Tbsp. Discard remaining fat. Combine reserved fat and flour in a medium saucepan over medium heat, and stir until smooth. Stir in reserved 1 cup broth, cider, and milk, and bring to a boil, reduce heat, and simmer, uncovered, 3 minutes, stirring constantly until thick and bubbly. Stir in remaining salt and black pepper. Serve gravy with skinned turkey. Makes 12 servings (6 oz. of turkey and 2 Tbsp. of gravy).

Amy Grant

CRANBERRY SAUCE

3 c. fresh cranberries

⅔ c. golden raisins

½ c. maple syrup

½ c. honey

¼ c. cider vinegar

½ tsp. ground allspice

Combine all ingredients in a large saucepan. Bring to a boil; reduce heat, and simmer 10 minutes. Serve warm. Makes 4 servings, ½ cup each.

Amy Grant

TURKEY TETRAZINI

¼ c. butter

¼ c. all-purpose flour

1 tsp. salt

¼ tsp. ground nutmeg

2 c. chicken broth or turkey stock

1 c. whipping cream

¼ c. dry sherry

⅓ c. freshly grated Parmesan cheese

½ lb. spaghetti, cooked

3 c. diced, cooked turkey
½ c. chopped green bell pepper
2 c. sliced mushrooms

Preheat oven to 350. Butter 2 ½-quart casserole. Melt butter in a saucepan and add the flour. Stir in salt and nutmeg. Stir in the stock or broth. Mix well. Simmer about 5 minutes, stirring until thick. Stir in cream, wine, and cheese. Combine the sauce with the cooked spaghetti, turkey, pepper, and mushrooms. Pour into the casserole and bake for 25 to 30 minutes.

Winnie Fiddler

TURKEY POT PIE

3 c. flour
¾ c. shortening
1 tsp. salt
cold water to mix

Mix flour and salt, and then cut in shortening until dough crumbles fine. Add enough water to mix. Roll the largest half of dough out to cover the bottom inside of a Pyrex baking pan or quiche pan. Reserve the remaining dough for the top crust. This intentionally has less shortening than a regular pie crust; it makes it stay together better and is easier to handle.

Filling:
1 can English peas
2 carrots, cubed
2 c. water
¼ tsp. thyme
¼ tsp. paprika
1 tsp. Morton's Nature's seasoning
2 c. chopped turkey, cooked
1 stalk celery, chopped
½ onion, chopped
2 chicken bouillon cubes

1 tsp. dried, crumbled parsley
salt and pepper to taste

Drain the juice off can of peas and cook juice with celery, carrots, and onion. Add the water, bouillon, seasonings, and turkey. Cook, just a few minutes, thickening with a paste of flour and water. Pour into crust. Add top crust; make a few slashes for steam to escape. Bake 1 hour at 350. Let set about 5–10 minutes, before cutting to serve.

Doris Novotny

HAM LOAF

2 lb. ground ham
1 lb. ground fresh pork
1 ½ c. bread crumbs
2 eggs, beaten
½ c. chopped onion

Glaze:
½ c. brown sugar
1 tsp. mustard
2 Tbsp. vinegar
1 Tbsp. water

Combine meat mixture, shape, and bake in loaf pan at 325 for 1 ½ hr. At end of 45 minutes, brush with glaze. Brush 3 or 4 times during the last 45 minutes.

Hot Sauce:
½ c. dry mustard
½ c. vinegar

Mix together and let stand overnight in refrigerator. Beat 1 egg, ⅓ c. sugar, dash of salt, and mustard mixture. Cook over water or in heavy pan until thickens. Cool mixture. Then add an equal amount of Hellmann's mayonnaise. Serve the ham loaf with the hot sauce.

Sharlene Hammons

CHALUPAS

3 lb. boneless pork roast
1 lb. pinto beans, soaked overnight
2 cloves garlic, chopped
2 Tbsp. chili powder
1 Tbsp. cumin
1 tsp. oregano
1 4-oz. can diced green chilies
1 Tbsp. salt, or to taste
water
corn chips
shredded cheddar cheese
chopped onion
shredded lettuce
chopped tomatoes
avocados, sliced or diced
hot sauce
sour cream

Combine pork, beans (after overnight soaking), garlic, chili powder, cumin, oregano, chilies and salt in large kettle. Add water to cover. Bring to a boil, cover and simmer about 6 hours. Break up meat and cook uncovered until thick, about 45 minutes. To serve, place a layer of corn chips on plate and top with meat mixture. Garnish with cheese, onion, lettuce, tomato, and avocado. Serve hot sauce and sour cream separately. Makes 10 servings.

Note: You can double this recipe if large enough pan. This freezes well.

Cyndy Cooper

GRILLED ORIENTAL PORK TENDERLOIN

Marinade:
½ c. peanut oil
¼ c. hoisin sauce
¼ c. soy sauce
½ c. rice wine vinegar
¼ c. dry sherry
½ tsp. hot chili oil
1 Tbsp. dark sesame oil
4 whole green onions, finely chopped
4 cloves garlic, minced
2 Tbsp. minced fresh ginger root
2–4 pork tenderloins, 3 lb. total

Combine all marinade ingredients and mix well. Pour over pork and marinate 3–4 hours at room temperature or overnight in the refrigerator.

Grill over medium flame for 8–10 minutes per side or until done, basting frequently with marinade. Makes 4–6 servings.

Jane Lodes

PORK CHOPS IN GRAVY

1 egg
2 Tbsp. water
8 pork loin chops (½-inch thick)
¾ c. seasoned breadcrumbs
2 Tbsp. Crisco oil
1 can condensed cream of mushroom soup, undiluted
1 can condensed French Onion soup, undiluted
¼ c. grated Parmesan cheese

First Lady Kim Henry's parents, Janiece and Monty Blain

In a shallow bowl, heat egg and water. Dip pork chops in egg mixture and coat with breadcrumbs. In a large skillet, brown chops in oil. Transfer to a greased 9x13 baking dish. Combine the soups and pour over chops. Sprinkle with cheese. Cover and bake at 325 for 1½-2 hours or until meat is tender. Serve with mashed potatoes. Makes 8 servings.

Janiece Blain

PORK CHOPS AND RICE

5 or 6 pork chops
1 ½ c. raw rice
tomato
1 c. chopped green pepper
½ c. chopped onion
celery salt
basil
garlic powder
marjoram
thyme
curry powder
1 can beef bouillon soup

Brown pork chops on both sides. Put rice in Dutch oven and place pork chops on top. On top of each pork chop, place a slice of tomato. Add the green pepper, onion, and spices. Pour can of beef bouillon and 1 can of water over the pork chops. Cover and bake at 350 for 1 hour.

Amy Mainord

Mongolian Pork Chops

6 10-oz. center-cut double pork chops

Mongolian Marinade:
1 c. hoisin sauce
1 Tbsp. sugar
1 ½ Tbsp. tamari soy sauce
1 ½ Tbsp. sherry vinegar
1 ½ Tbsp. rice vinegar
1 scallion, white and ⅔ of the green parts, minced
1 tsp. Tabasco sauce
1 ½ tsp. Lee Kum Kee black bean chili sauce
1 tsp. peeled and grated fresh ginger
1 ½ Tbsp. minced garlic
¼ tsp. freshly ground white pepper
¼ c. fresh cilantro leaves and steam, minced
1 Tbsp. sesame oil

Trim the excess meat and fat away from the ends of the chop bones, leaving them exposed. Put the pork chops in a clean plastic bag and lightly sprinkle with water to prevent the meat from tearing when pounded. Using the smooth side of a meat mallet, pound the meat down to an even 1-inch thickness, being careful not to hit the bones. Alternatively, have your butcher cut thinner chops and serve 2 per serving. To make the marinade, combine all the ingredients in a bowl and mix well. Coat the pork chops liberally with the marinade and marinate for 3 hours or up to overnight in the refrigerator. Place the chops on the grill and grill for 5 minutes on each side, rotating them a garter turn after 2 or 3 minutes on each side to produce nice crosshatch marks. It's good to baste with some of the marinade as the meat cooks. As with all marinated meats, you want to go longer and slower on the grill versus shorter and hotter, because if the marinated meat is charred, it may turn bitter.

Betty K. Fletcher

QUICK BAKED PORK CHOPS

¼ cup butter or margarine
1 c. rice, uncooked
1 can French Onion soup
1 can beef broth
4–6 pork chops

Melt butter in a frying pan, add rice and stir constantly over low heat until brown. Transfer to a 2 ½-quart casserole dish, add soup and broth and top with pork chops. Cover and bake at 350 for 1 ½ hours. Pork chops will be tender.

Kurstyn Mills

CINNAMON PORK CHOPS

4 bone-in pork chops, cut 1¼-1½ inches thick
vegetable oil
cinnamon
salt
½ c. ketchup
2 Tbsp. white wine vinegar
½ c. water
1 tsp. Worcestershire sauce

Brown chops in a lightly oiled pan. Place chops in a casserole. Salt and generously sprinkle with cinnamon. Combine liquid ingredients and spoon over chops, being careful not to wash off the cinnamon. Cover tightly with a lid or foil and bake at 325 for 3½-4 hours, depending on the thickness of the chops.

Gaye Etheridge

Ham Loaf

3 lb. ground ham
2 lb. ground pork
4 eggs
2 c. milk
2 c. crackers crumbs
Glaze:
1 c. brown sugar
1 tsp. dry mustard
½ c. vinegar
1 rounded Tbsp. of flour
½ c. cold water

Mix and cook glaze until thick. Mix ground ham, pork, eggs, milk, and cracker crumbs well and make into loaves. Spread ¾ of the glaze on top of loaves. Bake at 400 for 30 minutes and at 350 for 1–1½ hours. Spread remaining glaze over top before slicing and serving.

Clif and Gloria Scott

WHITE FIELDS

A place to call home.

Mary Jones, LPC, Executive Director

White Fields:
A Place to Call Home

Founded on principles of stability and permanence, White Fields is a long-term home for severely abused and neglected boys who are in the care of the Oklahoma Department of Human Services (OKDHS) Child Welfare Division. Tom Ward and Trent Ward's original inspiration for this challenging, but important, endeavor came from their family's desire to help those who are less fortunate–especially children.

Through volunteerism and a four-year research process, the Wards gathered information regarding the current placement options available for children in OKDHS' custody. They discovered that some children are unable to manage in foster care or adoptive homes and consequently make many moves within the OKDHS system.

The Wards concluded that Oklahoma needed a home for severely abused and neglected children that would follow a continuum of care model. White Fields was their answer. Its unique model allows eight to eighteen-year-old boys the opportunity to heal and make progress while maintaining established relationships with friends, caregivers, and role models. Boys start out in a twenty-four-hour supervised living situation. As they progress, they can move to community-style housing and independent living, all on White Fields' campus.

White Fields welcomed its first residents to its 140-acre campus in November of 2006. Each resident is welcomed with his own bedroom, a handmade quilt, toys, and sporting equipment upon arrival. They have the opportunity to attend an on-campus school and receive a specialized education focused on their specific academic needs and learning strengths. When appropriate, the boys have the option of attending public schools. Additional tutors and mentors are available to help them as they grow.

White Fields has strong values centered on the fundamental principle that everyone deserves to be and feel safe, both physically and emotionally. They appreciate each boy's strengths and differences, and believe each child has gifts that can grow through encouragement and development. Individualized care is provided to help each boy overcome trauma and gain self-worth.

White Fields' staff and volunteers strive to be positive role models for their residents. White Fields is lead by executive director Mary Jones, a licensed professional counselor. Mary has been working with Oklahoma children and families since 1990, and is a passionate advocate for children. She brings substantial experience to her role as executive director of White Fields.

> *"White Fields is a groundbreaking concept for the social services community," said Jones. "I fully support its core belief that children need strong, long-term bonds with their caretakers. I believe that through the development of hope, a good support network, and positive social skills, these children can begin to undergo transformations that will set their lives on improved paths and hopefully make a difference for future generations."*

Additional information about White Fields' mission and progress can be found at the organization's Web site at www.whitefieldsok.com.

Senator Inhofe's EPW Achievements

Senator James Inhofe

As chairman and now ranking-member of the Senate Environment and Public Works Committee, I have seen firsthand the successes of the federal highway system. As the author of the federal highway bill the president signed into law in August 2005, I am particularly proud of the increase in funding that Oklahoma received from the bill. Passage of this bill included about 32% more funding than the previous highway authorization bill for Oklahoma and ended Oklahoma's status as a 'donor state,' as our state will now receive more money than it sends to Washington in federal highway funding. Additionally, I secured over $300 million in funding for thirty-eight specific major highway projects around Oklahoma. This historic legislation also lessened the federal bureaucracy over highway trust funds by returning the decision-making process back to the states.

Through the Environment and Public Works Committee, I also had the privilege of being an integral part of the Energy Policy Act of 2005, where I included provisions to expand refining capacity and improve permitting processes so we can explore our domestic resources in an environmentally-conscious manner. Developing energy at home translates to energy security, ensuring stable sources of supply and well-paying jobs for American workers. Perhaps no place else in the country can appreciate this more than Oklahoma, where the oil and gas industry is experiencing a resurgence, contributing to a healthy economy at home. During the energy bill, I worked to include provisions that clarify environmental regulations so that oil and gas can be produced more efficiently as well as passing legislation to encourage the use of domestic biofuels in our cars and trucks.

I also authored legislation to reauthorize the Economic Development Administration (EDA). EDA assists our local communities in creating and retaining jobs and spurs economic growth. From 2003 to 2006, EDA has invested $17,578,107 in rural Oklahoma and has created 8,024 and saved 750 jobs in Oklahoma.

Through my position on the EPW Committee, I will also continue to make the Water Resources Development Act a top priority. This legislation provides Oklahoma with numerous water infrastructure project authorizations and policy improvements that are vital to the state and the nation's economy, public safety, and environment.

Senator Inhofe's SASC Achievements

In the midst of a global War on Terror, maintaining a strong national defense and supporting our brave servicemen, women, and their families are the highest responsibilities of the United States Congress. This includes meeting and exceeding the care needs of our wounded warriors and their families. I have been proud to serve in both the House and Senate Armed Services Committees where I have fought to provide the best equipment, force structure, training, and care for our military personnel fighting in harm's way.

In my position as second-ranking member of the Senate Armed Services Committee, I have had the opportunity to single-out and support Oklahoma's strong military installations and their surrounding communities. Oklahoma has a solid military foundation and I believe it serves both Oklahoma and the nation to promote the military contribution in our state. Oklahoma can proudly boast that it is the only state to go through all Base Realignment and Closure (BRAC) rounds without losing a single installation, and has actually gained new assignments as our military restructures. In the latest round, Ft. Sill added over 3,600 new jobs and Tinker Air Force Base added 355 jobs.

I have worked with the other members of Oklahoma's congressional delegation to increase money available for military construction and add funding in new research development for military programs. Recently, we were able to obtain a commitment from the U.S. Air Force for Altus Air Force Base to conduct centralized training of the new KC-X aircraft, replacing the present KC-135 mission. Additionally, the U.S. Army has moved its Air Defense Artillery School to Fort Sill, and is looking to further expand its involvement there with future artillery systems.

I will continue to serve Oklahoma and our nation from my position on the Senate Armed Services Committee, working to ensure that Oklahoma's military installations and supporting communities remain at the forefront of strengthening and supporting our nation.

Oatmeal Cake

Mix and let stand for 20 minutes:

1 c. oatmeal
1 stick butter
1 ½ c. boiling water

Mix:

1 c. brown sugar
1 c. white sugar
2 eggs
1 tsp. baking soda
1 tsp. salt
1 tsp. vanilla
1 tsp. cinnamon
1 ⅓ c. flour

Mix together and pour into mini Bundt pan. Bake 350 degrees for 40 minutes.

Topping for Oatmeal Cake:

Boil for 2 minutes:

6 Tbsp. butter
½ c. white sugar
¼ c. evaporated milk
1 tsp. vanilla

Let cool and beat until thick, then pour over cooled cake.

When I had trouble getting our four children to eat oatmeal in the mornings, this worked like magic.

Mrs. James M. (Kay) Inhofe

Lucas Sees Bright Future for Oklahoma Energy

Congressman Frank Lucas

Ever since a jet of black crude sprung out of the ground at Oklahoma's first commercial oil well in 1897, the state has been forever linked to the energy industry. We've watched fortunes made and lost from the boom and bust cycles of the oil patch, and we've seen the industry change from a rugged crew of roughnecks and roustabouts, to an industry of amazing technological advancements, like horizontal oil drilling and biodiesel made from switchgrass.

In the Third District, we have the unique perspective of both pumping oil out of the ground as producers and pumping gasoline into our tanks as consumers. And in Congress, I've worked to balance the needs of both interests.

The solution is to work toward a more stable energy sector, and to reduce the likelihood of the boom and bust days of the past. That's best achieved by creating a coherent, long-term energy policy and reducing our dependency on foreign sources of energy.

I supported the comprehensive energy bill that was signed into law that is helping lower fuel prices through energy conservation, exploration, and innovation. Since then I've worked in Congress to help enact a comprehensive policy that will increase and expand our local energy industry, and provide reasonable prices for Oklahoma consumers.

Marginal Oil and Gas Wells

The Energy Bill includes provisions for specific wells that are abundant in Oklahoma, called marginal wells. These wells produce only enough oil or gas to be marginally profitable, thus making them the wells most likely to be shut down when prices drop. These wells are the small business "mom and pop" operations of the oil and gas industry. Although they only produce on average about 3 barrels of oil per day, they make up about 85% of Oklahoma's oil production. About 70,000 of these wells are located in Oklahoma alone.

Keeping these wells producing is vitally important. They are operating on an economic shoestring, and once they're shut down, they're gone forever. That's why I have supported tax credits for marginal wells that are triggered when oil and gas prices are low. Since the tax credit would kick in only when prices drop, it will allow these smaller wells to remain profitable enough to keep pumping until the prices rise again, reducing the likelihood that they are lost forever.

Electricity and Renewables

The bill will also make Oklahoma's energy grid less susceptible to the blackouts that plagued the Northeast in the past, by promoting investment in the electric transmission grid, improving the reliability of electric transmission networks, and improving the transparency of electricity markets.

Other provisions in the bill important to Oklahoma include renewable energy grants and incentives, as well as biodiesel research and tax credits. The bill also extends and expands the wind energy tax credit, providing an incentive for wind energy production.

Step outside on any given day in Oklahoma and you'll realize we have a tremendous potential for producing wind energy. With the tax credit incentives and the upgrades to the infrastructure grid to transmit the electricity, Oklahoma is poised to be not only a wind energy producer, but a seller of that energy to other markets.

Oil and Gas Job Training

I can remember the days of the oil boom in the 1980s. Oil production skyrocketed, causing production companies to scramble for help on the rigs. As a result, many workers with little training fell victim to the dangerous environment. Sadly, these sites were being visited all too often by ambulances and medical helicopters.

Today, safety training is a critical element of a prospective oil field employee's resume. That's why I worked with local education officials at the High Plains Technology Center in Woodward to secure grants for job training in the oil and gas industry. The funds will be used to train students on realistic industry equipment the safety procedures to avoid the dangers of oil and gas industry work.

A sound energy policy will reduce our dependence on foreign countries for our oil and gas, it will make our electrical grid less susceptible to the blackouts that have plagued the Northeast, and it will both save the loss of jobs in the energy sector and create new jobs for manufacturing and technology. As Oklahomans, we have a unique perspective on the energy industry, and we'll continue to play a leading role in the energy sector in the next hundred years.

A Century of Construction Means Better Travel

Travel by horse and buggy would have been difficult enough, but Oklahoma's roads were certainly not designed for the new-fangled autos. Photos of roads in the era before a state-maintained highway system was built make it clear that the thoroughfares we take for granted impact our lives more than we can imagine.

At the time of statehood, the public was beginning to demand good roads, and the state's constitution directed the Legislature to create a state highway department; but even after the Oklahoma Department of Transportation (then known as the Department of Highways) was formed in 1911, counties remained in charge of road building and maintenance.

The agency was funded with a $1 voluntary tax on each of the state's 9,000 autos. Fewer than one-fourth of Oklahomans opted to pay the assessment. Nonetheless, the first highway commissioner, Sidney Suggs, proposed six main lines that would connect seventy-four of the state's seventy-seven counties.

Eventually, state and federal funding was set aside for highway construction and maintenance, and Suggs' six proposed highways were built—and all are still in use. The original Main Line No. 1 and Main Line No. 2 parallel present-day Interstates 35 and 40, including the Oklahoma City interchange now called the "Dallas Junction."

One of the first federal projects to be built in Oklahoma was a nine-foot-wide stretch of asphalt pavement running from Miami to Afton. That road became part of Route 66, the famed "Mother Road," Main Street of America. It was one of America's first interstate highways, although the system we now know as the interstate system was developed later.

Oklahoma had two distinctions when its interstates were built: The state was one of the first, some say *the* first, to connect an interstate highway to one in another state, and in the mid-1970s, with comple-

Dan Overland, Chairman of Oklahoma Transportation Commission

tion of I-40 in western Oklahoma, Oklahoma was one of the first to complete its rural system.

Today, ODOT maintains 30,000 lane miles of highway—enough to travel from Oklahoma City to Los Angeles and back eleven times—and 670 centerline miles of non-toll interstate. Oklahomans travel more than 65 million miles each year on highways.

Dan Overland was appointed by Gov. Brad Henry to the Oklahoma Transportation Commission and serves as chairman. As such, he helps oversee the Oklahoma Department of Transportation.

Oklahoma roads in the era before state-maintained highways

In Shawnee you'll find unique shopping, great dining, family-fun attractions and truly grand events! Enjoy a round of golf, explore the lavender farm or try your luck at one of our distinguished casinos.

Visit online today for your chance to Get Away & PLAY

Shawnee's Santa Fe Depot was built in 1902 as a stopping point for the Santa Fe Railroad. Inspired from European cathedral architecture, the limestone station includes a 60 foot clock tower, resembling a Scottish lighthouse. It opened as a museum in 1982 and contains collections of railroad and county history.

North of the Santa Fe Depot Museum, Beard Cabin is Shawnee's oldest dwelling built in 1891 by John Beard, founder of Shawnee and namesake for Shawnee's Beard Street.

Shawnee's Garment Factory opened in 1903 and is home to Roundhouse Overalls, named after the turntable-like train repair houses of the day. The overalls and other products are available at retail locations.

Owl Drug, on Shawnee's Main Street operated from 1895 until the late 1980's. It is now the Owl Shoppe, a soda fountain and gift shop.

Shawnee Milling Company, established in 1891 moved in 1897 to its current location as Shawnee Roller Mills. A fire demolished the mills in 1934 and a new facility was erected in 1935 and named Shawnee Milling Company.

Home to the first SONIC, in 1953 the Top Hat drive in restaurant was born and in 1959 they renamed it SONIC. Shawnee is home to the first SONIC as well as the celebrated 3000 SONIC.

The Aldridge opened in 1928 as an elegant hotel in the hub of Shawnee's social life. The Aldridge welcomed visitors such as Eleanor Roosevelt.

The Ritz Theatre was built in 1897 to 1899 and originally constructed as a dry goods store. Originally called The Cozy, the theatre opened in 1913. In 1926 the theatre was renamed The Ritz and Shawnee's first talking motion pictures were shown.

Mills Machines

Ninety-nine years in business indicates that something has been going right along the way. Mills Machine has been doing the correct thing since being founded in 1908. The company is built on a line of strong people and a history of innovation.

At the end of the Civil War, Samuel and Lucinda Mills were making a meager living in Bowling Green, Kentucky. Looking for greener pastures, they left in a covered wagon, first for Kansas, and then to the Indian Territory when the free land opened. W. H. (Homer) Mills, born in 1890, the youngest of nine, was born in Kansas and raised in the new state of Oklahoma.

*CEO and President
Chuck Mills and father David*

One day in 1908, at the age of eighteen, Homer came in from the fields and told his parents that he was tired of starving and was taking his tools and going to Shawnee to start a business. He founded Mills Repair Shop on Main Street with most of the business coming from the bicycle (the automobile was not readily available to the average person). The mechanically inclined Homer soon gained a reputation for being able to repair almost anything. He added guns to his growing list of things to be repaired while his brother, Frank, joined the business. After a couple of years Frank sold his share to Les Thompson for the grand price of $15.00.

An electric motor-driven central shaft powered the lathes, presses, and drills. A smithy with a hand-driven blower helped create the special shapes needed for repair of the motorcycles, guns, and custom machine parts. The picture above shows the shop around 1920.

In 1924 Homer bought out Les and changed the name of the company to Mills Machine Company. Around this time the oil boom hit Oklahoma with one of the world's largest oil fields in the booming town of Earlsboro, five miles East of Shawnee. Oklahoma Seismograph Company moved into Shawnee and decided that Mills Machine had the technical skills to repair the drilling rigs and bits. As the experience grew, Mills Machine began to manufacture bits and tooling for seismic crews in Oklahoma and beyond.

Boating in Benson Park.

ing facility was completed on the grounds, which includes a retail store. Benson Park Pecans provides harvesting, cracking, shelling, and a variety of pecans and gifts in the gift shop. Detailed information (including photos) of the grounds, store, process, history, and products can be found on the Web site at BensonPark-Pecans.com. Come visit Jim and Deann at the historic Benson Park; they're ready to meet all your pecan needs! Benson Park Pecans is located at 41502 Benson Park Road, Shawnee, OK, phone (405) 273–1235.

Homeward bound after a days outing at Benson Park, SHAWNEE, Okla.

Oklahoma BBQ

and Grilling

Van's Pig Stand History *and* Recipes

In 1928, Van opened his first pig stand in Wewoka, Oklahoma. It was a small little store serving barbeque, such as the pig sandwich and ribs. In 1929, a second pig stand opened in Seminole, Oklahoma, but was sold in 1935.

However, the Shawnee, Oklahoma, Van's Pig Stand was founded in 1930 and still is a favorite of locals and a traditional stop for all those returning to the area. This Van's Pig Stand is the oldest barbeque restaurant, owned and operated by the same family, in Oklahoma.

Our barbeque is slow smoked on a Southern Pride Pit with genuine Oklahoma hickory wood. This is evident by the smoke ring present on all our ribs and brisket. Our ribs and brisket are first marinated with our own secret "Rib Rub" before they are placed on the pit. The rub gives the ribs a hint of sweet, which is perfectly complimented by the hickory smoke flavor. The rub forms a nice "bark" on the brisket that makes it something to die for.

moved in to its first permanent home, Monnet Hall. The striking building of almost 47,000 square feet was built on Parrington Oval just to the north of the Carnegie Library Building.

On the exterior, the four-story stone building featured two large stone owls (symbols of Minerva, Roman goddess of wisdom), which appeared to look over the campus to the north and south from their niches at the peak of the roof. Thousands of law students passed through the halls of Monnet Hall, also known as the "Law Barn," and spent many hours in the classrooms and the impressive, high-ceilinged reading room. However, with continued growth came the need for more space.

In 1976, the College of Law moved into its current home located at 300 Timberdell Road at the south end of campus. In 2002, a major construction project providing an additional 80,000 square feet was completed. Included were a new library and a 250-seat courtroom with state-of-the-art technology. Extensive renovations and expansion of existing spaces combined function with aesthetic design to provide the perfect setting in which to study the law. The building that houses all of the Law Center functions was named Andrew M. Coats Hall in 2002 by the University of Oklahoma Board of Regents.

Today, the College of Law is home to more than 500 students, 42 full-time faculty members, numerous adjunct professors and administration and support personnel. Proudly counted among its graduates are many elected officials at the state and national levels, private legal practitioners, business leaders and educators. Graduates can be found across the nation and around the world utilizing the solid intellectual base shaped by their experiences during their three years of study at the University of Oklahoma College of Law.

Andrew M. Coats, a 1963 graduate who has served as District Attorney of Oklahoma County, Mayor of Oklahoma City, and the president of the Oklahoma Bar Association, became the eleventh Dean of the University of Oklahoma College of Law in 1996. "The fact that the University of Oklahoma College of Law provides a first-class legal education for our students is demonstrated by the very high percentage of our graduates who pass the Bar Examinations in Oklahoma and in other states across the country," stated Coats. "Our graduates are highly sought-after by law firms, corporate legal departments, and governmental entities throughout the southwest. A law degree from the University of Oklahoma carries great prestige and receives great respect."

Historical Moments

Freshmen Class Officers 1966 "Young Leaders of the Future". Seated, from left: Dan Little, vice president; David Boren, president; Prudence Little, secretary Standing from left: Jim Kirk, honor council; Chris Sturm, honor council; Blake Hoenig, treasurer

Ada Louis Sipuel with Amos T. Hall (NAACP attorney) and the famous Thurgood Marshall and Dr. H.W. Williamston (Oklahoma NAACP); Oklahoma girl became the most famous plaintiff in a series of lawsuits in 1940s that crumbled the barriers of desegregation in higher education in America. In 1992, Sipuel was appointed a member of the OU Board of Regents by Gov. David Walters.

Remembering some of the earliest OU law graduates.

348

The Oklahoma Bar Association

The legal profession is responsible for administration of the justice system in Oklahoma and has contributed significantly to the rich history of the state. Many of the state's governors, including Governor Brad Henry, civic leaders, and always a significant percentage of its legislators have been lawyers, as well as of course, its judges, attorneys general, and prosecuting attorneys. The profession is self-regulated through the Oklahoma Bar Association (OBA), a non-profit professional organization, under the supervision of the Supreme Court.

The mission of the OBA is to assist Oklahoma lawyers in providing justice for all. Its goals include fostering the highest ideals of integrity and competence among its lawyer members and improving the public's understanding of the legal system and the role of lawyers within it.

The OBA is older than the state, having been formed in 1904. In 1962, the lawyers of Oklahoma raised the money to move OBA headquarters out of rented space and build a beautiful new home, a marble building, located near the state capitol at 1901 N. Lincoln. An addition has since been made so that the building now affords 46,000 square feet of office space and meeting facilities. The headquarters property is owned by the Oklahoma Bar Foundation, a separate entity, organized by Oklahoma lawyers in 1946. The foundation, funded primarily by contributions from Oklahoma lawyers, is a 501 (c)(3) charitable organization supporting Oklahoma's justice system and is the third oldest bar foundation in the United States.

The OBA, under rules promulgated by the Supreme Court, supports the work of the Professional Responsibility Commission on matters of alleged misconduct and disciplinary action, and the work of the Board of Bar Examiners on bar examination and bar admissions matters.

The OBA is an "integrated bar," which means that a lawyer must be an OBA member in order to practice in the state. There are more than 11,000 active members in the state and more than 3,000 active members out of state, with a total membership, including inactive members, of almost 16,000. The OBA is governed by a seventeen-member Board of Governors, elected by its members. For more than sixty years, the presidents have been elected based on a geographic four-year rotation, from Oklahoma County every fourth year; from Tulsa County every fourth year; and from one of the other seventy-five counties in alternating years. In 2007, the state's centennial year, the president is Stephen D. Beam of Weatherford and the president-elect is J. William Conger of Oklahoma City.

Although many Oklahoma lawyers work as volunteers in OBA sections and committees, the scope of OBA activity is so extensive that it is necessary for it to maintain a large staff. There are about forty skilled and highly professional full-time employees who work under the direction of an executive director, a position currently held by John Morris Williams. The departmental organization includes administration, continuing legal education, General Counsel, Ethics Counsel, public information, and information services. In addition and not included in the forty-person work force just described are the staffs of the Oklahoma Bar Foundation, the Professional Responsibility Commission, and the Board of Bar Examiners. Annual membership dues paid by Oklahoma lawyers are the funding source to support the organization. Dues are set by the OBA House of Delegates, with the approval of the Supreme Court.

Each of the seventy-seven counties has a County Bar Association that elects and sends delegates to the OBA annual meeting to participate in the proceedings of the OBA House of Delegates, the body that formulates OBA policy. The seventeen-member Board of Governors meets monthly to execute and administer those policies. With rare exceptions the OBA and its House of Delegates meet only once a year, usually in mid-November, normally alternating the meeting site between Oklahoma City and Tulsa.

Two former OBA presidents have subsequently served as the leader of the nation's lawyers in the office of president of the American Bar Association (ABA). They are James D. Fellers of Oklahoma City, deceased, who served as OBA president in 1964 and as ABA president in 1975, and the author of this piece, William G. Paul of Oklahoma City, who served as OBA president in 1976 and as ABA president in 2000.

For more information about the OBA log on to its Web site at www.okbar.org/public.

CREAM CHEESE PIE

Line pan with graham cracker crust, unbaked.

Filling:

12 oz. cream cheese

2 eggs

¾ c. sugar

2 tsp. vanilla

Combine and whip till light.

Topping:

3 Tbsp. powdered sugar

1 tsp. vanilla

1 c. sour cream

Pour in crust and bake 15–20 minutes at 350 degrees. Remove and let cool 10 minutes. Pour in topping and bake 10 minutes. Refrigerate 5 hours.

Barbara Paul

Oklahoma Trial Lawyers Association

The Oklahoma Trial Lawyers Association is recognized as the first Trial Lawyer organization in America, and the forerunner of a national group. Drawing on their Oklahoma pioneer spirit, seventeen Oklahoma plaintiffs' attorneys met in secret in the Huckins Hotel in Oklahoma City one evening in 1943, and created the Negligence and Compensation Attorneys Association. Included in this group of passionate men devoted to representing individuals were Frank Seay, Paul Pugh, Claude Briggs, Homer Bishop, Lawrence Elder, Jim Rinehard, Charlie Schworke, and Jim Driscoll. While not as old as its proud state, OTLA is now sixty-four.

A good idea does not remain a secret long and a few years later a national organization, based on the Oklahoma experience, was begun and Seminole lawyer Homer Bishop became the first president of that group, which grew into the Association of Trial Lawyers of America and in 2006, became the American Association for Justice, AAJ. It now has over 75,000 members and is one of the most powerful organizations in Washington.

NACAA continued to grow in Oklahoma and became OTLA in the late 1950s. As its membership grew in the early '70s OTLA hired its first executive director and opened an office in Oklahoma City. Prior to that, the group president had operated the organization from his own office. In 1975, OTLA formed a political action trust, LEGAL, and was one of the first such PACs in the nation. It was devoted to espousing the views of individuals who were otherwise unrepresented.

OTLA now owns an office building in Oklahoma City near the state capitol where it holds seminars and other meetings for its several hundred members. It also publishes *The Advocate,* a quarterly magazine for lawyers. Its editors have included Appellate Court Judge Paul Brightmire, long time editors Jeff Greer and Mark Ashton, and current editor Gary Brooks.

The group has had fifty-eight presidents over its history, including some of the nation's leading plaintiff advocates. In 2007, Jennifer DeAngelias became its first woman president.

BUTTERMILK BROWNIES

Terry and Terri West

Batter:

1 c. margarine

⅓ c. cocoa

1 c. water

2 c. flour

2 c. sugar

1 tsp. salt

2 eggs, slightly beaten

½ c. buttermilk

1 ½ tsp. vanilla

Frosting:

¼ c. margarine

3 Tbsp. cocoa

1 tsp. vanilla

3 Tbsp. buttermilk

2 ½ c. powdered sugar, sifted

1 c. chopped nuts (optional)

Directions: Bring to boil margarine, cocoa, and water. Combine dry ingredients. Add eggs, buttermilk, and vanilla. Blend in cocoa mixture. Bake in 11x15 pan at 375 for approximately 40 minutes or until cooked through.

While batter is cooking prepare frosting. Bring to boil margarine, cocoa, and buttermilk. Reduce heat and stir in powdered sugar and vanilla. Fold in nuts if desired. Frost brownies while hot.

Terry and Terri West

Vegetables *and* Sides

MASHED POTATOES
The Famous Red Rock Mashed Potatoes

10 lb. red skin potatoes
1 lb. butter
3 lb. sour cream
2 ½ c. scallions, ¼-in bias
4 Tbsp. fresh cracked black pepper
3 Tbsp. salt

Wash potatoes. Cover with cold water about two inches above the potatoes. Cook until fork tender or until they break apart. Drain. Place in bowl to hold all and add all other ingredients and mix on medium until completely combined.

Red Rock Canyon

355

SCALLOPED PINEAPPLE

3 c. cubed French bread
⅓ c. melted butter
3 eggs, lightly beaten
1 c. sugar
1 20-oz. can crushed pineapple, undrained

Combine all ingredients. Spoon into 2-quart casserole dish. Bake at 350 for 45–50 minutes.

A great side for ham at Easter!

Dr. Scott Stewart and Robin Stewart

BROCCOLI OR ASPARAGUS SOUFFLÉ

(Your choice of vegetable)
20 oz. broccoli or asparagus, chopped
¼ c. butter
¼ c. all-purpose flour
2 c. milk
¾ c. grated Parmesan cheese
½ tsp. kosher salt
pepper to taste, about ½ tbsp.
¼ tsp. grated nutmeg (mol)
6 egg yolks, beaten
½ tbsp. cream of tarter
9 egg whites, beaten stiff

Preheat oven to 350. Cook chopped broccoli or asparagus, then set aside. Melt butter in saucepan; stir in the flour. Cook over high heat for 1 ½-2 minutes. Remove from heat. Add milk and whisk vigorously until lump free.

Combine each group and put in layers in baking dish (corn layer then chilies layer).

Bake at 350 for 45 minutes-1 hour.

This makes a very large casserole and is easy to cut in half.

Judge Robert Henry

BROCCOLI ELEGANT

1 ½ c. water
6 oz. pkg. cornbread stuffing mix
2 Tbsp. butter
2 Tbsp. flour
¾ c. milk
3 oz. pkg. cream cheese, softened
1 c. shredded cheddar cheese
¼ c. butter
2 10-oz. pkg. frozen broccoli spears, thawed
1 tsp. chicken-flavored bouillon granules
¼ tsp. salt
4 green onions, sliced
1 small can of sliced mushrooms
paprika for garnish

Combine water, ¼ cup butter, and packaged seasoning mix; bring to a boil. Remove from heat; stir in stuffing crumbs and let stand 5 minutes. Spoon stuffing around inside edge and bottom of a lightly buttered 9x13 baking dish, leaving a well in the center as if making a crust. Place broccoli in the well; set aside. Melt 2 Tbsp. butter in a heavy saucepan over low heat; add flour, stirring until smooth. Cook 1 minute, stirring constantly. Stir in bouillon. Gradually add milk; cook over medium heat, stirring constantly until thickened and bubbly. Add cream cheese and salt, stirring until smooth. Stir in onion. Spoon mixture over center of broccoli; sprinkle with cheese and paprika. Cover with aluminum foil and bake at 350 for 35 minutes. Remove foil and bake an additional 10 minutes. Makes 8 servings.

Honeysuckle Rose Gardens

PARMESAN CHEESE SMASHED POTATOES

3 lbs. red potatoes, cooked, unpeeled
1 tsp. Kosher salt
½ tsp. freshly ground pepper
1 ½ c. half-and-half
1 stick of butter
½ c. sour cream
½ c. freshly grated Parmesan cheese

With an electric mixer, mix all together until chunky-smooth.

Honeysuckle Rose Gardens

BAKED APPLES

Choose baking type apples, such as Roman Beauty, Jonathan, etc. Wash and core apples Either pare upper half of apples or slit around center. Place in baking dish; fill center of each apple with:

1 to 2 Tbsp. brown sugar
1 tsp. butter
⅛ tsp. cinnamon

Cover bottom of pan with water about ¼ inch deep. Bake uncovered at 375 until tender when pierced with fork. Time varies with apple size and variety (around 45 minutes). Baste syrup, from bottom of pan, over apples occasionally while baking.

Doris Novotny

LEMON RICE

1 ½ c. rice
2 ¼ c. chicken stock, hot
¾ stick butter
lemon peel strips from 1 lemon
1–2 Tbsp. lemon juice
1 c. whipping cream, warm
minced parsley
white pepper

Sauté lemon peel in butter about 3 minutes; remove peel, add rice and sauté another 3 minutes. Add hot stock and simmer covered about 15 minutes or until liquid is absorbed. Add lemon juice and one half of the cream. Stir and add remaining cream. Season with pepper and stir in parsley. Serve immediately, may be made ahead and reheated, but with out the parsley, which is to be added at the last minute.

Dr. Jon Reese

CRANBERRY WILD RICE

1 c. chopped onion
2 Tbsp. butter
1 can whole cranberry sauce

2 pkg. long grain & wild rice mix
1 ½ c. thinly sliced celery

Cook onion in butter in 10-inch skillet until tender, not brown. Add enough water to cranberry sauce to make 4 ¼ cups. Add cranberry sauce and contents of rice and seasonings to skillet; stir. Bring to a boil. Cover tightly and cook over low heat until all liquid is absorbed, about 25 minutes. Stir in celery.

Amy Mainord

RICE PILAF

1 c. rice (Uncle Ben's or long grain)
½ c. butter
1 c. vermicelli, broken up
1 ½ c. chicken broth
1 c. water
2 ½ Tbsp. Wyler's chicken granules
salt and pepper

Melt butter in a 2-quart pan. Add vermicelli to butter and stir constantly until browned. When browned, add broth and water. Bring to a boil, then lower heat. Simmer for 20 minutes until water is all absorbed and rice is soft. Turn off heat and let set for a few minutes. Stir once, and then serve.

Judy Kinnett

CORN CASSEROLE

½ c. butter
2 eggs, beaten
½ c. chopped green pepper
1 8 ½-oz. box cornbread mix
½ c. chopped onion
1 can cream corn
salt and pepper
1 can whole kernel corn
2 c. shredded Cheddar cheese

Sauté peppers and onions in butter; add corn, including liquid, eggs, and cornbread mix, salt and pepper. Pour mixture into greased 9x13 baking pan; top with cheese. Bake in 350 oven 30 minutes.

Mike and Jane Lodes

ITALIAN GREEN BEANS

2 (#10) cans green beans (2 gallons)
1 ½ lb. sausage
5 onions, diced
Italian seasoning, salt and pepper to taste
#2 ½ size can tomatoes

Brown sausage and reserve grease. Cook onions until soft. Put sausage in beans and add the onions tomatoes and seasonings. Makes enough to serve a large group.

Judy Kinnett

Zucchini Casserole

1 lb. extra large zucchini, chopped into chunks

1 lb. sausage

1 onion, diced

1 c. cracker crumbs

2 eggs

1 c. American cheese

1 c. Monterey Jack cheese

pinch of paprika

salt and pepper to taste

Rep. Fallin in Kitchen

Add chunks of zucchini to boiling, salted water. Cook until tender. Drain and mash. Add sausage and diced onion in skillet and cook until brown. Add drained zucchini, drained meat, cracker crumbs, eggs, American cheese, and salt and pepper. Bake at 350 for 30–35 minutes. Add Monterey Jack cheese and paprika and bake until cheese is melted.

Congresswoman Mary Fallin

Sweet Potato Puffs

4–6 sweet potatoes, peeled and cubed

Cook potatoes in water until tender. Mash potatoes and season with a little butter. You want mixture to stay stiff. Cool. Wrap about ¼ c. mixture around large marshmallow, roll in chopped nuts or crushed corn flakes. Repeat until mixture is gone. The number of puffs is determined by the number of sweet potatoes cooked. Place marshmallows in casserole dish, cover, and bake at 325 for 20 minutes. Uncover to slightly brown, basting with melted butter.

The Freed Family

Autumn Potatoes

2 ½ lb. baking potatoes
2 ½ lb. sweet potatoes
butter, brown sugar, and honey to taste
1 tsp. salt

Boil the potatoes until soft. Mash and add honey, butter, and brown sugar to taste.

Linda Praytor

Twice Baked Potato Casserole
A Diabetic Delight

6 medium unpeeled potatoes, baked
¼ tsp. salt
¼ tsp. pepper
1 lb. sliced bacon, cooked and crumbled
3 c. sour cream
2 c. grated cheddar cheese
2 c. grated mozzarella cheese
2 green onions, chopped

Cut baked potatoes into 1-inch cubes. Place half in a greased 9x13 baking dish. Sprinkle with half of the salt, pepper, and bacon. Top with half the sour cream and cheese. Repeat layers. Bake, uncovered at 350 for 20 minutes. Sprinkle with onions.

Deborah Nickell

JUDY'S SWEET POTATO CASSEROLE
Low Sugar

Filling:

2 lb. sweet potatoes, about 4, peeled and cut into 1-inch cubes

¼ c. Splenda brown sugar

½ c. I Can't Believe It's Not Butter-Light

2 eggs, lightly beaten

⅓ c. milk

1 tsp. vanilla extract

Topping:

4 oz. chopped pecans, about 1 cup

5 Tbsp. + 1 tsp. Splenda brown sugar

½ c. all-purpose flour

⅓ c. I Can't Believe It's Not Butter-Light, melted

Magician Jim Smithson performing at Pott County DHS Christmas Party

For filling, in large pot combine potatoes with enough cold water to cover; over high heat bring to a boil. Reduce heat to medium; simmer until potatoes are tender: 30 minutes. Drain; mash until smooth. Let stand until cooled slightly, 15 minutes. Preheat oven to 350. Butter 2-quart baking dish. In bowl, combine potatoes with next 5 ingredients. Spread mixture in baking dish. For topping, in large bowl combine pecans, sugar, and flour; stir in butter until mixture is combined. Sprinkle pecan mixture over potato mixture. Bake until top is browned and mixture is set in center, 40–45 minutes.

Makes 12 servings.

BEST SAUERKRAUT

2 jars sauerkraut, drained

½ c. packed brown sugar

⅓ c. cider vinegar

2 Tbsp. caraway seeds

2 c. water

Boil and cover. Simmer for 1 ½ hours.

3 medium onions

½ stick of butter

Sauté onions and pour into sauerkraut. Serve warm or chilled.

Winnie Fiddler

CUCUMBER WITH VINAIGRETTE

¼ c. sugar

¼ c. rice vinegar

2 Tbsp. fresh ginger, chopped

½ tsp. crusted red pepper flakes

1 English cucumber, thinly sliced

Combine and chill before serving.

Joann La'Valley

STUFFED EGGPLANT

6 oz. eggplant

2 oz. blended shrimp

1 oz. crabmeat

1 Tbsp. ricotta

1 Tbsp. breadcrumbs

½ Tbsp. garlic

1 oz. Mozzarella cheese

4 jumbo shrimp

Mix with Tbsp. blended shrimp, crabmeat, ricotta, bread-crumbs, garlic, and Mozzarella cheese until it is into a paste texture. Take the whole eggplant cut in half to about 6 oz. Take out the top part of the eggplant about halfway deep. Stuff the eggplant with the mixed paste; add the jumbo shrimp on top of the eggplant. Put the eggplant in a baking pan lightly oiled, in a 500 degree oven for 15 minutes or till the eggplant is soft around the edges. Serve with any of your favorite sauces or plain.

Laziee Mustani, Tony Veliu

SUMMER SQUASH CASSEROLE

6 yellow summer squash

½ c. chopped white onions

½ c. chopped green onions

1 clove garlic, minced

¼ c. chopped fresh parsley

½ stick butter

2 slices white bread

1 medium bowl ice water

1 egg

salt and pepper

1 c. cracker crumbs, or enough to cover casserole

Preheat oven to 350. Peel and cut squash into cubes. Boil until tender, about 5–7 minutes, and drain. Brown onion, garlic, and parsley in 2 Tbsp. butter seasoned with salt and pepper. Soak bread in ice water and wring out; chop fine. Add to onion and garlic mixture; cook, stirring for 2–3 minutes. Add drained squash and cook 2–3 minutes more, stirring. Remove from heat. Beat egg and add, allowing it to absorb into the mixture. Season with salt and pepper. Place in casserole dish or baking pan. Cover top with cracker crumbs and dot with remaining butter. Bake for 20–25 minutes, until the crumbs are brown.

Joann La Valley

SWEET AND SOUR BAKED BEANS

6 slices bacon, crumbled

1 lb. cooked hamburger, drained

1 lg. onion, chopped

1 (#2 1/2) can pork 'n beans

1 can red beans, drained

2 cans butter beans, drained

½ c. brown sugar

½ c. ketchup

2 Tbsp. liquid smoke

Mix all of the above ingredients and bake at 200 for approximately 1 hour and 20 minutes.

Elaine Chard

Jalapeno Hominy

4 cans yellow hominy, drained
1 can cream of mushroom soup
1 can cream of asparagus soup
4 cups shredded cheddar cheese
1 jar diced pimento, drained
1 small can chopped green chilies

Combine all of the above ingredients in large bowl; stir well. Spoon mixture into greased casserole. Bake, uncovered, at 350 for 20–25 minutes.

Mainord Family

Kate and Steve's Favorite Vegetarian Spaghetti Sauce

1 can chopped tomatoes (Muir Glen Organic are the best)
½ c. chopped onion
1 clove garlic
2 tsp. basil
1 tsp. oregano
½ tsp. cilantro
sea salt and pepper to taste
Add your favorite chopped vegetables:
½ c.   squash—yellow or zucchini
½ c.   red pepper (green or yellow-your favorite)
¼ c.   fresh spinach leaves
½ c.   steamed broccoli flowerets

Sauté garlic and onion in a tablespoon of olive oil until

transparent. Add vegetables and sauté about a minute. Add tomatoes and liquid to skillet. Stir in spices, cook over medium heat, stirring occasionally. Lower temperature and cover skillet. Simmer about 10 minutes. Serve with your favorite spaghetti, garlic bread, and salad.

Kate and Steve Blain

FAMILY FAVORITE CORN DISH

2 pkg. frozen corn

1 stick butter

3 Tbsp. flour

1 pt. half-and-half

Combine the corn, melted butter, flour in a dish. Add salt and pepper to taste. Completely cover corn mixture with the half-and-half. Cover and bake at 325 for 1½ hours. Delicious! Right off the Cob!

Penny S. Hague

Award winning entertainers Amy Grant and Vince Gill

SWEET POTATO-AND-TURNIP COMFORT CASSEROLE

"We call this one Comfort Casserole," says Amy, "because it's so warm and soothing."

2 lb. sweet potatoes, peeled and thinly sliced

2 lb. turnips, peeled and thinly sliced

2 c. shredded Swiss cheese, divided

3 Tbsp. butter, divided

1 tsp. dried thyme, divided

½ tsp. salt, divided

¼ tsp. pepper, divided

Preheat oven to 400. Butter a 1-quart baking dish. Arrange

half of sweet potatoes and turnips, alternating slices, in single layer in bottom of dish. Sprinkle with 1 cup Swiss cheese, 1 ½ Tbsp. butter, ½ tsp. thyme, ¼ tsp. salt, and 1/8 tsp. pepper. Repeat layering with remaining sweet potatoes, turnips, butter, thyme, salt, and pepper. Cover; bake 45 minutes. Uncover; sprinkle with remaining cheese. Continue baking until golden, 10–15 minutes. Garnish with thyme, if desired.

Amy Grant and Vince Gill

Zocalo Mexican Restaurant

Owner/Manager Sherry Seaberg serving Tecumseh mayor, John Collier and wife

A delightful stop just three blocks south of Highway 9 in downtown Tecumseh, Zocalo Mexican Restaurant serves up *must-come-back-for-more* signature dishes and an array of made-from-scratch traditional Mexican favorites. The atmosphere is warm, friendly, and inviting. The ingredients are fresh, the chips are light and served warm, and the overall experience is superb. A lovely little patio adds to the charm.

VEGETABLE QUESADILLA

It's unbelievable that vegetables can taste this good. Add fresh spinach if desired.

Owner Sherry Seaberg serving Phyllis Flora and author Ronnye Sharp.

Use all fresh ingredients.

1 10" flour tortilla
1½ c. broccoli, cauliflower, and baby carrots, cut in large pieces
¼ c. coarsely sliced red and green bell peppers
¼ c. mushrooms
1 tsp. seasoning mix (mix to taste: salt, garlic powder, pepper, chili powder, cumin)
¾ c. shredded cheddar cheese
¾ c. shredded Monterey Jack cheese
melted butter or vegetable spray

Sauté vegetables in butter until soft, add seasoning. Brush one side of tortilla with melted butter or vegetable spray. Lay oil-side down flat on griddle. Cover half with cheddar and half with Monterey Jack cheese. Layer the cooked vegetables on one half of tortilla and grill until cheese is melted and bottom is lightly browned. Fold in half and cut into 4 wedges, each with a fold to help hold wedges together. Serve with sour cream.

TACO SALAD

Layer into a corn tortilla taco shell:
¾ c. refried beans
¾ c. lettuce
¾ c. cooked and seasoned ground beef
¾ c. lettuce

Top with chopped tomato, cheddar, and Monterey Jack cheese. Serve with sour cream, salsa, and lime wedge.

Spinach Enchilada Dinner

The best spinach enchiladas are served at Zocalo Mexican Restaurant in Tecumseh. Made with fresh spinach and served piping hot,. there is no holding this dish in the kitchen or on the plate!

For Each Enchilada:
6" white corn tortilla
1 c. fresh spinach
¼ c. Monterey Jack cheese

Cover tortilla with cheese, place spinach across the center of the tortilla, packing it firmly, but not tight. Heat in a microwave to melt the cheese (about 30 seconds), fold the tortilla over and roll. Transfer to dinner plate. Cover with sour cream sauce, sprinkle with Jack cheese, and serve with rice and beans. (The restaurant heats the finished plate under very high heat until the cheese is bubbly and serves immediately.)

Senator Tom Coburn

The Senate committees on the judiciary, homeland security and governmental affairs; Indian affairs; and health, education, labor, and pensions all are charged with oversight of the subjects reflected in their names. However, the way in which the committees can best serve the country is by providing transparency in how your hard-earned tax dollars are spent.

The lack of transparency in the way government spends your money has allowed runaway spending to happen unchecked and out of the sight of American taxpayers. Consider the federal government spends roughly $1 trillion annually in federal grants, contracts, and earmarks. Yet, there had been virtually no way to track how this money was spent. In September 2006, President Bush signed into law the Federal Funding Accountability and Transparency Act, which I co-sponsored with Senator Barack Obama (D-IL). The bill requires the Office of Management and Budget to set up a "Google-like" Internet search engine of virtually all government spending. It is my hope this bill will provide taxpayers with a significant tool to hold elected officials accountable for the way their tax dollars are spent.

The bill garnered a wide array of support across the political spectrum because openness in government truly is a bipartisan issue. The Web site, www.federalspending.gov will fully be implemented in January 2008.

This transparency bill was an important first step toward changing the culture in Washington, D.C. Behavior in Washington will change now that politicians know their spending decisions will be open to public scrutiny. Every citizen in this country, after all, should have the right to know which organizations and activities are being funded with their hard-earned tax dollars. Only by fostering a culture of openness, transparency, and accountability will Congress come together to address the mounting fiscal challenges that threaten our country.

Oklahoma State Regents for Higher Education

The History of the Oklahoma State Regents for Higher Education and Chancellor of the Oklahoma State System of Higher Education

John Massey, Chairman

When the Eighteenth Legislature convened in January 1941, the governor met with legislative leaders, as well as institution heads, to discuss the enactment of legislation that would vitalize higher education. It became apparent that there was a majority sentiment in favor of an agency that could formulate and carry out a long-range plan for higher education in Oklahoma. In March 1941, Article XIII-A was passed by special election to establish the Oklahoma State Regents for Higher Education.

In June of 1942, a report was given to the governor entitled "A System of Higher Education for Oklahoma," defining the role of the Oklahoma state regents. It was prescribed that the board would consist of nine members appointed by the governor and confirmed by the Senate to serve nine-year terms. The regents would assume the role of coordinating board of control for all state institutions and have the powers of setting standards, determining functions, granting degrees, allocating funds, and setting tuition and fees.

Dr. Glen D. Johnson, Jr., Chancellor

Shortly after the passage of the act, the regents employed a small technical and clerical staff and established headquarters in the state capitol. The first state regents meeting was held on June 16, 1941. Members of the first board were: chairman, John H. Kane of Bartlesville; Dial Currin, Shawnee; Clee O. Doggett, Cherokee; W.E. Harvey, Oklahoma City; Wharton Mathies, Clayton; J.E. Peery, Minco; John Rogers, Tulsa; Ben F. Saye, Duncan; and Frank Buttram of Oklahoma City.

As a constitutional board, the Oklahoma State Regents for Higher Education called the selection of the chief executive officer, titled the chancellor as "undoubtedly the most important single responsibility of the State Regents." It was their belief that the chancellor would be the heart of the System and responsible to the Regents for administering its programs.

Their criteria for the position was: an individual whose academic background was unquestioned, who had broad administrative experience, and who could gain and hold the confidence of his associates and the general public. Additional criteria included an unbiased outlook, an ability to reconcile opposing educational philosophies into a rational and coherent program, and vision without being visionary.

In 1943, the State Regents selected Dr. Mell Achilles Nash as the first chancellor of the Oklahoma State System of Higher Education, serving from 1943 to 1961. The Regents viewed Nash as an excellent choice due to his experience in education, prior to becoming chancellor, including having served as president of the Oklahoma College for Women at Chickasha, superintendent of public instruction for Oklahoma, and president of the Oklahoma State Board of Education and the Oklahoma Education Association.

In 1961, Dr. E.T. Dunlap became the second chancellor of the Oklahoma State System for Higher Education and served until his retirement on January 1, 1982. At his retirement, the Oklahoma State Regents for Higher Education named him chancellor emeritus. Dunlap graduated from Southeastern Oklahoma State University in 1940, and then served as a teacher, county superintendent of schools, and high school inspector for accreditation for the Oklahoma State Department of Education. Dunlap was elected to the Oklahoma House of Representatives in 1946, chaired the Committee on Education and was the principal author of the Education Code, which was signed into law in 1949. From 1951 to 1961, he was president of Eastern Oklahoma State College in Wilburton.

In January 1982, Dr. Joseph (Joe) Leone was selected to serve as the third chancellor. Leone's service to higher education began in 1965 as an adjunct professor of education at the University of Oklahoma. In 1969, Leone's service continued at OU as chief administrative officer to the vice president for research and public service. Leone became president of Oscar Rose Junior College in 1972, a position he held until 1978. He was then employed at the State Regents as executive vice chancellor, a position he held until appointed as chancellor in 1982. Leone served as chancellor until April 1987.

Dr. Dan S. Hobbs served as interim chancellor of the Oklahoma State System of Higher Education from 1987 to 1988. Hobbs joined the

State Regents in 1961 as research assistant and became the educational programs officer and senior research officer in 1966. Prior to becoming interim chancellor, Hobbs served as senior vice chancellor of the Planning and Policy Research Division for seven years and as vice chancellor for academic affairs for eight years. Hobbs retired as senior vice chancellor emeritus from the State Regents in 1988, after twenty-seven years of service but remained active in higher education.

Dr. Hans Brisch was named chancellor by the Oklahoma State Regents for Higher Education in 1987, after a year-long national search. Charged with a change agenda to turn Oklahoma higher education around and improve its competitiveness, he consistently and aggressively implemented an agenda focused on student success, program quality, first-rate faculty, excellence, and efficiency. As a result of his hard work, student preparation for college entry, college retention, and college graduation rates all increased plus the system saw an eight-year growth in external research funding that ranked number one in the nation. Brisch retired as chancellor emeritus in 2003.

In January 2003, Dr. Paul G. Risser was named as the sixth chancellor of Higher Education. Risser has the distinction of having led two universities as president, Oregon State University (1996–2002) and Miami University of Ohio (1993–1996). In addition, he served as vice president for research and then as provost at the University of New Mexico (1986–1993), and as the chief of the Illinois Natural History Survey at the University of Illinois (1981–1986). Risser's years were marked with academic leadership, focusing on high-quality academic programs, fostering strong research success, and working closely with local and statewide communities to further higher education's goals. Risser served as chancellor until July 2006 and now serves as acting director of the Smithsonian's National Museum of Natural History and as the chair of the University of Oklahoma Research Cabinet that coordinates and facilitates research across the university's three campuses.

Dr. Phil Moss was named interim chancellor by the Oklahoma State Regents for Higher Education in June 2006. While serving as interim chancellor, Moss continued in his role as vice chancellor for academic affairs. In this position, he served as the chief academic officer for the Oklahoma State System for Higher Education and provided leadership across the divisions of Student Affairs, Pre-Collegiate Programs, and Collegiate Programs. In addition, he was responsible for the day-to-day

and long-range administration of academic projects and supervision of academic personnel. Moss' service as interim chancellor ended in January 2007.

In January 2007, Dr. Glen D. Johnson, Jr. became the eighth chancellor of the Oklahoma State System of Higher Education. As chancellor, Johnson leads a state system comprised of twenty-five state colleges and universities, ten constituent agencies, one higher education center, and independent colleges and universities coordinated with the state system. Johnson provides leadership on matters relating to standards for Oklahoma higher education, courses and programs of study, budget allocations for institutions, fees and tuition, and strategic planning. He is responsible for an annual higher education budget in excess of $1.4 billion as well as the state endowment fund, with a market value over $200 million. He is responsible for OneNet, the state's telecommunications network for government and education, as well as the Oklahoma Guaranteed Student Loan Program, which has guaranteed more than 1 million student loans exceeding $2.5 billion in insured debt. Johnson directs twenty statewide scholarship programs as well as other programs, including the State Regents' Summer Academies in Math and Science program and the statewide GEAR UP efforts.

Chancellor Johnson's goal for the State System is to increase the number of students with college degrees and to better prepare graduates to compete in a rapidly changing global economy, graduates who will be equipped to critically think, to analyze, to problem solve, with excellent math, verbal, and technological skills who will "add value" to the Oklahoma economy. Because the future success in Oklahoma is dependent on the investment in education and a settled workforce, the State Regents launched six initiatives to reach the goal of "more" students who are better prepared.

The first initiative reflects the growing need to maximize educational facilities and equipment throughout the state. Cooperative Alliances with CareerTech served more than 4,000 students in the fall 2006, who enrolled in specific technology center courses for college credit.

The second initiative is the Adult Degree Completion Program. Beginning in March 2007 most of Oklahoma's public universities began offering a degree completion program for working adults. It is an opportunity for Oklahomans to finish a bachelor's degree in a flexible format that's convenient for those who wish to attend college while working and/or raising a family.

The third initiative, concurrent enrollment, allows eligible high school students to take advantage of opportunities to earn college credit tuition free. Almost 8,000 students are enrolled concurrently in college classes while still in high school.

The fourth initiative began in the spring 2007 when the State Regents launched www.OKcollegestart.org, a comprehensive, Web-based information system for prospective and current college students. The Web site provides students with a "one-stop shop" for college planning and preparation. Through this site, students, parents, and high school counselors can perform several tasks, including financial aid and college applications, from one central location.

Making education more affordable through financial aid is the fifth initiative. Financial aid in Oklahoma is available from several different programs, all of which address the growing need for assistance. Even though Oklahoma's public colleges and universities continue to be among the most affordable in the nation, these programs serve a vital role in making education affordable for the citizens of Oklahoma. The Oklahoma Legislature, in cooperation with the governor, has offered the students of Oklahoma an educational promise through the very successful Oklahoma's Promise–Oklahoma Higher Learning Access Program (OHLAP). To date, more than 67,000 students from nearly 500 high schools throughout the state have enrolled in the program. It's called Oklahoma's Promise because students promise to meet the academic and conduct standards set by the State Regents and in return, the state of Oklahoma promises to provide free tuition to qualified students whose annual family income at the time they enroll in OHLAP is no more than $50,000. In 2006 nearly 70% of the high school seniors who enrolled in the program completed the requirements. On average, OHLAP students have higher high school grade point averages and ACT scores, perform better in college, and graduate at a higher rate than non-OHLAP students.

The sixth initiative focuses on Workforce and Economic Development. Oklahoma has been successful in developing alliances among higher education, government, and industry to address workforce needs, commercialization, and technology transfer. Currently, the State Regents have alliances in a variety of fields, including health, telecommunications, electrical, and aerospace.

The State Regents dedicated $4.5 million to institutions offering nursing and allied health care programs to address the growing health care worker shortage. The initiative is expected to produce an additional 300 registered nurses, 130 allied health professionals, and 15 additional master's level nursing faculty members annually.

Standing Regent Jimmy Harrell, Chancelor Dr. Glen Johnson, Chairman John Massey, Regent Bill Burgis

The Johnsons

Oklahoma's heritage is best reflected in its families that pass a sense of duty and public service from one generation to the next. The Johnson family of Okemah has served Oklahoma for over sixty years with the tradition of public service passing from father to son.

Glen Dale Johnson was born on September 11, 1911, in Melbourne, Arkansas. In 1920, the Johnson's moved to Paden, Oklahoma. In 1939, Johnson graduated from the University of Oklahoma Law School at Norman and settled in Okemah to practice law.

Johnson was elected to the Oklahoma House of Representatives in 1940, where he served as assistant democratic floor leader, an unheard of honor for a freshman House member. Johnson's service in the Oklahoma House coincided with the formation of the Oklahoma State Regents for Higher Education.

Following the Japanese attack on Pearl Harbor in 1941, Johnson enlisted in the United States Army. Johnson married Imogene Storms of Okemah in December 1942. In May 1946, he was discharged as a major and returned to Okemah to practice law.

Johnson ran for and was elected to the U.S. Congress from Oklahoma's 4th Congressional district as a Democrat in 1946. Johnson served in the freshman congressional class with fellow Oklahoman and later speaker of the House, Carl Albert; Massachusetts Representative, John F. Kennedy; and California Representative, Richard M. Nixon. Johnson considered running for re-election in 1948, but instead chose to run for the U.S. Senate. After losing the Democratic nomination, Johnson retired from Congress after serving only one term.

Johnson left Congress and continued his work in law. Johnson was the neutral arbitrator for the National Mediation Board in 1949 and 1950. He served as an attorney in the Office of the Solicitor for the U.S. Department of the Interior in Washington, D.C., from 1961 to 1967. Johnson was the chairman of the Oil Import Appeals Board representing the Department of the Interior from 1967 to 1969. Johnson completed his legal career by serving as the attorney in Solicitor's Office, Department of the Interior, assigned to the Muskogee, Oklahoma, field office from 1969 to 1972. Johnson later relocated back to Okemah, Oklahoma, where he remained until his death there on February 10, 1983.

The torch was passed to the next generation. …

Dr. Glen D. Johnson, Jr. was born on April 20, 1954, and followed his father's footsteps by first attending the University of Oklahoma where he graduated with honors with an undergraduate degree in political science and a Juris Doctor degree from the OU College of Law in 1979. He was a member of Phi Beta Kappa at OU and received the Letzeiser Award as one of OU's outstanding seniors.

Public service was always a part of Johnson's life. Johnson Sr.'s service, as well as good friend Carl Albert's, served as a role model for the younger Johnson. In 1980, he took his first steps toward public service when he was elected to the Okemah School Board and in 1982, at the age of 28, Johnson was elected to the Oklahoma House of Representatives. In 1990, at the age of 36, he was elected as the youngest sitting Speaker of the House of Representatives in the nation.

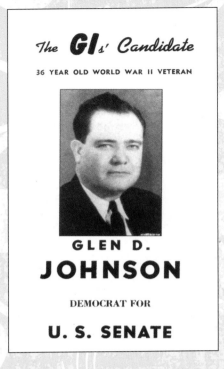

The GI's' Candidate

36 YEAR OLD WORLD WAR II VETERAN

GLEN D. JOHNSON

DEMOCRAT FOR

U. S. SENATE

Mrs. Johnson would play the piano in the back of a pick-up on the campaign trail while Mr. Johnson would greet people; Campaign poster of Johnson Sr.

Former coach Barry Switzer

OU Coach Bob Stoops holding championship trophy

OSU Library

Oklahoma State University History

Oklahoma Agricultural and Mechanical College was founded on December 25, 1890, twenty months after the Land Run of 1889, as a result of the Morrill Act. Since its birth, the school has remained true to its land-grant mission of teaching, research, and outreach. When the first students assembled for class in Stillwater on December 14, 1891, there were no buildings, no books, and no curriculum. Two years and six months later, after classes began in local churches, 144 students moved into the first academic building. The building, now called Old Central, still stands today and is home to the Oklahoma State University Honors College and the Oklahoma Museum of Higher Education.

On July 1, 1957, Oklahoma A&M College became Oklahoma State University. Although Stillwater remains the university's main campus, the OSU System has five branch campus locations: Stillwater, which includes the Center for Veterinary Health Sciences; OSU-Tulsa; OSU-Oklahoma City; OSU-Okmulgee; and the OSU Center for Health Sciences in Tulsa, which includes the OSU Medical Center. In addition to its branch campuses, OSU has a presence in all seventy-seven of Oklahoma's counties with OSU Extension Offices and seventeen agricultural experiment stations sprinkled across the state. OSU also is establishing a new sensor testing facility in Ponca City and a biosciences institute in Ardmore in partnership with the Noble Foundation.

Named Oklahoma's inaugural Truman Honor Institution for its production of Truman Scholars, the OSU System has an enrollment of around 32,000 with students from all 50 states and nearly 120 nations.

Oklahoma State University has more than 350 undergraduate and graduate degrees and options, as well as professional degree programs in medicine and veterinary medicine and its nine different colleges provide unmatched diversity of academic offerings.

Old Central - June 27, 1971, Old Central was placed on the National Register of Historic Places and 2006 it was designated as the future home of the OSU Honors College.

OSU conducts innovative research and technology transfer that enhance Oklahoma's economic vitality and its quality of life. Interdisciplinary collaborations with academic institutions, government agencies, private business, and industry ensure that contributions of faculty and student researchers to the development of new knowledge and its dissemination are pertinent and lasting.

Areas of emphasis include: alternative energies and conservation; animal based agriculture and biotechnology; environmental protection; food production and safety; health and medicine; manufacturing and advanced materials; national defense and homeland security; sensors and sensor technologies; and transportation and infrastructure.

Although OSU is a large, comprehensive university, its size does not minimize the personal attention given to each student. The individual is more than just a number at this university. OSU encourages all students, when they first enroll, to identify the college in which they wish to major. Once the student has identified his or her major department, he or she becomes a very important individual to the faculty and advisors of that department. Because the average number of students majoring in any one department is less than 150, the student can count on personal attention in a friendly environment.

The size of the university has many distinct advantages. OSU's 2 million-plus volume library, its modern research laboratories and equipment, excellent physical education, recreation and student union facilities, nationally-recognized residence halls programs, outstanding cultural events, athletics in the highly competitive Big 12 Conference, and more than thirty nationally-affiliated fraternities and sororities, all provide a stimulating educational and social environment.

Since its inception, Oklahoma State University has been a school rich in tradition. OSU students, alums, and fans are proud to wear the school colors of orange and black. Venues are described as a "sea of orange" during athletic events and the OSU mascot, Pistol Pete, has been nationally recognized. All OSU Cowboys/Cowgirls are connected through the university's traditions like homecoming, the annual ring ceremony, spirit songs, and the singing of the alma mater before and after most OSU gatherings. During the singing of the OSU Alma Mater students and alums lock arms and sway left and right.

In 1896, Oklahoma A&M held its first commencement with six male graduates. Today OSU graduates more than 5,000 annually and its alumni totals more than 200,000 worldwide. OSU graduates have

OSU Student Union and lovely campus

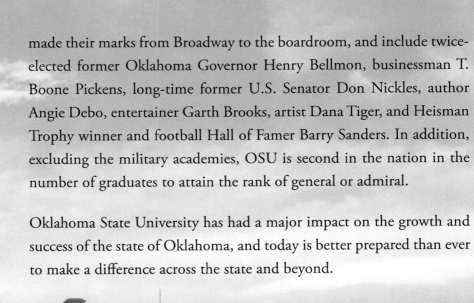

made their marks from Broadway to the boardroom, and include twice-elected former Oklahoma Governor Henry Bellmon, businessman T. Boone Pickens, long-time former U.S. Senator Don Nickles, author Angie Debo, entertainer Garth Brooks, artist Dana Tiger, and Heisman Trophy winner and football Hall of Famer Barry Sanders. In addition, excluding the military academies, OSU is second in the nation in the number of graduates to attain the rank of general or admiral.

Oklahoma State University has had a major impact on the growth and success of the state of Oklahoma, and today is better prepared than ever to make a difference across the state and beyond.

T. Boone Pickens

The future of Oklahoma State University Athletics will not be defined by a single facility or venue but by an assortment of new facilities that will form a state-of-the-art complex on the OSU campus.

The Athletic Village, to be located just north of Boone Pickens Stadium, will benefit every program in the Oklahoma State athletic department while providing OSU with cutting edge venues located in a convenient and comprehensive setting. And unlike most campuses in which facilities are added individually, Oklahoma State is in the enviable position of being able to put together a long-range facility blueprint that will allow the venues to compliment each other in an integrated fashion. While planning for the Athletic Village is still in the early stages and all artists' renderings are subject to change, the completed projects will include new venues for track, baseball, tennis, and soccer. The village will also house the Sherman Smith Training Center, the new indoor practice facility that will benefit every student-athlete on the OSU campus.

Owners Bob and Cherie Trousdale

417

Hal C. Smith

Restaurants

Oklahoma's Finest Dining

The RedHawks are the top minor league affiliate of the Texas Rangers, an affiliation dating to 1983.

Following the 2003 season, ownership transferred to the current group headed by Bob Funk and the result has been unparalleled success. Under the current ownership, attendance grew from 474,206 in 2004, to an Oklahoma record 542,095 in 2005. In 2006, it was 526,932.

The RedHawks play at AT&T Bricktown Ballpark, opened in 1998 as the first major project of an ambitious, publicly-funded civic improvement program at the center of Oklahoma City's downtown revitalization.

Located in a former warehouse district adjacent to downtown, AT&T Bricktown Ballpark fits in with a brick façade, classic dark green seats, upper deck, and statues of Oklahoma hall-of-famers Mickey Mantle, Johnny Bench, and Warren Spahn gracing the entrances.

The Brick holds 13,066, including the outfield berms. It has twenty-five suites on two levels and also offers club seats, a lounge, meeting space, new batting cages, and a high-tech scoreboard installed in 2007.

Blazers

Season Highlights

1992–93 By some accounts, the best team in franchise history. Posted impressive 25-4-1 home record. Fleury the first, and to date, only Blazers player to date to lead league in scoring. Prolific offensive team that could sometimes score at will. Only team in franchise history with two 40-goal and two 30-goal scorers on the same roster.

1993–94 More of a finesse team then a rugged team, the Blazers had to get tough in a hurry to play the Wichita Thunder. The Doug Shedden–coached Thunder would attempt to run roughshod over the Blazers in nearly every game. The hostilities came to a head December 22, 1993 in Oklahoma City. The Blazers and Thunder established a then CHL record of 336 penalty minutes in a game. Labeled " The Holocaust" by the "Voice of the Blazers" John Brooks, the Blazers went on to win 12–3.

1994–95 One year to the day after "The Holocaust," the Oklahoma City Blazers established numerous CHL records in a 16–1 rout of the Dallas Freeze. Joe Burton recorded six goals, only after rookie Michel St. Jacques recorded five. The 16 goals scored by the Blazers is still a league record today. St. Jacques went on to earn CHL Rookie of the Year honors, the only Blazer to ever receive that award.

1995–96 After a sluggish 4–4 start to the season, Doug Sauter, in his first season with the Blazers, overhauled his team, adding key players like Steve Moore and Tim Sullivan. From that point, the Blazers posted a 43–9-4 record, en route to the regular season championship and the team's first post season championship. The Blazer's led every offensive category, including goals, assists, points, penalty minutes, minors, majors, and power-play goals.

1996–97 The Blazers picked up where they had left off during the

'95-'96 season winning 10 of the first 12 games. With the successful regular season the Blazers earned another spot in the Central Hockey League Playoffs. In the first round of the playoffs the Blazers played league rivals the Wichita Thunder who they dominated in the regular season play. However, the Blazers were not as successful in the playoffs as they were in the regular season.

1997–98   The '97-'98 season brought change for the Blazers. This turned out to be the first season since the '93-'94 campaign that George Dupont wasn't in the roster. Several questions hung over the team, such as: How would the Blazers replace his offense? The Blazers did just fine. Joe Burton had his most prolific season as a Blazer, recording a league-record setting 74 goals and 124 points. Hardy Sauter chipped in 87 assists and 109 points, both records for scoring by a defenseman. This team is often forgotten when thinking about the best teams in franchise history. The Blazers went 19 consecutive games without a home loss in the regulation to start the season. This was the first taste of "The Mad Greek" Peter Arvanitis. He set a franchise record for penalty minutes with 403 and a league record with 35 major penalties.

1998–99   Definitely, a team that is a candidate for "arguably the best team in franchise history." This season the Blazers set franchise record for wins in a season (49) and most points (100). The Blazers led the league in goals (322), assists (518), points (840), and penalty minutes (108) en route to the team's third Adams Cup. The four consecutive 40-win seasons was a then record for the minor professional hockey in North America.

1999–00   This season the most defining moment for the Blazers came off of the ice. After several moths of posturing, bickering, and worry, the Blazers secured a long-term deal with the city of Oklahoma City to play hockey at the Cox Convention Center and newly named Ford Center. Coinciding with the lease was the introduction of Robert A. Funk to the sports community in Oklahoma City. Funk, owner of Express Personnel Services, purchased the Blazers from Chicago businessman Horn Chen. Following the purchase of the Blazers, Funk formed Express Sports, the premier provider of professional sports entertainment in Oklahoma City.

An overachieving bunch of players who gelled as a team was the key to the success of the Blazers this season. With achievements on and off the ice, the Blazers not only brought home the Western Division Championship, the Adams Cup Regular Season Championship, and the Ray Miron Cup Playoff Championship but also the North American Minor Professional Attendance Champions with an average of 9,096.

2001–02   The first season of the "new" Central Hockey League produced one result that appeared to be a constant for the Blazers: winning the Northwest Division. The new CHL has produced a better level of talent from top to bottom than any of the previous seasons. The Blazers came out of the gates on fire, winning 7 of their first 9 games. In script made for Hollywood, the '00-'01 CHL champion Blazers played the '00-'01 WPHL champion Bossier-Shreveport MudBugs in the first round of the playoffs. The bugs used two overtime wins to take the series 3–1.

Promise of a highly productive offensive season winked at the Blazers before the start of the season. The Blazers had three of the top scorers in CHL history on the same roster: Joe Burton, Hardy Sauter, and Jonathan Dubois. Add Blair Manning to the mix and the stage was set for positive results in the new building that they would call home, the Ford Center. However, the team results were not what the Blazers fans wanted. The Blazers would take home the Northwest Division Championship and the North American Minor Professional Attendance title the Blazers would soon fall the Memphis Riverkings in the first round of the Central Hockey League playoffs.

The first season without Joe Burton is one the Blazers would like to forget. The Blazers suffered offensively, scoring the fewest goals in franchise history (176) en route to missing the playoffs for the first time in the 12 seasons since the rebirth of the CHL.

LET'S GO BLAZERS

The struggles continued for the Blazers for the first 40-plus games of the season. The team had difficulty winning the big game and was under .500 until February 12 and not above .500 until February 19. Despite those troubles, the Blazers nearly made the post season. A 17–4-5 record over the last 26 games of the season put the Blazers in position to challenge the Tulsa Oilers for the fourth and final playoff spot in the Northern Conference. A 5–4 loss at Tulsa in the 63rd game of the season shut the Blazers out of the playoffs for the second straight season.

Similar to the season before, the Blazers began with a rough 2–6-2 record, but rebounded to make the postseason for the first time in the last two seasons. This team had to overcome its share of adversity, including call ups, lengthy suspensions, and immigration troubles. For the better part of the season the Blazers who struggled to score goals in each of the previous two seasons, averaged nearly four goals per game.

2006–07   The '06-'07 season was extremely exciting for the Blazers. The team finished the regular season 35–21–8, clinching a spot in the Central Hockey League playoffs. The playoffs ended for the Blazers in game 7 against the Colorado Eagles in the semi-final round of the Northern Conference series. Although the team did not bring home the championship cup our 15th season, there were many memorable moments, including clinching the Central Hockey League Attendance title for the 15th consecutive time as well as the North American Minor League Hockey attendance title.

The Blazers currently lead all of minor pro hockey in playoff attendance at 7,212 per game.

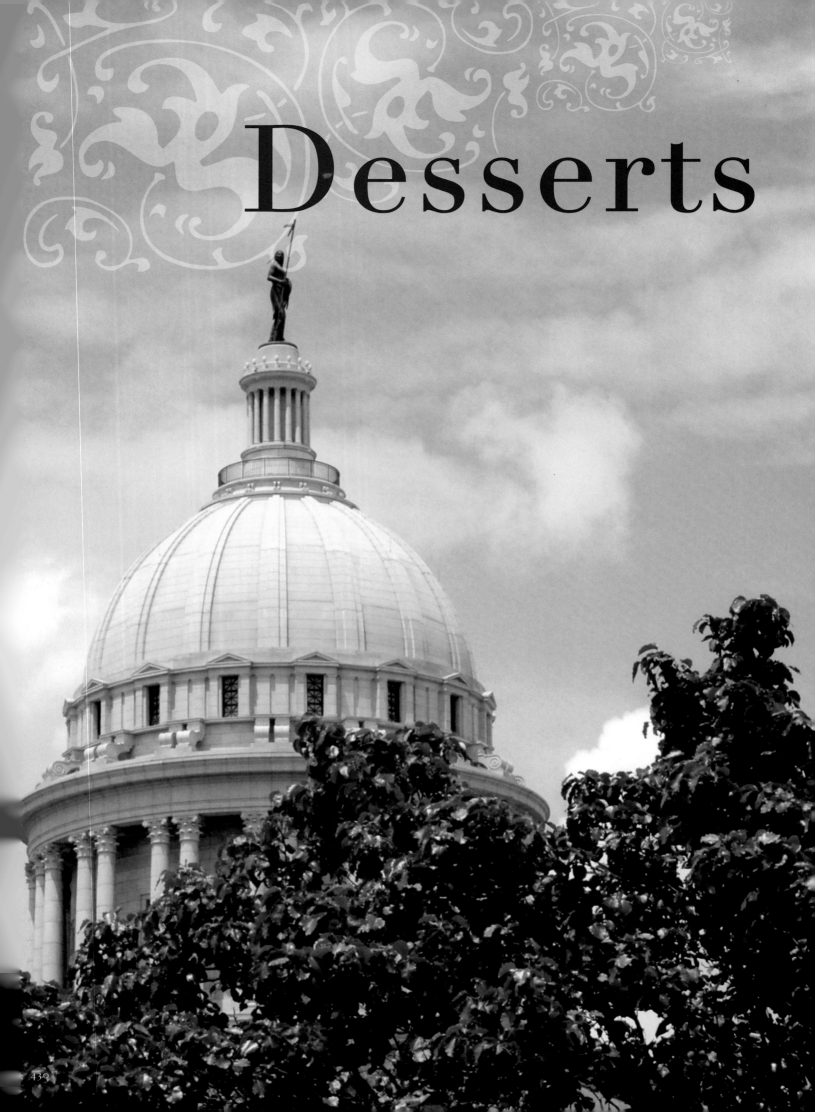

Desserts

MILLIONAIRE PIE

Place Pie Recipe in the middle of page with a photo of Astronaut John Herrington on each side of recipe. Cutline: Chickasaw John Herrington, Astronaut Cutline: Native American Pilot, John Herrington

1 baked pie shell
8 oz. cream cheese
2 c. powdered sugar
1 c. drained crushed pineapple
1 box dream whip or 1 ½ c. cool whip
nuts (optional)

Combine chilled cheese, sugar, chilled pineapple, and dream whip. Place in pie shell and chill.

John Herrington's mom

ALMOST SUGAR-FREE MILLIONAIRE PIE

Diabetic Version (Very low sugar and low fat)

8 oz. fat free cream cheese (room temperature)
¼ c. 1% or skim milk
1 large can crushed pineapple with juice (in own juice)
1 large box sugar-free instant vanilla pudding
1 c. pecans, chopped (I use ½ c.)
16 oz. lite or fat-free Cool Whip
2 regular-sized sugar-free or fat-free graham cracker crust (or 1 extra large)

Mix cream cheese, milk, and juice from pineapple until smooth with mixer. Stir in pineapple and nuts. Fold in Cool Whip. Pour into crust and chill.

Martha McMahan Lindgren
Trinnette Smith

Award-Winning Homemade Orange Sherbet

2 cans Eagle Brand milk
1 small can crushed pineapple, undrained
1 large bottle orange pop

Combine all ingredients into the ice cream can. Stir thoroughly. Fill the can up to the line with the orange drink. It should take about 20–25 minutes, depending on your ice cream maker. Enjoy!

Penny S. Hague

Choconut-Almond Cheesecake

1½ c. chocolate cookie/cracker crumbs
3 Tbsp. sugar
¼ c. butter or margarine, melted
4 8-oz. pkg. cream cheese, softened
3 large eggs
1 c. sugar
1 14-oz. pkg. flaked coconut
1 11.5-oz. pkg. milk chocolate morsels
½ c. slivered almonds, toasted
1 tsp. vanilla
½ c. semisweet chocolate morsels
toasted chopped almonds for garnish

Stir together first 3 ingredients; press mixture into bottom of a 10" spring form pan. Bake at 350 for 8 minutes. Cool. Beat cream cheese, eggs, and 1 cup sugar at medium speed until fluffy. Stir in coconut, milk chocolate morsels, ½ cup almonds, and vanilla. Pour into pan. Bake at 350 degrees for 1 hour. Cool on a wire rack. Semisweet morsels in a zip-top plastic bag; seal. Submerge bag in warm water until morsels melt. Snip a tiny hole in 1 corner of bag; drizzle chocolate over cheesecake. Cover and chill 8 hours. Chill up to 5 days, if desired. Garnish, if desired.

Jack and Donna Smith

AMARETTO CHEESECAKE

1 stick butter (melted)
1¾ c. graham cracker crumbs, ground
dash of cinnamon
¼ c. pecans, ground
3 eggs, beaten
2 8-oz. pkg. cream cheese, softened
pinch of salt
1 c. sugar
4 Tbsp. amaretto
½ tsp. almond extract
3 c. sour cream

Mix butter, graham crackers crumbs, cinnamon, and pecans together and press into spring form pan. Mix eggs, cream cheese, salt, sugar, amaretto, and almond extract together until smooth. Add sour cream and blend all together. Pour in pan and bake at 375 degrees for 45 minutes or until just set. Cool at least 5 hours. May be served plain or with favorite fruit topping.

Donna Smith

RED ROCK CANYON'S FAMOUS KEY LIME PIE

8 limes, zested
24 egg yolks
8 cans sweetened condensed milk
3 ½ c. Nellie's key lime juice

Zest lime in large mixing bowl using box grater. Add the sweetened condensed milk, eggs, and Nellie's lime juice. Thoroughly combine. Portion to each pie, be careful not to over fill. Place in 325 degree pre-heated oven for 10 minutes. Let set at room temperature for 10 minutes. Place in refrigerator for next day use. Makes 4 pies.

Note: Pies cannot be used the same day that they are baked!

Avis Scaramucci, owner
Nonna's Euro-American
Ristorante and Bar

435

Nonna's Euro-American Ristorante and Bar

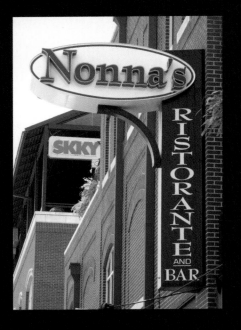

According to *Oklahoma City Downtown Monthly* magazine, Nonna's "unquestionably vies for the top spot among the metro's gourmet restaurants." *MetroFamily Magazine* gives it four out of four forks. Avis Scaramucci keeps the mood at her restaurant warm and upbeat while Executive Chef Shawn Davidson creates magic with pastas, meats, and seafood. Two premier dishes include the Nested Sea Scallops, pan seared with spinach and mushrooms and topped with citrus beurre blanc, and Mango BBQ Shrimp, which is wrapped in bacon and served with mango salsa. Blackberry Duck and USDA Graded Prime Tenderloin are some top choices from the meat menu. Nonna's received the Wine Spectator Award of Excellence in 2006, offering 200 selections on the wine list so that diners will find a special complement for every meal. First-time visitors may be unaware of the owner's prolonged effort to build a home for Nonna's in the city's Bricktown, an endeavor that *The Oklahoman* chronicled in a series of feature articles. Indeed, the more one knows about Avis' enterprising spirit, the more fascinating Nonna's becomes. The restaurant is just one of her Bricktown enterprises, which include the Purple Bar, a bakery, a Streetside Café, and the Painted Door gift shop. And newly opened in 2007, Painted Door gift boutique is also located in the beautiful Skirvin Hilton Hotel in Downtown Oklahoma City. She and her husband also own Cedar Spring Farms, where most of Nonna's herbs, edible flowers, and vegetables are grown. The Insalata Caprese and Tomato Bisque provide a great way to get acquainted with the harvest. Nonna's, located in a more than ninety-year-old warehouse, is three floors of part art gallery, bakery, fine dining, and pure fun! Valet parking available.

1 Mickey Mantle Drive,
Oklahoma City, OK
(405) 235–4410
www.nonnas.com

LEMON MERINGUE PIE

1 ½ c. sugar
¼ c. cornstarch
3 egg yolks, slightly beaten
2 Tbsp. margarine
⅓ c. lemon juice
1½ c. hot water
dash salt

In saucepan, mix sugar, cornstarch, and salt. Gradually blend in water. Bring to boil over high heat, stirring constantly. Reduce heat to medium; cook and stir 8 minutes more. Remove from heat. Stir small amount of hot mixture into egg yolks; return to hot mixture. Bring to boil, stirring constantly. Reduce heat to low. Cook and stir in lemon juice. Cover entire surface with clear plastic wrap and cool for 10 minutes. Pour mixture into cooled pastry shell.

Meringue:
3 egg whites
¼ tsp. cream of tartar
6 Tbsp. sugar

Beat mixture until it will hold peaks. Spread over pie and return to 400 degree oven until slightly brown.

Jennifer Freed

LAYNIE'S FAVORITE LAYERED DESSERT

1 c. flour
½ c. margarine, softened
1 ½ c. chopped nuts, divided
8 oz. cream cheese, softened
1 c. powdered sugar
1 c. cool whip

1 3-oz. vanilla instant pudding
2 ½ c. milk, divided
1 3-oz. chocolate instant pudding
remainder of 8 oz. cool whip
1 Hershey bar, grated (optional)

Combine flour, margarine and ½ cup nuts. Mix until crumbly.

Press into a 9x13 baking dish. Bake at 350 for about 15 minutes or until brown. Set aside to cool.

In a bowl, combine cream cheese and sugar. Add 1 cup of cool whip and spread over crust. Prepare vanilla pudding with 1 ¼ cups of milk. Pour over cream cheese layer. Chill until set.

Prepare chocolate pudding with 1 ¼ cups of milk. Pour over vanilla layer. Chill until set. Top with cool whip. Sprinkle remaining nuts and grated chocolate on top. Chill several hours

Kate Blain

Hawaiian Dessert

1 box orange cake mix
1 small pkg. instant vanilla pudding
1 3-oz. pkg. orange gelatin
4 eggs
1 ½ c. milk
½ c. vegetable oil
Filling:
1 20-oz. can crushed pineapple, drained
2 c. sugar
1 can mandarin oranges, drained
1 pkg. flaked coconut
1 c. sour cream
1 carton cool whip, thawed
toasted coconut

In large mixing bowl, combine first 6 ingredients, and mix well. Pour into two greased and floured round pans. Bake at 350 for 25–30 minutes. Cool. In separate bowl, combine pineapple, oranges, sugar, coconut, and sour cream. Set aside 1 cup of mixture. On one cooled cake, spread mixture and then place other cake on top. In the 1 cup mixture you set aside, fold cool whip and then spread over top and sides of cake. Sprinkle toasted coconut on top.

Angela Hodge

STRAWBERRY FROZEN DELIGHT

Combine:
1 c. flour
½ c. melted butter
¼ c. brown sugar
1 c. chopped pecans

Mix and spread on jelly roll pan; bake at 350 for 20 minutes, stirring every 5 minutes. Watch so that it doesn't burn.

In a large mixing bowl, combine and beat at high speed for 20 minutes:

1 c. sugar
2 large egg whites
2 tsp. lemon juice
1 10-oz. frozen strawberries, thawed, including syrup

Whip and fold in ½ pint whipping cream and spread half of nut mixture on bottom of 9x13 Pyrex dish. Spread strawberry mixture next and finish by covering with nut mixture. Cover with foil and put in the freezer until frozen. Can make several days in advance and leave in freezer until ready to serve. May garnish with a dollop of whipping cream and a strawberry, if desired.

Mary Sue Cochran and Susan Gau

Fresh Rhubarb Pie

For 8" pie:
2 c. sugar
¼ c. flour
3 c. cut-up rhubarb (about 3 large stocks)
¼ tsp. orange peel
1 Tbsp. margarine or butter
For 9" pie:
2 ¼ c. sugar
⅓ c. flour
4 c. cut-up rhubarb (about 4 large stocks)
½ tsp. orange peel
2 Tbsp. margarine or butter

Heat oven to 425. Mix sugar, flour, rhubarb, and orange peel in saucepan and heat until sugar has melted. Pour heated mixture into prepared pie crust. Add pats of butter over top of mixture. Cover with top crust, cut slits for venting. Bake for 40–50 minutes.

Susan Kemp

Chess Pie

1 ½ c. sugar
1 ½ Tbsp. white cornmeal
½ c. melted oleo
3 whole eggs
1 tsp. lemon juice
1 tsp. vanilla
¼ c. milk or cream

Mix each ingredient, as listed above. Pour into pie shell and bake at 350 degrees for 45 minutes. I especially like this filling in tart shells.

Jennifer Freed

Strawberry Pie

1 qt. strawberries (or more), washed and stemmed, but whole
2 Tbsp. cornstarch
1 c. sugar
1 c. water

Combine cornstarch, sugar, and water in saucepan and cook over medium heat until thick and clear. Add 1 lid almond extract, 3 Tbsp. strawberry Jell-o (dry), and red food coloring. Put fresh, dry berries into cooked shell. Pour filling over berries, being sure to cover all berries. Refrigerate.

Pie Crust:

Combine ½ c. oil with 2 Tbsp. milk and mix well. Combine 1 ½ c. flour, 2 Tbsp. sugar, and 1 tsp. salt. Add flour mixture to liquid mixture. Blend with fingers or fork. Pat into pie plate. Bake at 375 for 15 minutes. Cool slightly before adding berries.

The Freed Family

Banana Cream Cheese Pie

8 oz. cream cheese
4 c. whipping cream
1 c. sugar

Cream the above together and pour into a cooled pie crust lined with 4 bananas sliced and dipped in lemon juice. Top with blueberry or cherry pie filling. Keep in refrigerator.

This recipe makes 2 pies and is a good one to have over the holidays.

The Mills Family

CHOCOLATE TRIFFLE

1 brownie mix (no nuts)
½ c. Kahlua
3 small boxes instant chocolate pudding
14 oz. cool whip
6 Heath toffee bars, crumbled

Bake brownie mix according to package directions. After brownie has cooled, prick with fork and drizzle ½ cup Kahlua over top. Prepare pudding according to directions. Layer in bowl: ½ crumbled brownie, ½ pudding mixture, ½ cool whip, ½ Heath bars. Repeat and chill.

Joann Roberson

TORTILLA PIE DESSERT

10 flour tortillas
2 sticks butter
1 can pie filling, peach, apple, cherry, etc.
1 ½ c. sugar
1 ¼ c. water
cinnamon
vanilla

Fill tortillas with pie filling and roll up. Place in casserole dish. In saucepan heat butter, sugar, and water. Add cinnamon and vanilla to taste. Pour mixture over tortillas. Bake in 350 degree oven for 45 minutes.

Lisa Fulton

BANANAS FOSTER

2 ripe bananas, peeled
⅛ tsp. cinnamon
1 Tbsp. lemon juice
2 Tbsp. banana liqueur
2 Tbsp. butter
¼ c. white rum
¼ c. brown sugar
1 pt. vanilla ice cream

Slice bananas in half lengthwise. Brush with lemon juice. Melt butter and sugar in a skillet. Add bananas, sautéing them until just tender. Sprinkle with cinnamon. Remove from flame. Pour liqueur and rum over bananas; carefully and immediately ignite it, basting bananas until flame burns out. Serve over ice cream. Makes 4 servings.

Pat Sims

VANILLA PUDDING

1 c. sugar
dash of salt
⅓ c. flour (scant)
2 c. milk (do not use skim milk)
2 eggs
1 tsp. vanilla
hunk of butter (or margarine)

Sift together sugar, salt, and flour. Add just enough milk to form a pasty consistency; add one egg and mix well. Continue to add milk, stirring after each addition. Add remaining egg and mix well. Cook on low-medium heat, stirring constantly (mixture will burn if left unattended), until mixture thickens to desired texture. Remove from heat and add butter (or margarine) and vanilla. Stir and let sit till cooled.

Chocolate Pudding:

Same ingredients and procedure used for vanilla pudding plus ½ c. cocoa, sifted with other dry ingredients.

Recipe History:

This pudding recipe was used by my maternal grandmother (and probably my maternal great-grandmother) and has been passed down through the ages; three generations later, everyone still loves it. Both my immediate and extended family members have come to expect at least two homemade chocolate pies at family gatherings. Use the vanilla pudding for coconut or banana cream pie or banana pudding; it can't be beat!

Nieta St. Clair

BANANA PIE

1 can Eagle brand milk
4 large bananas, sliced
1 baked pie crust
½ c. chopped nuts
cool whip

Simmer can of Eagle brand milk in can in water to cover for 3 hours. Little bubbles should come up, but do not boil or simmer to long. It should be about the color of caramel. Fill pie crust with sliced bananas and cover with can of caramelized milk, covering all bananas. Sprinkle with nuts and top with cool whip.

Note: I usually cook 3 or 4 cans of milk at once and store in cabinet for later use. I usually make a circle of cool whip about 1½ " from edge of pie and 1 ½" wide. This is a very good pie.

Zac Cooper

CHOCOLATE ESPRESSO CRÈME BRULEE

2 c. whipping cream
1 Tbsp. finely ground espresso or powder
5 oz. bittersweet chocolate
6 egg yolks
3 Tbsp. granulated sugar
1 tsp. Mexican vanilla

Heat oven to 300 degrees. Mix whipping cream and espresso in a saucepan and bring to a simmer. Remove from heat and breakup chocolate into and whisk until smooth. Beat egg yolks, sugar and vanilla. Gradually add chocolate mixture to egg mixture. Strain, if necessary. Pour into ramekins. Bake in water bath for 40 minutes or until set. May refrigerate for up to 2 days.

Betty K. Fletcher

BUCHE DE NOEL

6 egg whites
6 egg yolks
¾ c. sugar
⅓ c. cocoa
1 ½ tsp. vanilla
dash of salt
Filling:
1 ½ c. heavy cream
½ c. powdered sugar
¼ c. cocoa
2 Tbsp. instant coffee
1 Tbsp. vanilla

Grease bottom of a 15x10 pan and line with waxed paper and grease again. Preheat oven to 375. Beat egg whites until soft peaks form; add ¼ cup sugar, 2 Tbsp. at a time, beating until stiff peaks form. Beat egg yolks, adding remaining ½ cup sugar. Beat for 4 minutes until thick. At low speed, beat in cocoa and vanilla. Gently fold the mixture into egg whites. Spread evenly in pan. Bake for 15 minutes until surface springs back. Sift powdered sugar on a 15x10 dish towel. Turn cake out on towel, lift pan off and remove the waxed paper. Roll up jelly roll fashion and allow to completely cool. Beat filling ingredients until thick. Unroll the cake and spread the filling on top; re-roll cake and sprinkle with powdered sugar.

Roberson Family

CHOCOLATE MOUSSE

Syrup:

2 c. sugar

¾ c. white corn syrup

½ c. water

30 oz. sweet German chocolate

½ lb. butter

1 c. egg yolks (1 doz.)

2 c. egg whites (1 doz.)

2 c. heavy cream

Melt chocolate and butter in double boiler. Separate egg yolks and whites. Cook syrup to 2 cups, which will spin an 8-inch thread. Beat 1 cup yolks till very stiff (5 to 8 minutes). Very slowly, pour 2 cups syrup into beaten egg yolks and continue beating. Add cooled, melted chocolate to above mixture. Beat 2 cups egg whites to soft peaks and fold into mixture. Strain. Cool mixture in refrigerator for 3 hours. Cover top with waxed paper to keep from crusting. Fold in 2 cups cream that has been whipped with 1 tsp. vanilla and ¼ c. sugar. Garnish with extra whipped cream and slivered chocolate.

Betty K. Fletcher

TIRAMISU

Yellow cake
Use your favorite cake recipe, purchased cake, or a yellow cake mix. I generally bake the cake in a 9x13 pan. You could also use the traditional ladyfingers or pound cake.

Soaking Syrup:
¾ c. coffee
¼ c. Kahlua or other coffee liqueur
Combine.

Frosting:
2 8-oz. pkg. cream cheese, room temperature
1 c. sifted powdered sugar
½ c. sour cream
1 c. whipping cream
2 Tbsp. Sweet Marsala
2 tsp. vanilla

Using mixer, beat cream cheese in large bowl until light. Gradually add sugar and beat until fluffy. Add creams, Marsala, and vanilla and beat until well blended. Cover and let stand at room temperature up to 1 hour.

Assembly:

6 oz. chopped semi-sweet chocolate

Using serrated knife, cut cake in half horizontally. Place one layer on serving platter with cut side up. Brush cake with half of the soaking syrup. Sprinkle with half the chopped chocolate. Spread with a third of the frosting. Top with remaining cake layer. Brush with remainder of soaking syrup. Sprinkle with remainder of chocolate. Spread remaining frosting over sides and top of cake. Cover and refrigerate. May be garnished with chocolate curls or fresh berries. Makes 12 generous servings.

Barbara Harjo

UPSIDE DOWN GERMAN CHOCOLATE CAKE

1 c. pecans
1 c. coconut
1 German chocolate cake mix
1 box powdered sugar
1 8-oz. pkg. cream cheese
¼ c. milk
caramel syrup

Sprinkle pecan and coconut in the bottom of greased and floured 9x13 cake pan. Mix cake mix, using directions on box. Pour over nuts and coconut. In separate bowl, blend together the sugar and cream cheese, and then add milk. Pour over cake. Bake in 325 degree oven for 1 hour and 15 minutes. Cut yourself a big slice, then pour or drizzle caramel over your cake and enjoy.

Amber Parsons

MOM'S CHOCOLATE ANGLE FOOD CAKE

¾ c. cake flour
⅞ c. sugar
¼ c. cocoa
Sift and set aside.
12 egg whites
1 ½ tsp. salt
1 ½ tsp. vanilla
½ tsp. almond flavoring

Judge Henry and mother Hazel Henry Searcy

Beat together until foamy. Gradually add ¾ cup sugar, about 2 Tbsp. at a time, continue beating until stiff peaks form. Gently and gradually fold in the sugar-flour-cocoa mixture over meringue until flour disappears. Put into ungreased tube pan.

Cut thru batter with knife. Bake at 350 for 30–35 minutes. Invert until cool.

Top the cake with cool whip and a large grated Hershey bar. Whipped cream, ¼ tsp. vanilla and 3 Tbsp. sugar may be used instead of cool whip. Spread on cool cake.

Judge Robert Henry

UNCLE ROBERT'S RASPBERRY SHORTCAKE

(Note: these "shortcakes" do not contain shortening. We're not sure what's in it anyway. These rely on good ol' cholesterol-laden heavy cream.)

2 c. of flour
1 Tbsp. baking powder (make sure it is fresh)
½ tsp. salt
2–3 Tbsp. sugar
2 Tbsp. good cocoa (like William Sonoma's or Penzey's fabulous cocoa powder)

Sift and stir these dry ingredients together. They must be well-mixed for even flavoring and even rising.

Add about 1 cup or so of good, heavy cream (whipping cream). The idea is to make a dough of workable consistency, but then, of course, don't work it too much. (This is a "quick bread" not a yeast bread). Roll out with flour and cut biscuits. Dip the biscuits in melted butter on both sides, and bake on an oiled sheet cake pan at 425 for 10 - 15 minutes. Cool.

Drizzle a plate with chocolate sauce, slice open the shortcakes, and top with sugared raspberries, or mixed berries (raspberries, strawberries and blueberries, e.g.). Top with sweetened whipped cream, and drizzle, if you like, with Bonny Doon's Framboise, or one of the other raspberry liqueurs. If you like, a creme anglaise can be used in stead of the chocolate sauce.

Judge Robert Henry

BLACK RUSSIAN CAKE

1 yellow cake mix
1 pkg. instant chocolate pudding
¼ c. vodka
¼ c. Kahlua
1 c. oil
½ c. sugar
¾ c. water
4 eggs

Preheat oven to 350. Beat all ingredients together for 4 minutes. Pour into greased and floured Bundt pan. Bake 50–60 minutes. Remove to plate. While still warm, punch holes in cake with fork and pour icing over the cake.

Icing:
¼ c. Kahlua
¾ c. powdered sugar

Beat until smooth. I usually double the icing recipe.

Rodney and Jennifer Freed

RUM CAKE

1 pkg. yellow cake mix
1 pkg. instant vanilla pudding
½ c. oil
½ c. rum
½ c. water
4 eggs
½ c. chopped pecans

Mix all the above ingredients, except for the pecans. Grease and flour Bundt pan. Sprinkle pecans in bottom of pan. Pour cake batter over pecans. Bake at 325 for 40–60 minutes, depending on oven. Prepare Glaze while cake is baking.

Glaze:

1 c. sugar

¼ c. water

¼ c. rum

½ c. oleo

Melt oleo in saucepan. Add sugar, water, and rum. Boil for 3 minutes. After cake comes out of the oven, pour glaze over cake, while it is still in the pan. Completely cool. Remove from pan.

Jennifer Freed

MIDORI CAKE

1 box yellow cake mix

1 3-oz. box instant pistachio pudding

4 eggs

½ c. plain yogurt

½ c. oil

¾ c. Midori liqueur

½ tsp. coconut flavoring

Mix all above ingredients and beat for 4 minutes on medium speed. Pour into well greased Bundt pan. Bake at 350 for 50–55 minutes. Cool about 15 minutes in pan, and then turn out onto cooking rack.

Midori Glaze:

2 c. powdered sugar

¼ c. Midori liqueur

½ pkg. cream cheese

2 Tbsp. butter

½ tsp. coconut flavoring

Mix all ingredients and beat at high speed until smooth and spreadable. Glaze while cake is slightly warm. Garnish with fresh kiwis and strawberries.

Marybeth Govin

PEACH CAKE

2 eggs

2 c. sugar

4 c. flour

½ tsp. nutmeg

½ tsp. allspice

1 tsp. salt

2 ½ cans peaches, chopped

2 tsp. soda

½ tsp. cloves

½ tsp. cinnamon

Mix well. Bake in a Bundt pan at 375 for 1 hour and 10 minutes or until done.

Suggested icings: Coffee Type or Cream Cheese Type.

Janiece Blain

ORANGE SLICE CAKE

2 c. sugar

3 ½ c. flour, divided

1 lb. orange slice candy, cut fine

2 sticks butter

4 eggs

1 box dates, cut

1 tsp. soda

2 c. chopped nuts

¼ tsp. salt

1 small can coconut

1 tsp. vanilla

½ c. buttermilk

Cream sugar and butter together. Dissolve soda in buttermilk. Add 1 egg at a time to creamed sugar and butter. Add flour and buttermilk. Fold in candy slices, dates, coconut, and nuts that have been coated with 1 cup of the flour (only 2 ½ cups goes in the batter.) Bake in greased tube pan 2 ½ hours in 250 degree oven. Pour 1 cup orange juice mixed with 2 cups confectioner's sugar over cake after taking from the oven but cool about 5 minutes. Cool in pan overnight. Good made in advance.

Georgia Welborn

CHOCOLATE CHUNK DRIED CHERRY CAKE

1 pkg. yellow cake mix with pudding

½ c. sugar

1 3.8-oz. pkg. devil's food instant pudding mix

4 eggs

¾ c. vegetable oil

½ c. water

1 8-oz. container sour cream

2 Tbsp. pure vanilla

5 3-oz. dark chocolate bars, divided. (Ghirardelli preferred.)

½ c. coarsely chopped dried cherries

1 Tbsp. butter

⅓ c. heavy whipping cream

1 small tub of cool whip

¼ c. powdered sugar

1 tsp. pure vanilla

Grease a 12-cup Bundt pan and dust with cocoa; set aside. Combine cake mix, sugar, and pudding mix in a large mixing bowl. Beat eggs and next 4 ingredients at medium speed with an electric mixer until blended. Gradually add oil mixture to dry ingredients; beat 2 minutes. Coarsely chop 3 chocolate bars; fold cherries, and chopped chocolate into batter. Pour batter into prepared pan. Bake at 350 for 1 hour or until a wooden pick inserted in the center comes out clean. Cool cake in pan on a wire rack.

Topping and Cream:

Coarsely chop 1 chocolate bar. Place chopped chocolate and butter in a small bowl, set aside. Bring whipping cream to a simmer in a small saucepan over medium heat. Remove and immediately pour over chocolate and butter. Whisk gently until smooth. Cool glaze 3 minutes or until slightly thickened. Drizzle glaze over cake. Coarsely chop remaining chocolate bar and sprinkle chopped chocolate over cake.

Mix the cool whip, vanilla, and powdered sugar together, whisk until smooth and fluffy. Pour in the center of the Bundt cake.

Honeysuckle Rose Gardens

ALMOND JOY CAKE

1 10-oz pkg. Duncan Hines milk chocolate cake mix with pudding
1 15-oz pkg. Duncan Hines home style coconut supreme frosting
1 6-oz pkg. mini-chocolate chips, reserve 2 Tbsp.
¼ c. chopped almonds, reserve 2 Tbsp.

Make cake as directed on package. Bake in 9x13 greased pan as directed. Mix coconut frosting, chocolate chips, and almonds together and frost cooled cake. Top with almonds and additional chocolate chips. Variation: For Mounds cake, substitute the milk chocolate cake mix with fudge cake mix and top with frosting, toasted coconut, and mini chocolate chips.

J.R. and Jan Ross

MAMA'S OATMEAL PIE

2 eggs, lightly beaten
¾ c. maple syrup

½ c. granulated sugar

½ c. packed brown sugar

½ c. milk

½ c. butter, melted

2 tsp. pure vanilla

1 c. flaked coconut

¾ c. rolled oats

½ c. chopped walnuts

1 9-inch pastry shell

In a large mixing bowl, combine the eggs, maple syrup, granulated sugar, brown sugar, milk, butter, and vanilla. Stir until the mixture is well-combined. Stir in the coconut, oats, and nuts. Pour filling into unbaked pastry shell. Bake in a 375 degree oven for 35–40 minutes, or until a knife inserted near the center of the pie comes out clean. Cool on a rack. Refrigerate for 2 hours. Serve with cinnamon whipped cream.

Linda Praytor

CINNAMON WHIPPED CREAM

In a chilled mixing bowl, combine 1 cup whipping cream, 2 Tbsp. sifted powder sugar, 1 tsp. vanilla, ½ tsp. ground cinnamon, and a dash of ground nutmeg. Beat with chilled beaters of an electric mixer on medium speed until soft peaks form.

Winnie Fiddler

FIZZY COLA CAKE

2 c. sugar

2 c. flour

1 ½ c. miniature marshmallows

½ c. unsalted butter

½ c. Crisco oil

3 ¼ Tbsp. Hershey's cocoa

1 c. Pepsi

½ c. buttermilk

1 tsp. baking soda

2 eggs, beaten

1 tsp. pure vanilla extract

Preheat oven to 350. Mix by hand sugar, flour, and marshmallows in medium bowl. Combine butter, Crisco, cocoa, and cola in saucepan and heat on low until melted. Pour over flour mixture and stir well. Add remaining ingredients and mix well. Spoon into greased 9x13 pan, making sure all is distributed evenly. Bake at 350 for 45 minutes. Remove to wire rack. Spread on cola topping while hot.

Fizzy Cola Topping:

½ c. butter

3 ¼ Tbsp. Hershey's cocoa

6 Tbsp. Pepsi

1 tsp. pure vanilla extract

1 box powdered sugar

1 c. chopped pecans or walnuts

About 10 minutes before the cake is done, combine butter, cocoa, and cola in medium saucepan and bring to a boil. Add in sugar. Remove from heat, stir in remaining ingredients. Mix until well combined. Pour over hot cake while still in pan. Will thicken as it cools.

Jan Ross

COCONUT CAKE WITH CARAMEL RUM SAUCE

Cake:

1 c. sugar

½ c. butter, room temperature

1 Tbsp. vanilla

½ tsp. almond extract

2 large eggs

1 c. flour

1 tsp. baking soda

½ tsp. salt

¾ c. sour cream

¾ c. plus 2 Tbsp. flaked coconut

¼ c. cream of coconut (such as Coco Lopez)

Preheat oven to 350. Spray 9-inch spring form pan with 2 ¾-inch sides with vegetable oil spray. Using electric mixer, beat sugar, butter, vanilla, and almond extract in large bowl until fluffy. Beat in eggs, one at a time. Sift flour, baking soda, and salt into medium bowl. Add to butter mixture and beat just until combined. Beat in sour cream, ¾ cup coconut, and cream of coconut. Pour cake batter into prepared pan. Sprinkle with remaining 2 Tbsp. coconut. Bake until cake is golden brown and tester inserted into center of cake comes out clean, about 55 minutes. Transfer pan to rack and cool completely. Using small knife, cut around sides of pan. Release pan sides.

Sauce:

½ c. sugar

2 Tbsp. water

1 Tbsp. dark rum

2 Tbsp. butter

½ c. whipping cream

Combine sugar and water in heavy small saucepan. Stir over low flame until sugar dissolves. Increase heat to high. Boil without stirring until syrup turns deep amber, brushing down sides of pan with wet pastry brush and swirling pan occasionally. Remove from heat. Carefully add rum (mixture will bubble vigorously). Return pan to heat and bring to boil. Whisk in butter. Add whipping cream and boil until sauce is reduced to ¾ cup, about 3 minutes. Remove from heat. Wrap cake tightly and store at room temperature. Refrigerate sauce. Warm sauce over low flame before using.

Cut cake into wedges. Serve with warm caramel rum sauce.

Jane and Mike Lodes

GOVERNOR'S KEATING'S FAVORITE APPLE CAKE WITH CARAMEL SAUCE

Frank and Cathy Keating

¾ c. butter

2 c. granulated sugar

3 eggs

2 c. all-purpose flour

2 tsp. ground cinnamon

2 tsp. baking soda

½ tsp. ground nutmeg

½ tsp. salt

4 ½ c. peeled, finely chopped apples (Granny smith or McIntosh)

1 tsp. vanilla extract

Preheat oven to 350. Cream butter and sugar in a large bowl. Beat in eggs, one at a time. Sift together dry ingredients and add to egg mixture, alternately with apples. Stir in vanilla. Pour into two 8-inch, greased, cake pans and bake for 40–50 minutes. Cool in pan for 5 minutes before cutting into squares. Serve warm with caramel sauce. Makes 8 servings.

CARAMEL SAUCE:

¾ c. butter

1 c. granulated sugar

1 c. packed brown sugar

¾ c. heavy cream

1 ½ tsp. vanilla extract

2 Tbsp. dark rum (optional)

Combine all ingredients in a saucepan. Bring to a boil over medium heat, stirring constantly. Immediately remove from heat and spoon over individual servings of warm cake.

Frank Keating

Award Winning Bread Pudding with Praline Sauce

4 Tbsp. unsalted butter, softened, plus 2 sticks (½ lb.), cut in small pieces

1 loaf country-style Italian or French bread, thinly sliced and toasted

5 eggs

3 c. milk

1 ½ c. plus 3 Tbsp. sugar

¼ tsp. salt

3 Tbsp. vanilla extract

1 ½ c. raisins

1 c. chopped pecans, lightly toasted

1 tsp. cinnamon

½ tsp. freshly grated nutmeg

Praline sauce:

2 sticks (½ lb.) unsalted butter

1 c. (packed) brown sugar

1 c. heavy cream

Terri Shipley

Combine all of the ingredients in a saucepan and bring to a boil over high heat. Reduce the heat and simmer for 5 minutes. Serve warm. Makes 16 servings.

Preheat the oven to 350. Butter a 9x13 glass baking dish with the softened butter. Set aside. Tear the toast in bite-sized pieces and place in a large bowl. In another bowl, whisk the eggs with the milk, 1 ½ cups sugar, and the salt. Beat in the vanilla. Pour the mixture over the bread and set aside until it is completely absorbed. Meanwhile, in a medium bowl, toss the raisins with the pecans. In a small bowl, mix the cinnamon, nutmeg, and the remaining 3 Tbsp. sugar. Fold the raisins and pecans into the moistened bread and transfer to the prepared baking dish; pat down evenly. Sprinkle the spiced sugar and the diced butter over the bread pudding and cover with foil. Set the baking dish in a larger pan of hot water and bake for 50 minutes-1 hour, or until the pudding feels firm and a knife inserted in the center comes out clean. Remove the foil and let sit for 10 minutes. Serve in squares with the praline sauce spooned on top.

Terri Shipley

HEAVENLY CHERRIES

Lerlene Hill, retired owner of Kathey's Kitchen

1 c. chopped pecans

3 c. vanilla wafers, crumbled

1¾ sticks butter, melted

2 cans eagle brand milk

juice of 4 lemons

2 cans pitted cherries, drained

1 pt. whipped cream

1 can coconut flakes

Mix butter and crumbs, press in a 7x11 dish and a 3x5. Mix milk, lemon juice, drained cherries, and pecans; fold whipped cream in gently. Pour in crumbed dish. Sprinkle with coconut. Let stand 24 hours. Makes 15 servings.

Lerlene Hill

STRAWBERRY CAKE WITH STRAWBERRY CREAM CHEESE FROSTING

solid vegetable shortening for greasing the pans

flour for dusting the pans

1 pkg. plain white cake mix

1 pkg. strawberry gelatin

1 c. mashed fresh strawberries with juice (1½ c. whole berries)

1 c. vegetable oil, such as canola, corn, safflower, soybean, or sunflower

½ c. whole milk

4 large eggs

1 c. frozen unsweetened grated coconut, thawed

½ c. chopped pecans

Strawberry Cream Cheese Frosting:

1 8-oz. pkg. cream cheese, at room temperature

1 stick butter, at room temperature

3½ c. confectioners' sugar, sifted

1 c. fresh ripe strawberries, rinsed, capped, and mashed to make ½ c., then drain well

½ c. frozen unsweetened grated coconut, thawed

¾ c. chopped pecans

Place a rack in the center of the oven and preheat the oven to 350. Lightly grease three 9-inch round cake pans with solid vegetable shortening, then dust with flour. Shake out the excess flour. Set the pans aside. Place the cake mix, strawberry gelatin, mashed strawberries and juice, oil, milk, and eggs in a large mixing bowl and blend with an electric mixer on low speed for 1 minute. Stop the machine and scrape down the sides of the bowl with a rubber spatula. Increase the mixer speed to medium and beat for 2 minutes more, scraping the sides down again if needed. The strawberries should be well blended in the batter. Fold in the coconut and pecans. Divide the batter among the prepared pans and place them in the oven; if your oven is not large enough, place two pans on the center rack and place the third pan in the center of the highest rack. Bake the cakes until they are light brown and just start to pull away from the sides of the pan, 28–30 minutes. Be careful not to overcook the layer on the highest oven rack. Remove the pans from the oven and place them on wire racks to cool for 10 minutes. Run a dinner knife around the edge of each layer and invert each onto a rack, then invert again onto another rack so that the cakes are right side up. Allow them to cool completely, 30 minutes more. Meanwhile, prepare the frosting. Combine the cream cheese and butter in a medium bowl with an electric mixer on low speed for about 30 seconds. Stop the machine and add the sugar and drained strawberries. Blend the frosting on low until the sugar has been incorporated. Then raise the speed to medium and mix the frosting another minute or until the frosting lightens and is well combined. Fold in the coconut and pecans. To assemble, place one cake layer right side up on a serving platter. Spread the top with frosting. Add another cake layer, right side up, and frost the top. Repeat this process with the third layer and frost the top. Use the remaining frosting to frost the sides, working with clean, smooth strokes. Serve at once or chill the cake for later serving. Place this cake, uncovered, in the refrigerator until the frosting sets, 20 minutes. Cover the cake with waxed paper and store in the refrigerator for up to 1 week. Or freeze it, wrapped in aluminum foil, for up to 6 months. Thaw the cake overnight in the refrigerator before serving.

Dr. Kent Thomas and Connie Thomas

BRITAN'S RED VELVET COOKIES

1 box Duncan Hines red velvet cake mix
2 eggs
½ c. oil

The Mills family

Mix all ingredients together. This will make a cookie dough. Roll into balls and place on lightly greased cookie sheet. Flatten slightly. Bake at 375 about 8–10 minutes. The top of the cookie will crackle.

CREAM CHEESE FROSTING:

8 oz. cream cheese, softened
¼ c. butter or margarine, softened
2 tsp. milk
1 tsp. vanilla
4 c. powdered sugar

Beat cream cheese, margarine, milk, and vanilla in medium bowl with electric mixer on low speed until smooth. Gradually add powdered sugar and beat on low until smooth.

Britan Mills

AMY GRANT'S MUD PUDDLES

¼ c. sweet butter
1 11½-oz. pkg. (2 c.) milk chocolate chips*
1 14-oz. can sweetened condensed milk
2 c. all-purpose flour

Glaze:

1 c. powdered sugar

½ tsp. vanilla extract

2–4 tsp. milk or water

Best selling contemporary Christian music singer songwriter Amy Grant and husband famous singer songwriter Vince Gill

Heat oven to 350 degrees. Melt butter and chocolate chips in 2-quart saucepan over low heat, stirring constantly, until smooth (5–10 minutes). Remove from heat. Add condensed milk; stir until smooth. Add flour; mix well. Shape rounded teaspoonfuls of dough into 1-inch balls. Place 1 inch apart onto ungreased cookie sheets. Bake for 6–8 minutes or just until set. (*Do not overbake.*) Cookies may appear slightly under-baked. Cool completely. Meanwhile, combine powdered sugar and vanilla extract in small bowl. Gradually stir in enough milk for desired glazing consistency. Drizzle over cookies. Makes 5 dozen cookies.

*May substitute semi-sweet real chocolate chips.

A family tradition from singer Amy Grant

KAREN MILLS PINEAPPLE COOKIES

1 egg

1 tsp. vanilla

2 c. flour

½ c. coconut

½ tsp. salt

2 tsp. baking powder

1 ¼ c. sugar

⅔ c. Crisco

¾ c. drained crushed pineapple

Mix all ingredients together well and drop by spoonfuls onto cookie sheet and bake at 325 until lightly brown.

Karen and Chuck Mills

Mexican Wedding Cookies

½ c. butter
1 c. flour
1 tsp. vanilla
2 Tbsp. powdered sugar
1 c. chopped pecans

Cream together butter and sugar until light. Add vanilla, flour, and pecans. Roll dough into 1-inch balls or finger shape. Place on greased baking sheet and slightly flatten balls. Bake at 300 for 25–30 minutes. Roll in additional powdered sugar while warm. Let cool, roll again in powdered sugar. Be careful to bake only until a light brown color. Cookies may be stored for several days with a light dusting of powdered sugar before serving. Makes 25–30 cookies.

Doris Novotny

Apricot Coconut Cream Pie

1 refrigerated piecrust
Filling:
1 envelope unflavored gelatin
1 c. apricot nectar
2 16-oz. cans apricot halves, drained
½ c. sugar
¼ c. cornstarch
¼ tsp. salt
1 ¾ c. milk
1 egg yolk, beaten
1 Tbsp. margarine or butter
½ tsp. vanilla
¼ c. coconut, toasted*
Topping:
1 c. whipping cream

Joan and Bill Perry

1 Tbsp. sugar

¼ tsp. vanilla

2–3 Tbsp. apricot preserves, melted

½ c. coconut, toasted*

Heat oven to 350. Prepare pie crust according to package directions for one-crust baked shell using 9-inch pie pan. Bake at 350 for 9–11 minutes or until light golden brown. Cool completely. In small bowl, sprinkle gelatin over ¼ cup of the apricot nectar; let stand to soften. Set aside. In another small bowl, cut 1 can of the apricot halves into small pieces. Set aside. In blender container of food processor bowl with metal blade, combine remaining ¾ cup apricot nectar and remaining can apricot halves. Cover; blend until smooth. In medium saucepan, combine ½ cup sugar, cornstarch, and salt; mix well. Stir in milk and apricot mixture. (Mixture will look curdled.) Cook over medium heat until mixture thickens and boils, stirring constantly. Boil 2 minutes, stirring constantly. Remove from heat. Blend a small amount of hot mixture into egg yolks. Gradually stir yolk mixture into hot mixture in saucepan. Cook over medium heat until mixture comes to a boil, stirring constantly. Cook 2 minutes stirring constantly. Remove from heat; stir in margarine, ½ tsp. vanilla, and softened gelatin. Fold in ½ cup toasted coconut. Refrigerate about 30 minutes or until slightly thickened. Fold in apricot pieces. Spoon into cooled, baked shell. Refrigerate about 45 minutes or until filling is partially set. In large bowl, beat whipping cream until soft peaks form. Add 1 Tbsp. sugar and ½ tsp. vanilla; beat until stiff peaks form. Gently fold in apricot preserves. Pipe or spoon whipped topping mixture over cooled filling. Garnish with ½ cup toasted coconut. Refrigerate 3–4 hours or until set. Store in refrigerator. Makes 18 servings.

Joan Perry

ELVIS PRESLEY CAKE

yellow cake mix

2 c. sugar

15 oz. can crushed pineapple

Bake cake in a 9x11 pan, according to box directions. While cake is hot, punch holes in it with a meat fork. Cook pineapple and sugar for 3 minutes and pour over hot cake.

Frosting:

1 box powdered sugar

8 oz. cream cheese

1½ c. chopped pecans

1 stick butter or oleo

1 tsp. vanilla

Mix well and spread on cooled cake.

In memory of her Mam-maw Mildred "Stevenson" Thomas. She always told me when you make this recipe that it is good and rich, just like Elvis!

Randy and Suzanne Gilbert

LEMON SQUARES

Combine:

2 c. flour

1 c. butter

½ c. powdered sugar

Press into 9x13 pan and bake at 350 degrees 20–25 minutes.

While baking, beat:

6 whole eggs

3 c. sugar

¾ tsp. salt

9 Tbsp. lemon juice

rind of 2 lemons

Sift into egg mixture:

6 Tbsp. sifted flour

1 Tbsp. powdered sugar

Fold in by hand. Pour over crust. Bake 30–34 minutes. remove and sprinkle with powdered sugar. Cool and cut in 2½-inch squares.

Lerlene Hill

PECAN TASSIES

3 oz. cream cheese
1 c. flour
½ c. butter

Let cream cheese and butter soften at room temperature; blend together and stir in flour. Chill about one hour. Shape into 2 dozen 1-inch balls; place in ungreased 1¾- inch muffin pans. Press dough against bottom and sides.

Filling:
1 egg
¾ c. brown sugar
1 Tbsp. soft butter
1 tsp. vanilla
⅔ c. coarsely broken pecans
dash of salt

Beat together egg, sugar, butter, vanilla, and salt until smooth, and then add pecans. Put equal amounts into each crust-lined muffin pan. Bake on bottom rack of slow oven at 325 for 30 minutes or until filling is set. Loosen edges with a knife. Remove from pans to cool.

Jennifer Freed

APRICOT BALLS

1½ c. dried apricots, ground
⅔ c. Eagle Brand
2 c. coconut
finely chopped nuts (optional)

Roll into balls, then in powdered sugar. Cover.

Amy Mainord

Bourbon Balls

½ c. butter
4 c. powdered sugar
1 c. finely chopped nuts
¼ c. bourbon
1 6-oz. pkg. milk chocolate chips
3 Tbsp. half-and-half

Put butter in a bowl and microwave on high until melted (about 1–2 minutes). Refrigerate until chilled. Shape into 1-inch balls and again refrigerate until firm. Combine chocolate chips and half-and-half in small bowl and microwave on medium-high until chocolate melts (1 ½ minutes), stirring once or twice. Stir until smooth. Drizzle chocolate over balls and chill. They can be put in small paper cups.

Jennifer Freed

Velvet Rum Balls

12 oz. pkg. chocolate chips, melted
½ c. sour cream
¾ c. powdered sugar
1 ½ c. vanilla wafers, crushed
2 Tbsp. light or dark rum
¼ tsp. salt

Mix all of the above ingredients. Chill. Roll into balls, and then roll in powdered sugar.

The Freed Family

Aunt Bill's Brown Candy

Photo: Bill and Joan Perry

3 pt. white sugar
1 pt. whole milk (or cream)
¼ lb. butter
¼ tsp. soda
1 tsp. vanilla
2 lb. nut meats, chopped fine

Pour 1 pint sugar in heavy aluminum or iron skillet and place over low heat. Begin stirring with wooden spoon, and keep sugar moving so it will not scorch. It will take over half an hour to completely melt this sugar, and at no time let it smoke or cook so fast that it turns dark. It should be about the color of light brown sugar syrup. As soon as you have the sugar heating in the skillet, pour the remaining 2 pints of sugar together with the pint of milk into a deep heavy kettle and set it over low heat to cook along slowly while the sugar melts in the skillet. As soon as all the sugar is melted, begin pouring it into the kettle of boiling milk and sugar, keeping it on very slow heat and stirring constantly. Now the real secret of mixing these ingredients is to pour a stream no larger than a knitting needle and to stir across the bottom of the kettle all of the time. Continue cooking and stirring until the mixture forms a firm ball when dropped into cold water. After this test is made, turn off the heat and immediately add the soda, stirring vigorously as it foams up. Soon as the soda is mixed, add the butter, allowing it to melt as you stir. Now, set off the stove, but not outdoors or in a cold place, for about 20 minutes, then add the vanilla and begin beating. Use a wooden spoon and beat until the mixture is thick and heavy, having a dull appearance instead of a glossy sheen. Add the broken pecan meats and mix. Turn into tin boxes or into square pans where it may be cut in squares when cooled slightly.

Joan Perry

Cashew Meringues

4 egg whites

1 tsp. vanilla

4 c. powdered sugar, sifted

2 c. cashews or mixed nuts, chopped

12 vanilla caramels

2 tsp. milk

¼ tsp. cream of tartar

In a large mixing bowl, allow egg whites to stand at room temperature for 30 minutes. Add vanilla and cream of tartar. Beat at medium speed until soft peaks form (tips curl). Gradually add powdered sugar, beating on medium speed just until combined. Beat for 1–2 minutes more or until soft peaks form. (Do not continue beating to stiff peaks.) Using a spoon, gently fold in the cashews or nuts. Drop mixture by rounded tsp. about 2 inches apart onto greased cookie sheet. Bake cookies at 325 degrees for about 15 minutes or until edges are very lightly browned. Transfer cookies to a wire rack; cool. In a small saucepan combine the caramels and milk. Heat and stir over low heat until the caramels are melted. Place cookies on a wire rack over waxed paper and drizzle caramel mixture over cookies. If desired, sprinkle with additional chopped nuts. Let stand until caramel mixture is set.

Note: Prepare meringues, but do not drizzle with caramel. Place in airtight storage container with waxed paper between layers. Seal, label, and store up to 3 days. Drizzle with caramel mixture before serving.

Donna Smith

English Toffee

2 c. sugar

½ lb. oleo

½ lb. butter

½ c. sliced almonds

Yellow Daisy Layer Cake

2 c. Shawnee best all-purpose flour
1 Tbsp. baking powder
1 tsp. salt
1⅓ c. sugar
½ c. shortening, softened
1 c. milk
1 tsp. vanilla
2 eggs

Preheat oven to 350. Sift together flour, baking powder, salt, and sugar. Add shortening, ⅔ cup milk, vanilla and mix to a smooth stiff batter. Add eggs, ⅓ cup milk, and mix to a smooth, soft batter. Pour into two 8-inch greased cake pans. Bake at 350 for 25–30 minutes. After cooled, frost as desired.

Shawnee Sugar Cookies

2 ½ c. Shawnee's best all-purpose flour
1 c. (2 sticks) butter
1 ½ c. powdered sugar
1 egg
1 tsp. soda
1 tsp. cream of tartar
2 tsp. vanilla

Preheat oven to 350. Soften butter at room temperature in 2-quart mixing bowl. Add sugar and beat until creamy. Add remaining ingredients to bowl and mix into dough. Chill completely. Dough can be dropped by teaspoons on greased cookie sheet and flattened with the bottom of a glass dipped in sugar or rolled flat and cut using your favorite cookie cutters. Bake at 350 for 10–15 minutes. Makes approximately 40 2-inch cookies.

The EXG Story

Growing up with a farm work ethic, when the opportunity to become a ranch owner presented itself in 1989, Bob Funk was enthusiastic and innovative as he began the process of changing another industry. Bob's first love in the cattle business was Limousin cattle and he has been a stalwart of that breed since he first invested his time, money, and energy into it. Express Limousin is preparing for its fifteenth annual Limousin production sale later this fall and each new sale adds another chapter to a success story second-to-none in that breed.

The historic and fertile Express Ranch is rich in heritage as it borders the north side of the North Canadian River. From 1866 to 1886 over 35,000 cowboys drove 3,000,000 Texas Longhorn cattle, from Texas to the northern markets up the Chisholm Trail. One of the main points of history on the trail was on the land known today as the main headquarters where all Express cattle sales are held. The most dangerous point on the trail for horses, cattle and cowboys was the crossing of the North Canadian River at the south end of the Express Ranch. The cattle were rested along the valley by the banks of the river and the hill on the north side of the ranch, where the Funk family home now sits, was the favorite campsite for many cowboys riding up the trail.

More than a decade ago, an important chapter of Angus history began as Bob Funk and Jarold Callahan negotiated the purchase of the B&L Ranch near Shawnee, Oklahoma, and the B&L Angus cow herd from the Oklahoma Cattlemen's Association Foundation. With that transaction, Angus cattle became a major part of the growth and expansion of the Express Ranches enterprise.

After his tenure in academia as both a teacher and judging coach and a successful leadership role in the Oklahoma Cattlemen's Association, Jarold Callahan joined Express Ranches as the Chief Executive Officer and the pace began to pick up. Uniquely located with ideal access to both a high percentage of the nation's cow herd and a high percentage of the nation's feedlot capacity, Express has become a crossroads for all segments of the beef industry. Five production sales each year share Express Angus and Limousin genetics with all types of cattlemen. The Express Scholarship program is the platinum standard of all junior incentive programs as it moves into its second million of award presentations. Bob Funk believes in America's youth.

Express Ranches is an active participant in every phase of the beef production process and has fed as many as 50,000 head of cattle per year. Even the relatively recent acquisition of the historic UU Bar and Mora Ranches located just outside of Cimarron, NM, has added over 150,000 acres of high-altitude rangeland to Express Ranches. A production unit of commercial cows and calves plus 4,000 to 5,000 yearlings each summer will result in the testing of Express genetics under these semi-arid conditions that are not unlike many of Express' commercial customers to the south and west of them. The genetics being developed, tested, and marketed by Express are required to satisfy the needs of every step in the production chain. Carloads of bulls shown at the Denver Stock Show and the sale of junior project cattle that compete in every level of competition force an ongoing emphasis on phenotype and structural soundness in the Express breeding programs. As the focus of the industry has shifted to added value from carcass genetics, the Express Ranch herd sires have set the standard for the industry with young sires set to push the bar even higher.

Ranking as the second largest seedstock operation in America, based upon sales records compiled by Cattle-Fax and published by NCBA, Express will sell more than 4,800 head of Angus, Limousin, and Lim-Flex genetics during the coming year. As the demand for bulls with the recognized EX brand and prefix has grown, Express has followed the lead of its founder and become an industry innovator in the development of a "franchise" approach to seedstock marketing with the formation of the EXG program. The first "franchisee" to enter the EXG program was Marc Rowland and his Rolling R3 Ranch in 2001. In 2003, Jim Barksdale added his Riverdale Ranch Limousin operation to the EXG family. Presnell Plantation from Indiana has stepped forward to become the latest addition to the EXG program for 2005.

In addition to its bull sales each spring and fall, Express Ranches is among the industry's largest sources of bulls sold at private treaty. Bred and open commercial females sell as part of the Express bull sales and customer sales hosted and managed by Express provide the opportunity for purchasers of Express genetics to sell both purebred and commercial females for premium prices. As the demand for bulls that feature Express genetics expands with each passing year, Express has become the beef industry's largest source of seedstock females through the sale of the sisters to the industry leading Express bulls. Ride the Chisholm Trail, stop at Oklahoma's own Express Ranches and let them show you why they are "The Outfit to Tie To."

Oklahoma Heart Healthy Cuisine

INTEGRIS
Health.®

Mission

The INTEGRIS Health mission is to improve the health of the people and communities we serve.

Organization

INTEGRIS Health is the state's largest Oklahoma-owned health care corporation and one of the state's largest private employers (about 9,000 employees statewide) with hospitals, rehabilitation centers, physician clinics, mental health facilities, fitness centers, independent living centers, and home health agencies throughout much of the state.

It is a not-for-profit corporation governed by a 13-member board of directors made up of business and community leaders from across the state. INTEGRIS is managed by President and Chief Executive Officer Stanley F. Hupfeld, with the assistance of senior staff in the areas of physician services, facility operations, strategic services, and finance.

History

The Beginning

Baptist Memorial Hospital opened its doors in 1959 as a 200-bed facility in Oklahoma City. On the city's south side, South Community Hospital opened in 1965 as a 73-bed facility.

1970s

In 1972, Baptist Memorial Hospital became Baptist Medical Center and increased the number of patient beds to more than 500. In 1974, con-

struction started on the south campus, eventually bringing patient capacity to nearly 400. The Baptist Burn Center, now known as the INTEGRIS Paul Silverstein Burn Center, opened in 1975. It was the first adult burn care center in the Sooner state. Another historic beginning came three years later, with the adult cochlear ear implant at Baptist.

1980s

In 1980, Baptist opened the first labor/delivery and recovery rooms for moms-to-be in Oklahoma City. And in 1983 and 1984, two special institutes were formed—the Oklahoma Heart Institute (later renamed the INTEGRIS Heart Hospital) and the Oklahoma Transplantation Institute (later renamed the Nazih Zuhdi Transplant Institute). Also in 1983, the first cochlear implant ever performed on a child took place at Baptist.

The first human heart transplant performed in Oklahoma was done by Nazih Zuhdi, M.D., in 1985. That same year, the first cancer center in Oklahoma opened its doors at Baptist—the Cancer Center of the Southwest, later renamed the Troy & Dollie Smith Cancer Center.

In 1986, the Henry G. Bennett Jr. Fertility Institute opened, and Oklahoma City's first in-vitro fertilization baby was born at Baptist Medical Center. Transplant breakthroughs continued with the first heart-lung transplant in Oklahoma performed by Nazih Zuhdi, M.D., in 1987.

The late '80s brought a whirlwind of activity to the south campus as well. The newly re-modeled Central Oklahoma Cancer Center opened in 1988, as did the Sleep Disorders Center of Oklahoma. In 1989, the Jim Thorpe Rehabilitation Hospital began as a 10-bed rehab unit inside South Community Hospital.

1990s

In the '90s, the transplant program at Baptist expanded to include other organ systems, with a liver transplant being performed in 1992. Meanwhile, South Community Hospital changed its name to Southwest Medical Center that year. And a groundbreaking was held for a freestanding rehabilitation hospital in 1993. The new 60-bed Jim Thorpe Rehabilitation Hospital opened its doors to its first patient in 1994. Since then, it has grown to include 124 rehab beds at the south campus and 43 beds at Baptist. It attracts patients from throughout the state, and even across the nation.

Also in 1994, Oklahoma Healthcare Corporation, the parent corporation of Baptist Medical Center, merged with Baptist Healthcare of Oklahoma to form a new organization named Oklahoma Health System. This merger created a network of health care facilities across the state.

One year later, Southwest Medical Center merged with the newly formed system and the new organization was renamed INTEGRIS Health.

Originally opened in 1965, Southwest Medical Center became part of INTEGRIS Health in 1995

INTEGRIS Rural Facilities

In addition to INTEGRIS Baptist Medical Center and INTEGRIS Southwest Medical Center in Oklahoma City, INTEGRIS Health operates numerous rural facilities throughout the state. In fact, approximately 6 out of every 10 Oklahomans live within 30 miles of a facility or physician included in the INTEGRIS Health organization.

INTEGRIS Baptist Regional Health Center–Miami, OK

INTEGRIS Baptist Regional Health Center is licensed for 123 beds and has more than 40 physicians and mid-level providers on its medical staff. The hospital provides a host of inpatient and outpatient services including critical care and surgical services, comprehensive rehabilitation, geriatric behavioral health, diabetes management, hospice, home health care, and home medical equipment.

INTEGRIS Bass Baptist Health Center–Enid, OK

The INTEGRIS Bass Baptist Health Center campus includes 207 licensed beds throughout three facilities. The hospital enjoys the distinctions of being the only non- profit, faith-based hospital in Enid and having served the Enid area longer than any other general hospital.

INTEGRIS Blackwell Regional Hospital–Blackwell, OK

INTEGRIS Blackwell Regional Hospital is a 53-bed hospital located in Kay County in north-central Oklahoma in Blackwell. In addition to Blackwell, the service area includes the communities of Ponca City, Nardin, Tonkawa, Lamont, Medford, Deer Creek, and South Haven, Kansas.

INTEGRIS Canadian Valley Regional Hospital–Yukon, OK

INTEGRIS Canadian Valley Regional Hospital consists of approximately 128,000 square feet and includes 44 inpatient beds as well as a medical office building. The hospital has 30 private medical surgical rooms, a 10-bed women's unit and a newly constructed four-bed intensive care unit.

INTEGRIS Clinton Regional Hospital–Clinton, OK

INTEGRIS Clinton Regional Hospital is a 64-bed acute care facility located in the heart of western Oklahoma. With some of the finest phy-

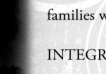

sicians in the state, INTEGRIS Clinton Regional Hospital takes care of families with the utmost care and skill available.

INTEGRIS Grove General Hospital–Grove, OK

Conveniently located in the heart of the city, INTEGRIS Grove is easily accessible by major highways from any point in the Grand Lake area.

INTEGRIS Marshall County Medical Center–Madill, OK

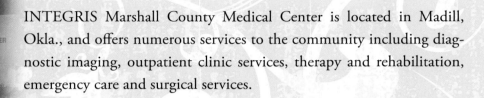

INTEGRIS Marshall County Medical Center is located in Madill, Okla., and offers numerous services to the community including diagnostic imaging, outpatient clinic services, therapy and rehabilitation, emergency care and surgical services.

INTEGRIS Mayes County Medical Center–Pryor, OK

INTEGRIS Mayes County Medical Center is located in Pryor, Okla., in Mayes County. INTEGRIS Mayes County Medical Center is an 88-bed hospital serving Mayes County and the surrounding areas.

Centers of Excellence

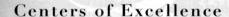

The entities that comprise the INTEGRIS Health organization offer a wide range of sophisticated inpatient, outpatient and ancillary services. Specialized Centers of Excellence have been developed though various entities affiliated with INTEGRIS Health to provide a high standard of care to patients within the region.

INTEGRIS Heart Hospital

INTEGRIS Henry G. Bennett Jr. Fertility Institute

Hough Ear Institute

INTEGRIS Hyperbaric Medicine and Wound Care Center

INTEGRIS Jim Thorpe Rehabilitation Services

INTEGRIS Nazih Zuhdi Transplant Institute

INTEGRIS Oncology Services

INTEGRIS Paul Silverstein Burn Center

INTEGRIS Sleep Disorders Centers of Oklahoma

INTEGRIS Stroke Center of Oklahoma

INTEGRIS Women's and Children's Services

INTEGRIS
MDA
Neuromuscular Center
SOUTHWEST MEDICAL CENTER

Team Hope

The Muscular Dystrophy Association (MDA) is a national voluntary health agency combating neuromuscular diseases that affect both children and adults. More than 2,000 Oklahomans are being assisted by MDA with medical expenses, equipment, support groups, summer camps and other resources.

Patients with more than 43 different neuromuscular diseases are cared for in the comprehensive MDA Neuromuscular Center at INTEGRIS Southwest Medical Center, staffed by neuromuscular specialists from INTEGRIS and the University of Oklahoma Department of Neurology.

It is the only such center in Oklahoma offering a level of care usually available only in major metropolitan areas. The unique partnership between INTEGRIS Health, Muscular Dystrophy Association and the OU Department of Neurology provides Oklahomans and people living

in surrounding areas expert care much closer to home—where it is most convenient.

In 2006, the INTEGRIS MDA Neuromuscular Center earned designation as an MDA/ALS Center, one of only 37 such centers in the United States to provide specialized care for people with ALS (Lou Gehrig's disease).

Once a month, "Team Hope," a group of professionals consisting of nurses, therapists, dieticians, psychologists and neurologists, comes together to concentrate solely on the needs of Oklahoma families affected by ALS. Currently, more than 160 people with ALS from around the state and the region are being followed in the clinic.

Dr. Beson with ALS patient

By managing symptoms aggressively and providing support and education, the center's medical director, Brent Beson, M.D., and his staff hope to help patients explore every opportunity to improve both their quality and quantity of life until a cure is found.

Note From the Medical Director

My name is Brent Beson and I am the medical director of the MDA Neuromuscular Center at INTEGRIS Southwest Medical Center in Oklahoma City. I am a native of Illinois, but I was raised in Oklahoma since the age of three. I graduated from Bridge Creek High School in Blanchard, Okla. From there, I went to college at Oklahoma City University and obtained a Bachelor of Science degree Summa Cum Laude in biochemistry.

My medical training was pursued at the University of Oklahoma Health Sciences Center. I enjoyed a competitive residency in adult neurology at Baylor College of Medicine in Houston, Texas. Then, I completed a fellowship in neuromuscular disease and clinical neurophysiology at Washington University in St. Louis.

My interest in neuromuscular disease started at a young age when I was a volunteer with the Muscular Dystrophy Association summer camps. Spending time with people with neuromuscular disease made a huge impact on my life. That is where I learned about muscle disease in detail and shaped my future for becoming a neurologist.

It seemed during my training in Houston and subsequently in St. Louis, that large numbers of people were coming from Oklahoma to be seen in consultation. It seemed very appropriate for me to dedicate my passion toward a Center of Excellence within Oklahoma City. That became a reality, working with INTEGRIS Health.

The success of the center has been dramatic. We have become a regional center of which Oklahomans are very proud. The partnership created through INTEGRIS, MDA, and the University of Oklahoma Health Sciences Center Department of Neurology has been a very important one. We have three physicians who come from the university to the center to assist in the care of patients throughout the region. This is successful in part because of a multi-disciplinary, comprehensive team approach modeled after other centers throughout the country.

Community Health Fair

I am married to my high school sweetheart, Wendy, and we have two children, Caitlin and Nicholas. We currently enjoy living in Newcastle near the area where we grew up. Wendy plays a very active role in the center as a neurology nurse whose special interest is caring for patients with amyotrophic lateral sclerosis. She works with the ALS Support Group and has shared in the passion of this center from its creation.

Brent A. Beson, M.D.
Medical Director
MDA Neuromuscular Center
INTEGRIS Southwest Medical Center

Other Clinical Services

Hospice of Oklahoma County Inc.–An affiliate of INTEGRIS Health, the hospice is a non-profit agency dedicated to providing physical, emotional and spiritual care for the terminally ill and their families.

INTEGRIS Mental Health Inc.–One of the state's largest mental health provider networks. INTEGRIS Mental Health offers a complete family of services provided by highly qualified professionals in inpatient, outpatient and clinical settings. Services range from day programs for children and adolescents to adult and geriatric inpatient services.

James L. Hall Jr. Center for Mind, Body and Spirit–An educational organization dedicated to improving health by increasing awareness of the healing power of the connection between mind, body and spirit.

Community Services

The scope of the INTEGRIS mission reaches far outside hospital walls and into the very lives of the citizens we serve through our many community services.

Baptist Community Clinic–The largest, free, all volunteer clinic in the state opened in 1993. The clinic is open to the public three nights a month and is operated by at least 40 volunteers consisting of physicians, nurses, pharmacists and clerical workers.

Health Essentials–A comprehensive and progressive health and wellness program. It's truly a one- source health resource. From seminars and health screenings to newsletters and a medical library, Health Essentials was created to give people the information they need to stay healthy.

Hispanic Health Fair–The Hispanic Health Fair is an annual event hosted by INTEGRIS Health and the American Red Cross. The program was developed to reach the rapidly growing Hispanic community. Free health screenings are provided along with essential health and service information.

Men U (Men's Health University)–This annual event is designed to educate men on the importance of taking care of their health. Men U offers free health screenings including cholesterol, glucose, blood pressure and cancer screenings, as well as physician presentations on men's health issues. Men U is one of the first of its kind in the country.

Women's Health Forum–Each September INTEGRIS Health invites the public to a two-week event consisting of special seminars, workshops and luncheons focusing on a variety of health-related topics. Medical experts from within INTEGRIS and across the country serve as speakers and share their knowledge on everything from exercise and nutrition to the latest medical technology and breakthroughs.

Hispanic Health Fair

Two of our volunteers

Services for Children

Basic Educational Empowerment Program—BEEP was created to help at-risk youth learn how to succeed in today's world. All students who begin the Junior BEEP program are referred from the Oklahoma County District Attorney through programs such as STRIVE, Youth Cornerstone, and Weed and Seed. These students meet four days per week working on modules to help them receive their GED. After creating a five year personal strategic plan, students may enroll in any program that will help them attain a job specific skill.

Camp Funnybone—Camp Funnybone is an annual five-day camp held in partnership with the International Center for Humor and Health. The participants learn clowning skills that are taught in a way that builds their sense of self-worth, increases their awareness of the value of other people, improves their ability to relate with others, and teaches children resilience through the healing art of laughter. Fit Kids Coalition—More than 40 Oklahoma organizations founded a coalition to voice and promote positive, rapid change in the fight against childhood obesity. Among the main objectives of the coalition are to achieve change through the Oklahoma Legislature with the Fit Kids Act of 2004, and to achieve change within school districts across Oklahoma.

Camp Funnybone

Western Village

On Your Own—A one-of-a-kind, innovative, day-long program in which doctors and other health care professionals take a look at life and health issues facing today's young people, specifically high school juniors and seniors. Interactive presentations on sexual health issues, nutrition and relationships are presented. Dr. Mary Ann Bauman, who helped pioneer the On Your Own concept, is the featured speaker and moderator for this event.

Positive Directions Mentoring Program—This program is a business/school partnership that began in 1991 that encourages employee volunteers and other community members to become mentors at three targeted Oklahoma City elementary schools. The objectives are to build self-esteem, establish positive relationships, help children overcome negative behaviors and improve the student's classroom participation.

Western Village Academy Inc.—Western Village is Oklahoma's first charter elementary school, and the first charter elementary school in the nation to be totally operated by a hospital corporation. Chartered in July 2000, the school is nestled amidst predominately low-income family housing. A few years ago Western Village Elementary School was deteriorating and threatened with closure. Today it is a thriving center of community activity with a strong base of family involvement. Children are taught through an art-based curriculum that encourages individual learning and creative problem solving. INTEGRIS commits to having one mentor for every student.

Positive Directions Mentoring Program

Services for Seniors

INTEGRIS Third Age Life Center—Two locations serve the Oklahoma City area: 5300 N. Independence and 4200 S. Douglas. INTEGRIS Third Age Life Center is one of the leading senior information and referral assistance centers in Oklahoma dedicated to the development and care of seniors. Services include support groups, workshops, educational seminars, health screenings, resource and lending library, Medicare and insurance counseling, social events, cyber café and volunteer opportunities. Some of the programs offered include the Healthy Heart Walkers Club and the "Young at Heart" Senior Prom.

Award-Winning Chef

Who says hospital food has to taste lousy? INTEGRIS Health has an award-winning chef who proves otherwise on a daily basis by providing tasty and nutritious meals to patients, employees and visitors. Marcelo Miranda is the executive chef at INTEGRIS Baptist Medical Center. He was also named the 2006 "Chef of the Year" by Culinary Arts of Oklahoma.

Each year, the Oklahoma chapter of the American Culinary Federation, ACF, recognizes an outstanding culinarian who works and cooks in a full-service dining facility. This person must demonstrate the highest standard of culinary skills, advance the cuisine of America and give back to the profession through the development of students and apprentices.

Chef Marcelo, as he's called, does all these things and more. He volunteers time to teach cooking classes to students at Platt College and participants of the Job Corp program located in Guthrie, Okla. He also serves the Oklahoma community as a whole by featuring a heart healthy recipe on KWTV-News9 in Oklahoma City each week.

Chef Marcelo has almost 20 years experience in the hospitality industry at the Westin Hotel and Gaillardia Golf and Country Club in Oklahoma City, and several reputable restaurants and hotels in California. He has been with INTEGRIS since 2002.

Miranda received his formal training in Brazil and at the Culinary Institute of America in Napa Valley, Calif. He is a member of the Escoffier Society, the American Boscuse d'Or Academy and the Les Toques Blanches International Club.

Chef Marcelo's unique gourmet cuisine has won him several top awards, including three silver medals from the American Culinary Federation National Championship. He says each new award is just as exciting to receive, and he is truly honored and humbled by this newest distinction.

The ACF developed the "Chef of the Year" award back in 1963. Since then, it has grown in prestige and become the highest honor annually bestowed by the ACF.

Mediterranean Skillet Steaks

Ingredients:

16 oz of lean beef tenderloin
1 1/2 teaspoon fresh oregano
1 teaspoon fresh basil
salt and pepper to taste
1/4 tablespoon extra-virgin olive oil
3 clove garlic
2 tablespoon crumbled feta cheese
1 tablespoon fresh lemon juice
1 tablespoon kalamata olives

Instructions:

Sprinkle both sides of the steaks with the oregano, basil, salt and pepper; rub the seasonings into the meat. Combine the oil and garlic in a large nonstick skillet. Cook over medium heat for about 1 minute, or until the garlic starts to sizzle. Add the steaks to the skillet and cook for about 5 minutes on each side for medium-rare. Remove from the heat and sprinkle with feta, lemon juice and olives; serve with your favorite starch.

Servings: About 4-5

Nutrition Information: One serving provides 192 calories, 22 grams protein, 10 grams fat, 4 grams saturated fat, 2 grams carbohydrate, 0 grams fiber, 68 mg cholesterol and 272 mg sodium.

Polenta with Wild Mushroom Sauce

Ingredients:

1 1/3 cups yellow cornmeal
1/2 teaspoon salt
4 cups water
1 tablespoon olive oil
2 garlic cloves minced
2 thyme sprigs
1 rosemary sprig
6 1/2 cups thinly sliced
   shitake mushrooms, (about 1 lb.)
1 cup canned crushed tomatoes
1/3 cup dry white wine
3 tablespoons balsamic vinegar
1/8 teaspoon salt
1/8 teaspoon pepper
2 tablespoons chopped parsley
3 tablespoons grated parmesan

Instructions:

Place cornmeal and 1/2 teaspoon salt in saucepan. Gradually add water stirring constantly with whisk. Bring to a boil, reduce heat to medium and cook 15 minutes stirring frequently. Spoon into 8 1/2 x 4 1/2 inch loaf pan coated with cooking spray. Press plastic wrap onto surface. Chill 2 hours until firm. Heat oil in skillet. Add garlic, thyme sprigs, rosemary sprig. Cook 3 minutes until garlic begins to brown. Stir in mushrooms and next 5 ingredients. Bring to a boil, cover, reduce heat and simmer 15 minutes. Discard thyme and rosemary. Add parsley, cook uncovered 5 minutes. Sauté polenta in frying pan coated with cooking spray until golden (or spray with cooking spray and bake in hot oven until golden and crisp on outside). Serve with mushroom sauce.

Servings: 4

Nutrition Information: One serving (= 1/4th of recipe) provides 295 calories, 10 grams protein, 6 grams fat, 1.5 grams saturated fat, 50 grams carbohydrate, 2 grams fiber, 4 mg cholesterol and 560 mg sodium.

Asparagus Frittata

Ingredients:

1 Tbs. olive oil
1 medium onion, chopped
2 garlic cloves, minced
3 cups coarsely chopped asparagus
2 cups egg substitute
1 Tbs. fresh basil leaves, chopped
1/2 cup shredded low-fat mozzarella cheese
1 Tbs. bread crumbs
Salt and pepper to taste

Instructions:

Heat oil in a 12-inch nonstick frying pan over medium-high heat. Sauté onion, garlic and asparagus, stirring occasionally until vegetables are soft, 5 to 6 minutes; set aside. In medium bowl, beat egg substitute; add cooked vegetables, basil, cheese, bread crumbs, salt and pepper. Set aside. Spray frying pan with nonstick cooking spray; pour in egg mixture. Cover and cook over medium heat, occasionally uncovering and gently lifting sides of frittata with spatula to let uncooked egg run under cooked part to set. Continue cooking and lifting sides until center is nearly firm, 4 to 5 minutes. Remove pan from heat; remove lid. Cover pan with large round plate or pizza pan; carefully flip pan and plate over together. Remove pan from plate; carefully slide frittata, uncooked side down, back into pan. Cook until bottom turns golden, 4 to 5 minutes. Slide frittata onto serving platter. Serve immediately garnished with lemon wedges.

Servings: 4

Nutrition Information: One serving (= 1/4th of recipe) provides 155 calories, 16 grams protein, 7 grams fat, 2.4 grams saturated fat, 10 grams carbohydrate, 3 grams fiber, 11 mg cholesterol and 250 mg sodium.

Recipes by Chef Marcelo

ASPARAGUS FRITTATA

1 Tbsp. olive oil
1 medium onion, chopped
2 garlic cloves, minced
3 c. coarsely chopped asparagus
2 c. egg substitute
1 Tbsp. fresh basil leaves, chopped
½ c. shredded low-fat mozzarella cheese
1 Tbsp. breadcrumbs
Salt and pepper to taste

Heat oil in a 12-inch nonstick frying pan over medium-high heat. Sauté onion, garlic, and asparagus, stirring occasionally until vegetables are soft, 5–6 minutes; set aside. In medium bowl, beat egg substitute; add cooked vegetables, basil, cheese, breadcrumbs, salt, and pepper. Set aside. Spray frying pan with nonstick cooking spray; pour in egg mixture. Cover and cook over medium heat, occasionally uncovering and gently lifting sides of frittata with spatula to let uncooked egg run under cooked part to set. Continue cooking and lifting sides until center is nearly firm, 4–5 minutes. Remove pan from heat; remove lid. Cover pan with large round plate or pizza pan; carefully flip pan and plate over together. Remove pan from plate; carefully slide frittata, uncooked side down, back into pan. Cook until bottom turns golden, 4–5 minutes. Slide frittata onto serving platter. Serve immediately garnished with lemon wedges. Makes 4 servings.

Nutrition information: One serving (= 1/4 of recipe) provides 155 calories, 16 grams protein, 7 grams fat, 2.4 grams saturated fat, 10 grams carbohydrate, 3 grams fiber, 11 mg cholesterol and 250 mg sodium.

MEDITERRANEAN SKILLET STEAKS

16 oz. of lean beef tenderloin

1 ½ tsp. fresh oregano

1 tsp. fresh basil

salt and pepper to taste

1/4 Tbsp. extra-virgin olive oil

3 cloves garlic

2 Tbsp. crumbled feta cheese

1 Tbsp. fresh lemon juice

1 Tbsp. kalamata olives

Sprinkle both sides of the steaks with the oregano, basil, salt and pepper; rub the seasonings into the meat. Combine the oil and garlic in a large nonstick skillet. Cook over medium heat for about 1 minute, or until the garlic starts to sizzle. Add the steaks to the skillet and cook for about 5 minutes on each side for medium-rare. Remove from the heat and sprinkle with feta, lemon juice and olives; serve with your favorite starch. Makes 4–5 servings.

Nutrition information: One serving provides 192 calories, 22 grams protein, 10 grams fat, 4 grams saturated fat, 2 grams carbohydrate, 0 grams fiber, 68 mg cholesterol and 272 mg sodium.

POLENTA WITH WILD MUSHROOM SAUCE

1 ⅓ c. yellow cornmeal

½ tsp. salt

4 c. water

1 Tbsp. olive oil

2 garlic cloves, minced

2 thyme sprigs

1 rosemary sprig

6 ½ c. thinly sliced shitake mushrooms (about 1 lb.)

1 c. canned crushed tomatoes

⅓ c. dry white wine

3 Tbsp. balsamic vinegar

⅛ tsp. salt

⅛ tsp. pepper

2 Tbsp. chopped parsley

3 Tbsp. grated parmesan

Place cornmeal and ½ teaspoon salt in saucepan. Gradually add water, stirring constantly with whisk. Bring to a boil, reduce heat to medium, and cook 15 minutes, stirring frequently. Spoon into 8 1/2 x 4 1/2 inch loaf pan coated with cooking spray. Press plastic wrap onto surface. Chill 2 hours until firm. Heat oil in skillet. Add garlic, thyme sprigs, and rosemary sprig. Cook 3 minutes until garlic begins to brown. Stir in mushrooms and next 5 ingredients. Bring to a boil, cover, reduce heat, and simmer 15 minutes. Discard thyme and rosemary. Add parsley, cook uncovered 5 minutes. Sauté polenta in frying pan coated with cooking spray until golden (or spray with cooking spray and bake in hot oven until golden and crisp on outside). Serve with mushroom sauce. Makes 4 servings.

Nutrition information: One serving (= 1/4 of recipe) provides 295 calories, 10 grams protein, 6 grams fat, 1.5 grams saturated fat, 50 grams carbohydrate, 2 grams fiber, 4 mg cholesterol and 560 mg sodium.

OKLAHOMA HEART HOSPITAL

Serving the State Leading the Nation

Dr. John Harvey (top)
Dr. Ron White (bottom)

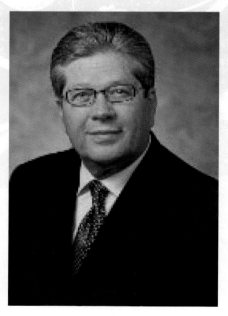

Oklahoma ranks number one for heart disease in the country. A staggering statistic. The rate of diabetes, high blood pressure, and high cholesterol are increasing at an alarming rate. In general, Oklahomans smoke too much and are inactive with poor diets. Plus, our rich and diverse cultures of Native Americans, African Americans, and Hispanics, face high levels of cardiovascular disease and have not been well educated about how to protect themselves.

The Oklahoma Heart Hospital was designed to fight heart disease head on. Just five years ago the hospital was only a dream. OHH is leading the nation in patient satisfaction, quality measures, and cardiovascular innovation. Oklahoma Heart Hospital was the first all-digital hospital in the nation and we continue to advance its technological capabilities. Within the walls of the hospital there are centers of excellence in the Oklahoma Heart Hospital. All of these entities are part of what makes the structure of OHH unique.

Many of the physicians, nurses, technologists, and support staff are Native Oklahomans. They take pride in helping serve, support, and heal their neighbors. The mantra of the hospital is "Serving the state, leading the nation." OHH serves with quality and compassion. Consistently the hospital receives awards for excellence in care. Many patients have become friends, visiting on occasion just to say hello and thank you.

Of this extraordinary group of cardiologists, vascular and thoracic surgeons, a majority are from right here in Oklahoma from places like

Dr John Randolph, heart surgeon, with long-time patient

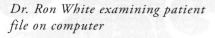

Dr. Ron White examining patient file on computer

Seminole, Anadarko, and El Reno. They lead an exceptional group called the Oklahoma Cardiovascular Associates (OCA). This group is made up of forty physicians who specialize in the prevention, diagnosis, and treatment of all forms of cardiovascular disease. Although the Oklahoma Heart Hospital is located in Oklahoma City, our physicians travel throughout rural Oklahoma seeing patients where they live. The reach of OCA is far, spanning from as far west as Guymon and Sayre, north to Ponca City and Blackwell, east to Hugo and Antlers as well as south to Healdton and Ardmore. Many of our physicians serve the citizens of their hometowns too. Drs. Ronald White and John Randolph have a clinic in Seminole. Dr. Phil Adamson sees patients in El Reno. Dr. Jim Melton travels to Anadarko to see patients. Our physicians care about the people of Oklahoma and it shows.

The vision of better cardiovascular health care for the people of Oklahoma was conceived many years ago, before even one piece of land was turned or a foundation was poured. A group of physicians dreamed of a better way to treat patients; a more focused approach that would lead to better outcomes. Sisters of Mercy at Mercy Health Center listened to that dream, and with their heritage of a pioneering spirit, bought into the idea. The Oklahoma Heart Hospital, the first free-standing heart hospital in the state, was itself a pioneer. Never before in Oklahoma had a group of cardiovascular physicians formalized a plan to partner with a hospital to create a center of excellence for patients with heart disease. Celebrating five years of success and its anniversary in 2007, that same pioneering spirit has led these physicians to do even more for the state. Plans have been completed on the expansion of the Oklahoma Heart Hospital and the creation of a brand new heart hospital to serve even more Oklahomans.

Being patient-focused does weigh heavily on bedside care, but our focus extends beyond our clinical staff. Food for our patients is just as important in their recovery as the medicine and nursing care. While food cannot heal, it can and does comfort. A patient at the Oklahoma Heart Hospital is able to choose the time they eat, as well as the entree. Every patient room has its very own menu with choices for breakfast, lunch, and dinner. When you are ready to eat, just simply pick up the phone and order. Food is delivered within 15 minutes, hot and fresh. Breakfast includes some favorites like good old-fashioned oatmeal and Cream of Wheat and some new favorites like the Oklahoma Omelet made with Canadian bacon, peppers, onions, tomatoes, mushrooms, and low-fat cheddar cheese. From burgundy beef stew and classic chicken Caesar salads to grilled tuna steak and café sandwiches the OHH menu is diverse and sure to please just about everyone. But save room for one of many wonderful desserts like caramel apple cake and blueberry coffee cake made from scratch daily by the hospital's pastry chef. Everything is prepared with the heart patient in mind; low-fat and non-dairy, low or no sodium, but with taste at the forefront. Some of our patients are required to be on a specialized diet. If that is the case, our Food and Nutrition Department will assist the patient in the substituting of an appropriate alternative.

HUCKLEBERRY COFFEE CAKE

½ c. stick margarine, softened

4 oz. low-fat cream cheese

1 c. sugar

1 egg

1 c. all-purpose flour

1 tsp. baking powder

½ tsp. baking powder

½ tsp. salt

1 tsp. vanilla extract

2 c. fresh or frozen huckleberries or blueberries

cooking spray

2 Tbsp. sugar

1 tsp. ground cinnamon

Nutrition Information per serving:	
Calories:	209
Fat:	5.3 grams
Saturated fat:	1.0 gram
Cholesterol:	24 mg
Carbohydrate:	3.7 grams
Sodium:	188 mg

Preheat oven to 350. Beat margarine and cream cheese at medium speed with an electric mixer until creamy. Gradually add 1 cup sugar, beating well. Add egg; beat well. Combine flour, baking powder, and salt; stir into margarine mixture. Stir in vanilla. Fold in berries. Coat a 9-inch cake pan with cooking spray; pour batter in pan. Combine 2 Tablespoons sugar and cinnamon; sprinkle over batter. Bake at 350 for 45 minutes-1 hour; cool on wire rack. Makes 10 servings.

BEEF BURGUNDY STEW

12 Servings

1 ½ lb. lean boneless round steak

cooking spray

1 tsp. vegetable oil

½ tsp. dried thyme

2 large cloves garlic, minced

2 bay leaves

3 c. Burgundy or other dry red wine

¼ c. tomato paste

½ c. plus 3 Tbsp. water, divided

2 ½ c. quartered fresh mushrooms (about ½ lb.)

12 small round red potatoes, quartered (about 1 ½ lb.)

6 medium carrots, cut into 1-inch pieces (about 1 lb.)

2 small onions, quartered (about ½ lb.)

2 10½-oz. cans low-sodium chicken broth

3 Tbsp. cornstarch

¼ c. chopped fresh parsley

1 ¼ tsp. salt

¼ tsp. pepper

Nutrition Information per serving:	
Calories:	220
Fat:	3.7grams
Saturated Fat:	1.1grams
Cholesterol:	36 grams
Protein:	16.8 grams
Carbohydrate:	20.9 grams
Fiber:	3.1 grams
Sodium:	312 grams

Trim fat from steak; cut steak into 1-inch pieces. Coat a Dutch oven or large pot with cooking spray; add oil, and place over medium-high heat until hot. Add steak, and cook until browned on all sides, stirring often. Drain and wipe drippings from pot with paper towel. Return steak to pot, and place over medium heat. Add thyme, garlic, and bay leaves; cook 1 minute. Add wine and tomato paste; bring mixture to a boil. Cover, reduce heat, and simmer 1 ½ hours or until steak is tender. Add water and next 5 ingredients; bring to boil. Cover, reduce heat, and simmer 40 minutes or until vegetables are tender. Remove and discard bay leaves. Combine cornstarch and remaining water; add to stew. Cook, stirring constantly, 2 minutes or until thickened. Stir in parsley, salt, and pepper. Makes 12 1-cup servings.

GRILLED YELLOW FIN TUNA WITH BALSAMIC GLAZE

4 5–6 oz. fresh yellow fin tuna steaks
Glaze:
¼ c. balsamic vinegar
¼ c. virgin olive oil
1 tsp. minced garlic
1 tsp. basil leaves
1 tsp. ground pepper

Chefs Damian Laguna,
Shametra Roland,
Fernando Acuna

Roast garlic in a sauté pan with 1 tsp. of olive oil until light brown. Combine all ingredients in a bowl. Brush glaze on tuna steaks with a pastry brush. Place tuna steaks on grill. Grill each side for 3 minutes or until done. Makes 4 servings.

OKLAHOMA OMELET

Dr. John Harvey with wife, Kim
Harvey, who volunteers her time to
help at Oklahoma Heart Hospital

2 oz. diced onions
2 oz. diced tomatoes
2 oz. diced green pepper
2 oz. sliced ham
2 oz. mushrooms
2 oz. fat free shredded cheddar cheese
3 oz. egg beaters

Spray pan with Pam spray, place onion, tomato, green pepper, mushroom, and ham on grill; sauté for 2 minutes.

Remove mixture from pan and place aside.

Spray pan, add eggs, cheese, and sautéed ham and vegetables, cook until egg is done. Flip over each side of the egg and serve.

John R. Harvey, M.D., F.A.C.C.
and his wife Kim

CARAMEL APPLE CAKE

1 ½ c. apple sauce
2 ½ c. flour
½ tsp. baking soda
2 tsp. baking powder
1 ½ tsp. cinnamon
2 Tbsp. Molly Mcbutter
1 ½ c. sugar
½ c. liquid egg substitute
½ c. fat-free sour cream
¾ c.   evaporated milk
non-stick cooking spray
Topping:
¼ c. oatmeal
⅓ c. brown sugar

Nutrition Information per serving:	
Calories:	305
Fat:	.9 grams
Saturated fat:	.2 grams
Cholesterol:	.8 mg
Protein:	6 grams
Carbohydrate:	69 grams
Fiber:	2 grams
Sodium:	313 mg

Preheat oven to 350. Mix apple sauce, evaporated milk, sugar, and egg substitute until incorporated. In a medium bowl, stir or sift together until thoroughly mixed: flour, baking soda, baking powder, cinnamon, and Molly Mcbutter. Using electric mixer, gradually add flour mixture to apple sauce mixture and blend with mixer until all flour has been added. Spray 9x13 glass baking dish with non-stick spray. Pour cake mixture on dish. In a small bowl, combine oatmeal and brown sugar and sprinkle over top of cake batter. Drizzle 5–6 Tablespoons more caramel topping over top. Bake at 350 for 20–30 minutes. Makes 12 servings.

Positively impacting human life
through exceptional healthcare

People Make the Difference

In a world of technological advances, the power of healing still begins just as it did one hundred years ago… in the hands of dedicated healthcare professionals.

Compassion, understanding, a gentle touch, an open heart for those in need… That's what you found in Shawnee, Oklahoma in 1906, the year before statehood, and that's what you'll find today at Unity Health Center.

Shawnee has been dedicated to supporting a local medical facility beginning in 1906 with a ten bed, privately owned general hospital. Through the years there were a number of hospitals in the area at various locations, including several privately owned facilities, a federally owned hospital operated by the US Indian Health Service, a municipally owned hospital, and a county owned facility.

The hospital of today for the Greater Shawnee area is Unity Health Center, a non-profit organization governed by a 16 member board with the region's best interest in mind. A sound fiscal policy has helped ensure the strong financial performance of Unity for the past three decades.

Unity Health Center was created in 2002 when Shawnee Regional Hospital (opened in 1967 as Shawnee Medical Center Hospital) joined forces with Mission Hill Memorial Hospital (built in 1964). Together, the two entities found that they could provide even better healthcare services for the region.

Healthcare in Shawnee is known for many 'firsts' dating back to 1906 when Shawnee was home to one of the first organized schools of nursing at Shawnee General Hospital. In the past four decades, healthcare professionals in Shawnee continued to be technology pioneers with the first Ultrasound, Computed Tomography, MRI and Digital Cardiac Cath Lab in the area. And today, Unity has the only Cancer Center in the region. This Cancer Center was started in 1968.

From the board, administrators and staff at Unity Health Center, here's to another one hundred years of healthcare for our friends and neighbors in the Greater Shawnee area.

UNITY
HEALTH CENTER
—— SHAWNEE, OKLAHOMA ——

Fast Tortellini Soup
by Carrye Wells, RD/LD, Unity Health Center

Servings: 16

1 tablespoon olive oil

1 medium onion, chopped

2 cups zucchini, chopped

2 cups carrots, frozen, sliced

1 can tomatoes, canned, chopped

2 cans low sodium chicken broth

2 cups corn, frozen

1 tablespoon garlic, minced

1 tablespoon basil, chopped

1 teaspoon seasoned salt

9 ounces cheese tortellini

¼ teaspoon pepper

In a 5 quart Dutch oven, heat oil. Add **onion, zucchini, carrots,** and **garlic.** Cook stirring often, until onion is limp, about **5 minutes**.

Add **basil, tomatoes, pepper, seasoned salt,** and **broth.** Heat until boiling, about **10 minutes**.

Stir in **tortellini** and **corn.** Reduce to medium heat and simmer until tortellini are tender, about **5 to 6 minutes**.

Per Serving (excluding unknown items):
91 calories; 2g Fat (19.9% calories from fat); 5g Protein; 14g Carbohydrate; 2g Dietary Fiber; 11mg Cholesterol; 247mg Sodium. Exchanges: ½ Grain (Starch); ½ Lean Meat; ½ Vegetable; ½ Fat; 0 Other Carbohydrates.

One hundred years ago, people cooked with fresh or canned vegetables from the garden. Today, you can still cook with healthy vegetables from the garden, canned or frozen, depending on how much time you have.

In 1907, the pace was slower. No one counted calories because people worked physically demanding jobs. Actually, it was physically demanding just to stay alive! Today, our lifestyles are dramatically different so we at Unity want to present a recipe that combines yesterday and today… fresh vegetables and tortellini… served up hot and fast for your family!

Loving Care Home Health

Loving Care

Loving Care In-Home Health Services is a family owned and operated Oklahoma business providing health care services to people in central Oklahoma.

Loving Care opened for business in 1997 in Noble as a Medicare licensed home health agency. In 1999, Loving Care started providing hospice services as a Medicare certified hospice provider. Private Duty nursing services have been offered since '97.

Rick and Billie Woods, husband and wife, started the operation in a second story room of their residence. The husband and wife team have worked together to build Loving Care into a 5-office, 180-employee company covering 13 counties in central Oklahoma. Loving Care has been recognized locally by the state of Oklahoma (OFMQ) as a top provider of home health services and nationally by the Federal Medicare program as a "TOP 25%" provider of home health services in the nation as recently as 2007. Loving Care is also proud of the "99% satisfied" patient satisfaction reports generated from all past patients or their representative(s).

The core of Loving Care's evolvement stems from a business model that never takes its eye off quality of nursing. Mrs. Woods, an RN of many years, instills the philosophy of patient care first and foremost in her staff. Ask any nurse at Loving Care what her boss expects and she would probably say, "Treat every patient as if they were a family member you care about immensely."

Loving Care is a true family-run operation with the three adult children of Rick and Billie each managing a location of the business. Mrs. Woods' sister, Joan, is a RN and Director of Hospice services. Tammy and Lisa (daughters) are both RNs functioning as Directors of Nurses. Mark (son) worked as a paramedic for ten years before he and his wife, Annette, opened the Shawnee branch of Loving Care in 2001. Annette is a RN and Director of Nurses at the Shawnee location.

Family members feel communication is a key to all Loving Care locations providing consistent, high-quality service. Constant, around-the-clock communication is a necessary ingredient to a high-quality service company. For that reason, Mr. and Mrs. Woods mandate that all family members involved in the company are always on-call to deal with issues that are part of business.

Loving Care provides home health, hospice, and private duty services to people of all ages and backgrounds regardless of ability to pay.

Wontons

3 lb. skinless chicken breasts
2 bunches green onions, chopped
8 Tbsp. soy sauce
3 tsp. minced fresh ginger
2–3 pkg. wonton wrappers

Grind chicken in food processor then add onions, soy sauce, and ginger to processor and continue until mixed well. Place in a bowl and place in refrigerator for 4–8 hours. The longer in the fridge, the stronger the flavor. Remove from refrigerator and place a teaspoon size or larger drop onto a wonton wrapper. Fold wrapper as directed. Seal the edges with cornstarch mixed with water. Deep fry until golden brown and serve with sweet and sour sauce.

Billie Woods

Dr. Tony Haddad with nurse *Dr. Tony Haddad with receptionist* *Mark Woods looking over chart with Dr. Scott Stewart*

SWEET AND SOUR SAUCE

2 c. sugar

2 c. water or 1 c. apple cider vinegar

squirt of ketchup

quarter size piece of fresh ginger, peeled

1 large clove garlic

salt and pepper

dash of soy sauce

dash of tiger Sauce

cornstarch

Simmer slowly for 1–2 hours. When ready to serve, remove the ginger and garlic clove then thicken with cornstarch. The recipe is a 2 to 1 ratio and you can make as large an amount as needed.

Billie Woods

eric's Pharmacy

Eric's Pharmacy

Eric's Pharmacy opened in Shawnee on March 1, 1995. Eric Winegardner and his pregnant wife, Demita, started the pharmacy with high hopes and visions of success. The initial business plan of Eric's Pharmacy was modeled after Ken's Discount Pharmacy in Norman where Eric worked while in pharmacy school. Six months after opening, the pharmacy was moved to Mission Hill Hospital (now Unity Hospital, south campus) where it remained for seven years. The pharmacy was moved into the Family Medical Specialists building in 2002.

Eric's Pharmacy began as a one-man operation but soon evolved into a two-man operation in the summer of 1995. Brent "Briff" Brown began working at the pharmacy while attending Shawnee High School and has been the veteran pharmacy technician ever since. Eric's Pharmacy now employs ten people. A new state-of-the-art pharmacy is in the works with groundbreaking planned for the summer of 2008. The new pharmacy will feature a double drive-thru and promises to be one of the "premier" pharmacies in the state of Oklahoma.

Eric Winegardner,
Owner/Pharmacist

The pharmacy features services such as patient counseling, drive-thru, compounding, nursing home consulting, administration of influenza and other vaccines, and delivery service. A state-of-the-art medication-filling robot (Script Pro) was added in 2006, and allows the pharmacists to have more time to spend with customers and patients. Offering expanded pharmaceutical care along with providing timely, knowledgeable, friendly services has made Eric's Pharmacy a prosperous business.

Eric attributes his success to a "deep-seeded faith" and a competent, reliable staff of support personnel. Former employer Jared Summers (Plantations, Royal Pipes & Tobaccos of Norman) encouraged the idea, provided financing, and provided emotional support during the first years of business. Eric says he understands the incredibly high failure rate of start-up businesses but encourages young pharmacy graduates to "explore your options and carefully consider the possibilities." Eric's Pharmacy has been a rotation site for pharmacy students at OU College of Pharmacy since 1999, and considers it "a pleasure" to work with the new generation of pharmacists. It also allows him to "test-drive" the students and to hire the best students for summer help or full-time employment.

SMCC
SHAWNEE MEDICAL CENTER CLINIC

About forty years ago, a group of physicians from ACH Hospital and Broadway Hospital saw the need to form a group practice to provide top-notch medical care to the people in Shawnee and surrounding areas. These physicians were among the best in their specialties. They specialized in internal medicine, general surgery, family practice, pediatrics, and allergy.

Later in the 1960s, ACH Hospital and Broadway Hospital merged to form the Shawnee Medical Center Hospital and the Shawnee Medical Center Clinic was born. The group of physicians who founded SMCC were Dr. Jerold Kethley, Dr. Frank Howard, Dr. James Louden, Dr. A.M. Bell, Dr. John Hayes, Dr. Jake Jones, Dr. Roy Kelley, and Dr. August Gauchat.

The clinic first opened its doors on December 4, 1967, by renting space at the hospital's west end. On April 15, 1977, construction of a new building for the clinic began. On May 8, 1978, SMCC officially moved into the two-story structure at its present location. The new location had over 46,000 square feet, which was more than twice its former site. It also housed a pharmacy, a laboratory, and a number of diagnostic machines to serve the twenty physicians.

Over the years, more physicians, specialties and ancillary services have been added. In 1994, SMCC further expanded and added another 22,000 square feet. The extra footage provided space for optometry, more doctors' offices, and expanded areas for laboratory, radiology, physical therapy, and administrative offices.

The latest expansion came in 2000, when an additional 8,800 square feet were added to house an expanded pediatric department, a training room, and medical records. Our current total footage is more than 80,000 square feet. And our latest ancillary services include Imaging, CAT scan, and Nuclear Medicine.

Oklahoma:
A Mansion Affair

Governor's Lunch

Jambalaya w/ Creole Rice

Grilled Chicken Marsala

Quiche Florentine w/ Tomato Soup

Lasagna Al Fronza w/ Salad

Blue Cheese Steak Salad

Tuesday Luncheon

Honey Glazed Sea Bass
On a Bed of Asian Slaw
With Braised Baby Bok Choy
Banana Foster's Crepe Cake

Walt Disney Luncheon

Salad Course
Tossed Baby Greens with
Sugar Curried Pecans
With Strawberry Balsamic Vinaigrette
Okra corn cake
Main Course
Grilled Buffalo Ribeye
With Wild Mushroom in
a Port Wine Sauce
On top Butternut Squash Risotto
Dessert Course
Native Oklahoma Sunset
White Chocolate Mousse
with Raspberry Sauce

Menu

Aperitif
Champagne and Rose water Granita
First Course
Strawberry and Bitter Greens Salad
Fresh Strawberries, Sugared Cayenne Walnuts,
With Blue Cheeses
Tossed in a Champagne Vinaigrette
Second Course
Seared Diver Scallops a top Caramelized Leeks
With a spicy Orange Marmalade Drizzle
Third Course
Raspberry Sorbet
Forth Course
Steak Saltimbocca
Beef pounded thin and then stuff with
a sautéed mixture of Crimini
Mushrooms, Baby Spinach, and Italian Cheeses
Roasted Asparagus in Truffle Oil
Potato Dauphine
Thinly sliced potatoes smothered in heavy
cream and thyme with layers of
Italian Cheese
Fifth Course
Fresh Berries in a Mint Glaze
White Sponge cake layered in Sabayon Cream

Dinner Menu

Frito Chili Pie
Chicken Tetrazzini
Coconut Crusted Shrimp
California Club Sandwich w/ Asparagus Soup
Cheesy Taco Soup w/ Flautas

OMRF Dinner Menu

Hors d' Oeuvre
Parmesan Crisps with roasted green onion pesto
Mozzarella and Cherry Tomato Skewers
Painted Shrimp with 3 Sauces
Salad Course
Panzanella Salad over Rustic Bread
Soup Course
Roasted Tomato Soup surrounding a
Seared Diver Scallop topped with a Lobster Crisp
Main Course
Chicken Provencal with Ribbon Vegetables
Roasted Parsnip Puree in Au jus
Dessert Course
Trilogy of Sorbet
Served in an Almond Tulle Cookie

Dinner Menu

First Course
Stacked Caprice Salad
Second Course
Sautéed Lobster with Spicy Corn Cake
With a Creole Cream Sauce
Third Course
Beef Tenderloin Au Poivre
Caramelized Shallots and Asparagus
With Garlic Swiss Char
Fourth Course
Trilogy of Sorbet

F.O.M. Luncheon

Steak Saltimbocca
Grilled Rosemary Shrimp Skewer
Cannelloni of Asparagus
Lasagna of Vegetables
Chef's Dessert Trio

FILET OF BEEF WITH GORGONZOLA HERB SAUCE

3 Tbsp. olive oil, divided

½ lb. fresh shiitake mushrooms,

stemmed, sliced

3 garlic cloves, minced

1 ½ c. hipping cream

1 c. crumbled Gorgonzola cheese (about 4 oz.)

2 tsp. minced canned chipotle in adobo

1 tsp. fresh de-stemmed thyme

8 6-oz. filet mignon steaks

1 Tbsp. unsalted butter

Heat 2 tsp. olive oil in heavy large skillet over medium heat. Add shiitake mushrooms and sauté until soft, about 4 minutes. Add garlic and thyme; stir 1 minute. Add whipping cream and bring to boil. Reduce heat to medium and simmer sauce until thickened, about 4 minutes. Stir in Gorgonzola cheese and chipotles. Season sauce to taste with salt and pepper.

Sprinkle steaks with salt and freshly ground black pepper. Heat remaining 1 Tbsp. olive oil and butter in another heavy large skillet. Cook steaks in skillet until brown on both sides and cooked to desired doneness, about 5 minutes per side for medium-rare. Re-warm sauce. Transfer 1 steak to each of 8 plates. Pour sauce over steaks and serve.

Chef Dereck Nettle

STRAWBERRY AND BLUE CHEESE
SALAD

1 bag triple washed spinach or rinsed and dried already

2 Tbsp. butter

1 c. brown sugar

2 c. walnuts

6 oz. blue cheese, crumbled

1 pt. fresh strawberries

1 c. bacon vinaigrette

kosher salt and freshly ground black pepper

¼ c. chives, chopped

Place butter into sauté pan; heat on medium till melted. Add brown sugar and cook till granules have dissolved, then add walnuts. Quickly toss nuts and then set aside to cool. Slice strawberries, place in a bowl, and add vinaigrette. Toss spinach, blue cheese, chives, and cooled walnuts together, slowly adding the strawberry mixture.

Salt and pepper to taste.

Chef Dereck Nettle

The First Lady in the kitchen with Executive Chefs Derek Nettle and Russell Humphries.

BUTTERNUT SQUASH SOUP

2 2-lb. butternut squash, halved lengthwise, seeded
1 c. butter
1 onion, diced
2–4 c. chicken stock
1 pt. heavy cream
pinch of grated nutmeg
pinch of red pepper flakes
honey
salt and freshly ground black pepper

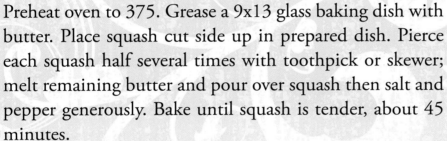

Preheat oven to 375. Grease a 9x13 glass baking dish with butter. Place squash cut side up in prepared dish. Pierce each squash half several times with toothpick or skewer; melt remaining butter and pour over squash then salt and pepper generously. Bake until squash is tender, about 45 minutes.

Sauté the diced onion. When the squash is done cooking, using a large spoon, scrape squash into the pot; discard peel. Add 1 cup chicken stock, 2 cups whipping cream, red pepper flakes, and nutmeg; then puree until smooth. Add additional stock to reach desired consistency. Simmer and stir soup over medium heat for 8 minutes or until heated through. Season to taste with salt and pepper.

Chef Dereck Nettle

Lieutenant Governor Jari Askins

It was November 9, 2006–just forty-eight hours after I was elected to serve as your Lieutenant Governor–that Oklahoma's centennial year celebration kicked off in the City of Tulsa with ten days of activities and events. This was quickly followed by our centennial float, *Oklahoma Rising,* being seen by 38 million people in the United States plus millions more in 150 countries around the world watching the Macy's 2006 Thanksgiving Day Parade in New York City.

The national attention to our grand celebration continued on New Year's Day, January 1st, when the world watched two magnificent Oklahoma floats lead off the Tournament of Roses Parade in Pasadena, California.

From coast to coast and now in literally hundreds of Oklahoma cities and towns, celebrations are taking place each month, culminating with a tremendous Centennial Celebration on Statehood Day, November 16, 2007.

Oklahoma is a proud state with a rich heritage. We are a dynamic, culturally diverse state full of hard-working, friendly people. It's a wonderful place to live and raise a family and a great destination stop for first-time visitors.

Oklahomans have been courageous people who dare to dream big. Over our first century, the world and the nation have been touched by our remarkable determination, compassion, and accomplishments.

Our great state has achieved so much in the past 100 years. I have a deep belief, however, that Oklahoma's best days are still ahead. Our state is on the rise and the economy is booming. Oklahoma's business climate is among the best in the nation. Yet, there is still much to accomplish. We have an exciting future with many new successes ahead in our next 100 years. I invite you to be an active participant in one of the more than 1,000 centennial projects and activities in communities all across our state.

Oklahoma's favorite son, Will Rogers, once said: "Oklahoma is the heart, it's the vital organ, of our national existence." I agree. And, what better year for Oklahoma to celebrate this fact on the national and world stages than during our Centennial Celebration.

It is an honor to represent my fellow citizens both in state and across America during this historic time in the life of our state. As we commemorate the centennial, let us reflect on our glorious heritage and then look to the future with excitement and anticipation for all that Oklahoma will be for the generations to follow.

CHOCOLATE CHIP BUNDT CAKE
Lt. Governor Jari Askins' family favorite recipe

1 butter cake mix
1 small box of vanilla pudding
5 oz. chocolate syrup
8 oz. sour cream
4 eggs
1 tsp. vanilla
¾ c. vegetable oil
⅔ c. chocolate chips

Mix all ingredients together. Pour into greased Bundt pan. Bake cake for 1 hour at 325. After the cake has cooled, sprinkle sifted powdered sugar over the top of the cake.

Lieutenant Governor Jari Askins

Oklahoma
Favorites

GRANNY'S CHICKEN FRIED STEAK

4 8-oz. rib eye steaks, fat trimmed
6 Tbsp. flour
½ tsp. salt
½ tsp. pepper (coarse ground)
1 ½ tsp. Lawry's season salt
½ tsp. paprika
½ tsp. garlic powder
2 eggs, lightly beaten
1 Tbsp. olive oil

Toby Keith and Hal Smith at the "Toby Keith's I Love this Bar & Grill" ribbon cutting, with Gov. Brad Henry and Fred Hall, Chamber of Commerce official, looking on. A favorite of Toby's is the chicken fried steak

Combine flour, salt, pepper, season salt, paprika, and garlic powder in bowl. Rinse and pat dry steaks. Dip in eggs and dredge in flour mixture, shaking off any excess flour. Heat 1 Tbsp. oil in skillet over medium-low heat. Add steak, turning frequently until desired doneness. Makes 4 servings.

COUNTRY WHITE GRAVY

3 Tbsp. poultry drippings (may use bacon or sausage also)
¾ c. milk
3 Tbsp. flour
1 tsp. salt
dash pepper (or to your liking)
¾-1 c. milk

Place drippings in medium skillet. In a jar with a tight-fitting lid, or a small bowl, combine ¾ cup milk, flour, salt, and pepper. Shake until well combined in jar or mix thoroughly in bowl. On medium heat, stir into drippings. Cook, stirring constantly until desired consistency. It should be thick and bubbly. Add additional milk if necessary. Makes 1 ½ cups.

Hal Smith

GARLIC-GRUYERE MASHED POTATOES

3 lb. Yukon Gold potatoes
¼ c. butter
¾ c. hot milk
½ c. sour cream
¾ tsp. salt
¼ tsp. pepper
3–4 garlic cloves, minced
1 c. shredded Gruyere cheese
2 green onions, sliced (slice 2 more for garnish if desired)

Peel potatoes, cut into chunks, and cook in boiling water for 15–20 minutes. Drain well. Return potatoes to pan and mash with potato masher or place in mixer bowl and whip potatoes. Add butter; stir in hot milk and next 4 ingredients. Mash/whip again to desired texture. Stir in 1 cup cheese and 2 sliced green onions. Garnish with more cheese and onions if desired.

Linda Praytor

Oklahoma Macaroni and Cheese

1 lb. small shaped pasta, like elbows or penne
4 c. milk
4 Tbsp. butter
6 Tbsp. flour
1 tsp. paprika
pinch of salt
pepper to taste
4 c. grated Gruyere cheese
3 Tbsp. grated low-fat or regular cheddar cheese

Preheat oven to 350 degrees. In a large pot, cook pasta following package directions. Drain and place in a large bowl. Bring milk to a boil in another pan, set aside. Melt butter in another pan. Add flour slowly to butter, whisking over a low heat for 5 minutes. Avoid browning. Remove from heat. Add milk to butter-flour mixture and blend well. Add ½ tsp. paprika, salt, and pepper to taste. Return pan to heat. Cook over a medium heat, stirring constantly, about 5 minutes, until thickened. Pour over pasta and mix thoroughly. Butter a 9x13 baking dish and fill with prepared pasta. Sprinkle grated Gruyere cheese, remaining paprika, and pepper over top. Place dish on a foil-covered baking sheet. Bake for 20–25 minutes. Remove from oven and turn the oven up to broil. Sprinkle cheddar cheese evenly over the top and place under broiler, with the rack on the lowest setting, for 3–4 minutes, or until slightly golden. Serve hot.

J.R. and Jan Ross

Cajun Fried Turkey the Okie Way

Bob and Sharon Stewart prepare Cajun turkey for family gathering.

If you have never tasted fried turkey, you are in for a special treat, but caution must be observed when frying turkeys.

12–14 lb. turkey
melted butter
Italian salad dressing
Tony's Creole seasoning
propane burner
cooking pot that will hold 5 gal. oil
leather gloves
thermometer
5 gal. peanut oil
hook for lifting turkey in and out of oil

Note: Turkey must be well thawed, dried, and contain no ice or water.

Using either poultry injection kit or 50cc plastic syringe, inject approximately 100 cc Italian dressing into the breast, legs, and under the skin of thawed turkey. Rub entire outside of turkey with melted butter. Sprinkle generously with Tony's Creole seasoning.

Heat oil to 350 degrees, slowly submerge turkey into oil, being extremely careful not to let the oil boil over. Fry 4 minutes per pound of turkey. Turkey will be a golden brown. Turn off propane burner and immediately remove turkey from oil. Due to the expense of the peanut oil, it is a good idea to fry several turkeys for friends and neighbors. You can start your own Cajun tradition.

Caution: Place burner away from any flammable materials and/or buildings. Fry only fully thawed and thoroughly dried turkey. Do not let oil come in contact with flame at any time. Keep temperature a constant 350 degrees.

Bob and Sharon Stewart

FRIED FISH

fish fillets (bass, catfish, or crappie)
Tabasco sauce
Shawnee's Best yellow corn meal
salt and pepper

State Auditor and Inspector Jeff McMahan and wife Lori McMahan

Mix salt and pepper to taste with corn meal. Dip (don't soak) fresh fish fillets in Tabasco sauce. Roll the wet fillets in corn meal mixture. Deep fry in oil until golden brown. I prefer peanut oil.

VENISON CHILI

2 lb. ground venison
1 lb. fatty hamburger meat
1 medium onion, chopped
salt and pepper
1 envelope William's chili seasoning
1 small can ranch style beans (optional)
1 can stewed tomatoes
1 large can tomato juice

Brown onion and meat with salt and pepper, drain fat. Add chili seasoning and stir. Add beans, tomatoes, and tomato juice and bring to a boil. Reduce heat and simmer for 20–30 minutes.

Jeff and Lori McMahan

NONNA'S COCONUT CREAM PIE

*Avis Scaramucci with Author
Ronnye Sharp*

Basic Cream Pie
¾ c. sugar
⅓ c. flour
⅛ tsp. salt
2 c. milk
1 ½ tsp. coconut extract
1 c. shredded coconut
2 Tbsp. butter
2 eggs

Heat milk to scald and add butter. Next combine sugar, flour, salt, coconut extract, and beaten eggs in a bowl. Then gradually add the hot milk mixture to the above combined ingredients, stirring constantly until filling is smooth. Add shredded coconut. This filling will be a little "runny" until it cools. Pour mixture into baked pie shell—top with meringue and toast coconut if desired.

SINGLE PIE SHELL

1 ½ c. sifted all-purpose flour
½ tsp. salt
½ c. shortening
4–5 Tbsp. cold water

Sift together flour and salt. Cut in shortening with pastry blender or fork until pieces are size of small peas. Gradually sprinkle water to the flour/shortening mixture until all is moistened. Gather up with fingers; form into a ball. On lightly floured surface roll until ⅛-inch thick. Transfer to pie plate fitting loosely onto bottom and sides.

If *baked* pie shell is needed, prick bottom and sides well with fork. Bake at 450 degrees until pastry is golden, 10–12 minutes.

Nonna's Restaurant and Bakery

PEAR HONEY

9 c. pears
juice of 1 lemon (about 4 tsp.)
1 c. crushed pineapple
5 c. sugar

Wash, peel and core pears; slice before measuring. Put through a food chopper. Combine pears, pineapple, and juice; add sugar. Cook over slow heat, stirring frequently. Cook about 45 minutes until desired consistency. Pour into jars; seal while hot.

Doris Novotny

INDIAN TACOS
Just like at the fair!

1 lb. ground beef
1 tsp. salt
dash of Tabasco sauce
grated cheese
chopped tomatoes
1 onion, minced
¼ tsp. pepper
pinto beans
shredded lettuce

Combine meat, onion, Tabasco sauce, salt ,and pepper in

a skillet and brown. Cover and let simmer while making the fry bread.

Fry Bread:
2 eggs
4 c. all-purpose flour
2 tsp. baking powder
1 c. milk
¾ tsp. salt

Beat eggs; add milk. Stir in flour, salt, and baking powder, mixing well together. Roll out to desired thickness on floured board, probably less than ½ inch. Cut into desired shapes and cut a slash in center of each. Fry in deep oil until brown. Drain on paper towels. These are crisp tacos. Layer each taco with beans, meat, shredded lettuce, and chopped tomatoes. Sprinkle with grated cheese. Serve hot with picante sauce. You can also add chopped onions to top of lettuce.

Doris Novotny

CORNMEAL DUMPLINGS

1 hambone simmered until meat falls from
  the bone easily
1 c. chopped onions
1 c. ham meat from bone cut into bit size pieces
2 c. white or yellow cornmeal
1 tsp. salt
1 tsp. black and 1 tsp. red pepper

Place hambone in large Dutch oven and cover with ample amount of water. Simmer until meat falls away from the bone. Take meat from bone and reserve.

Combine cornmeal, salt, black and red pepper. Add ham

and onions. Pour scalding broth over the cornmeal-ham mixture, starting with a cup of broth, adding more as needed to make a mixture stiff enough that you can form into dumplings the size of a lemon. Drop dumplings as you form them, into the simmering ham broth. Simmer from 20–25 minutes. Avoid stirring or moving dumplings around as they might disintegrate into the broth. Serve as any side dish but good with Mexican food too.

This was my grandmother and mother, Plezzie Webb Woodruff's, old-time Oklahoma recipe.

Barbara Brown

BANANA PUDDING

2 small pkg. instant vanilla pudding
3 c. milk
1 can Eagle Brand milk
1 c. sour cream
16 oz. tub cool whip
vanilla wafers
3 bananas, or more, to taste

Beat vanilla pudding mix with milk for 1- 2 minutes. In separate bowl, mix Eagle Brand, sour cream, and cool whip together; add to pudding mixture. Layer vanilla wafers, bananas, pudding mixture, in that order, in a large Pyrex dish. Refrigerate.

Ronnye Sharp and Jennifer Freed

GEORGIA WELBORN'S FRIED PIES

2 c. flour
½ c. milk
2 tsp. baking powder
1 Tbsp. sugar
1 egg, beaten with milk
pinch of salt
¼ c. Crisco
1 tsp. cream of tartar

Mix and roll out like pie crust and cut around a small bowl. Spoon fruit into crust, fold over, and pinch down sides. Freeze on cookie sheet. After frozen and ready to use, take out of freezer and deep fry frozen pie in Crisco oil until brown. I usually use a cast iron skillet. Drain on paper towel and put back on cookie sheet and drizzle with glaze. Bake at 350 degrees for about 10 minutes.

Glaze:

Powdered sugar, vanilla, and hot water. For filling I usually use cherry or apple pie filling or boil apricots and sweeten them.

Georgia Welborn

CHOCOLATE PIE

4 lg. egg yolks
1 c. sugar
¼ c. cornstarch
½ tsp. salt
2 ½ squares semi-sweet chocolate or ¼ c. cocoa
2 c. milk

1 tsp. vanilla

½ stick margarine

Combine sugar, cornstarch, and salt. In saucepan, melt chocolate and milk. Add sugar mixture and bring to boil. Cook 3–4 minutes. Add small amount to beaten egg yolks and then add back to pan on stove. Bring to boil. Cook 3–4 minutes. Take off stove and add vanilla and margarine. With hand mixer, beat until creamy. Put pudding into cooked pie shell. Top with meringue or whipped topping.

Freed Family Favorite

BETH SIMPSON'S CHOCOLATE CAKE

Preheat oven to 400 degrees.

Cake:

2 sticks of margarine

5 Tbsp. unsweetened cocoa

1 c. water

2 c. flour

2 c. sugar

½ c. buttermilk

2 eggs

1 tsp. baking soda

1 tsp. vanilla

In medium saucepan, bring margarine, cocoa, and water to a boil, cook for 4 minutes and remove from heat. In large mixing bowl, combine flour and sugar to mix well. Gradually add hot mixture while continually beating. Then add in remaining ingredients, mixing well. Pour into greased and floured baking pan(s) and bake at 400

Preheat oven to 450 degrees. Sift together flour, baking powder, salt; cut in shortening until like coarse crumbs. Add milk and mix lightly to make a soft dough. Knead lightly on floured surface and roll to ½ inch thickness. Cut dough to desired size and place on lightly greased baking sheet or pan with sides touching. Bake at 450 for 10–12 minutes. Makes 18 2-inch biscuits.

OKLAHOMA STYLE OKRA WITH TOMATO SAUCE

Jeanie McCain Edney, Deputy Director Oklahoma Centennial Commission

4 slices bacon
5 c. fresh okra, sliced
1 medium onion, chopped
1 medium green bell pepper, chopped
½ tsp. salt
¼ tsp. fine black pepper
½ tsp. ground cumin
½ tsp. garlic powder
2 8-oz. cans tomato sauce
cooked rice

Sauté bacon until crisp. Remove to paper towel and allow to drain. Reserve drippings in skillet. Sauté okra, onion, and green pepper in drippings until just tender. Crumble bacon and add bacon, salt, pepper, cumin, garlic powder, and tomato sauce to vegetables. Stir gently. Cover and simmer for 30 minutes, stirring occasionally. Serve over rice. Makes 6 servings.

Jeanie McCain Edney

OKLAHOMA OKRA PATTIES

4 c. fresh or frozen (thawed) okra
½ c. olive oil
3 eggs
1 medium onion, chopped
½ c. water
1 ½ tsp. salt, or to taste
pepper to taste
1 c. flour

Wash the okra and drain. Remove stems and cut into ½-inch slices. Salt okra. Blend eggs, onion, and water with salt and pepper. Add okra, then add flour and mix well. Heat oil in large skillet over medium-low heat. Put okra slices in heated oil. Turn okra while cooking until crispy and lightly browned, about 8–10 minutes. Drain on paper towels. Green tomatoes may also be prepared this way, chopped not sliced.

Jan Ross

QUICK CUCUMBER PICKLES

½ c. white vinegar
2 rounded tsp. sugar
1 tsp. mustard seed
1 tsp. salt
1 clove cracked garlic
1 tsp. dried dill or 2 Tbsp. fresh dill leaves
1 bay leaf
4 cucumbers, sliced in thinly at an angle

Heat a small saucepan over medium heat. Add vinegar,

sugar, mustard seed, salt, and garlic to the pan and cook until it begins to simmer and sugar dissolves. Toss the dill, bay leaf, and sliced cucumbers together in a heat-proof bowl. Pour the simmering liquid over the cucumbers and stir to cover. Chill and serve.

Linda Praytor

CUCUMBER WITH VINAIGRETTE

¼ c. sugar

¼ c. rice vinegar

2 Tbsp. fresh ginger, chopped

½ tsp. crusted red pepper flakes

1 English cucumber, thinly sliced

Combine and chill before serving.

Honeysuckle Rose Gardens

Country Hall of Famer Vince Gill

VINCE GILL'S HOMEMADE PIZZA PIE

Dough:

1 pkg. dry yeast

½ c. warm water

2 ¼ c. flour

¾ tsp. salt

1 tsp. sugar

1 egg

2 tsp. vegetable oil

Sauce:

¼ c. vegetable oil

1 14 ½-oz. jar pizza sauce

1 6-oz. can tomato paste
1 clove garlic, crushed
2 tsp. sugar
1 ½ tsp. dried oregano
1 tsp. dried basil
½ tsp. crushed red pepper flakes

Toppings:
pepperoni, sliced thin
mushrooms, sliced thin
onion, chopped
Mozzarella cheese, shredded
Parmesan cheese, grated
green and black olives, chopped

Combine yeast and warm water for dough, stirring until dissolved. Add 1 cup of the flour, salt, and sugar and mix well. Add egg and oil, stirring until mixture reaches a smooth consistency. Stir in 1 cup of flour to keep dough from sticking (add extra ¼ c. if needed). On lightly floured surface, knead dough until smooth and elastic. Place in a greased bowl and cover with a towel. Let dough rise in a warm place for about 1 hour or until it doubles. Let dough reach room temperature before shaping. Preheat oven to 350 degrees. To assemble, gently stretch dough to fit a greased 16-inch pizza pan. Crimp edge to form a rim and brush dough lightly with oil. Bake without toppings until just lightly browned. Mix pizza sauce, tomato paste, garlic, sugar, oregano, basil, and pepper flakes. Spread evenly over crust. Arrange your choice of toppings, except the cheese, over top and bake at 350 degrees for 15 minutes. Sprinkle mozzarella and Parmesan on top and bake for 5–10 minutes more, or until cheese is melted. Serve hot! Makes 2–4 servings.

Vince Gill

Oatmeal Raisin Cookies

1 c. Crisco
1 c. sugar
1 c. brown sugar
2 eggs
1 ½ c. flour
1 tsp. salt
1 tsp. vanilla
1 tsp. soda
1 tsp. cinnamon
3 c. quick oats
1 c. chopped pecans
1 c. raisins (boil in water with a little butter)

Cream Crisco and sugars; add eggs. Mix well. Add flour, salt, soda and cinnamon. Blend in nuts, raisins and vanilla; add oats last. Drop by teaspoonful on cookie sheet. Bake at 350 degrees for 10–12 minutes.

Carla Hill

Super Hot Fudge Sundae Sauce

14 ½-oz. can of evaporated milk
2 c. sugar
4 squares unsweetened chocolate (4 oz.)
¼ c. butter
1 ½ tsp. Mexican vanilla
¼ tsp. salt

Combine milk and sugar in saucepan. Bring to full rolling boil, stirring constantly. Boil at least one full minute. Add chocolate, stir until melted. Beat over heat until smooth. Remove from heat and stir in butter, vanilla, and salt. Serve hot or cold. Store in refrigerator. Pop in microwave for instant hot fudge.

Betty K. Fletcher

CHUNKY RED CHILI
Toby Keith's favorite recipe form the restaurant he co-owns, Hatch Valley Chile Co.

15–20 dried big red chili peppers

2 c. water

3 cloves fresh garlic

1 tsp. Mexican oregano

1 Tbsp. oil

3 lb. cubed pork

3 bay leaves

Soak chilies in water for 90 minutes. In a blender, puree chilies, water, garlic and half the oregano. Press through a strainer; keep the liquid and discard the rest. In a stew pot, heat the oil over medium heat. Add the pork and brown. Add the chili liquid, bay leaves and remaining oregano. Stir and bring to a boil. Reduce heat and simmer 30 minutes, or until pork is tender. Salt to taste. Serve with tortillas. Makes 8 servings.

Country Music Award Winner Toby Keith

RAW APPLE CAKE

½ c. Crisco

2 c. flour

½ tsp. salt

1 c. dates

Lou Kerr, President of Centennial Commission

2 c. sugar

2 tsp. cinnamon

4 c peeled and chopped apples

1 c. nuts

2 eggs

1 tsp. soda

Cream shortening and sugar. Add remaining ingredients, one at a time. Bake in 9x13 greased pan at 325 for 1 hour.

Sauce for cake:

1 c. sugar

2 Tbsp. flour

½ tsp. nutmeg

½ tsp. cinnamon

¾ c. water

2 Tbsp. butter

¼ c. Whiskey (old #7 or less)

1 tsp. vanilla

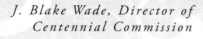

J. Blake Wade, Director of Centennial Commission

Mix gradually, bring to a boil. Boil 2–4 minutes. Remove and add vanilla. Pour hot over individual servings or can pour over entire cake.

If you don't use whiskey, increase water to 1 cup.

Mrs. Robert S. Kerr, Jr.

FRESH STRAWBERRY PIE

10-inch baked pie shell

6 c. of strawberries

1 ½ scant c. sugar

4 ½ Tbsp. corn starch

1 ½ Tbsp. lemon juice

Wash and stem berries; drain on paper towel. Take out enough whole berries to fill and stand in bottom of pie plate, set aside. Take rest of berries and mash. Mix sugar, lemon, and corn starch together and add to mashed berries. Cook about 10 minutes until thick and clear; cool.

Put whole berries on bottom of baked pie shell and cover with cooked cool berries, refrigerate until firm. Top with fresh whipped cream.

J. Blake Wade

OKLAHOMA'S BEST PECAN PIE

5 egg yolks
1 c. sugar
1 c. white Karo syrup
4 Tbsp. butter
1 ½ c. broken pecan meats
5 egg whites, well beaten
vanilla to taste

Cream butter, sugar and egg yolks. Add syrup, vanilla, and pecans and stir well. Fold in egg whites. Pour mixture into unbaked pastry shell and bake slowly at 325 for 1 hour until custard-like in consistency. Serve with ice cream and a few pecans sprinkled over the top, or whipped cream.

Excellent Pie Crust:
2 c. flour
½ tsp. salt
⅓ c. butter
⅓ c. white vegetable shortening
ice water (about ⅓ c.)

Mix salt into flour. Work both shortenings into flour with pastry mixer or by crossing two knives against each other.

Bits of shortening should be pea-sized. Moisten dough with ice water by stirring with a fork. Pat into 2 balls (for 2 crusts) wrap in wax paper and chill thoroughly. This dough handles easily and bakes very well.

Ronnye Perry Sharp

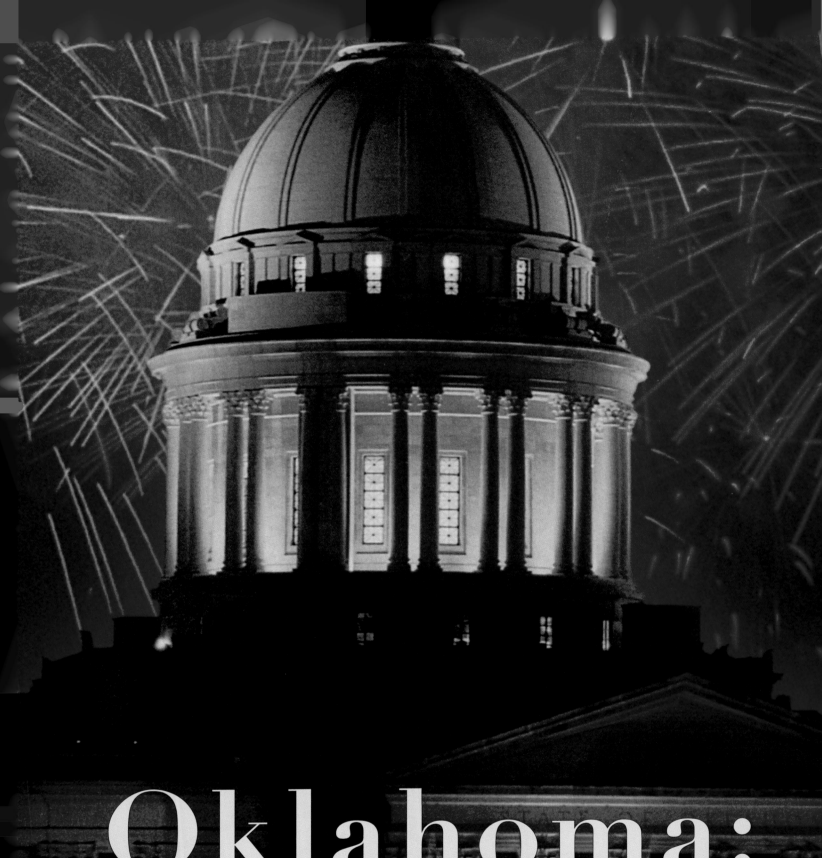

Oklahoma:
Celebrating *the* First Century

Celebrating the First Century

by Bob Burke

The year-long celebration of Oklahoma's first 100 years was the celebration of a lifetime. Grand-scale plans in all seventy-seven counties, from town to town and border to border, were designed to entertain, honor, captivate, and commemorate. Thousands of projects built fountains, monuments, parks, and cultural facilities, while programs and festivals enhanced local traditions. Oklahoma's rich and diverse heritage was highlighted by libraries, schools, museums, businesses, families, and historical societies.

The centennial was kicked off in Tulsa in November 2006, with expos, exhibits, concerts, a parade, and fireworks. The centennial float, "Oklahoma Rising," made its way down Broadway in New York City in the Macy's 2006 Thanksgiving Day Parade. On January 1, 2007, Oklahoma marched onto television screens around the world with two magnificent floats in the Tournament of Roses Parade. The U.S. Postal Service unveiled a new postage stamp to commemorate the centennial.

Two major events in the fall of 2007 brought great pride to Oklahomans. The Centennial Expo in Oklahoma City "filled in" for the Oklahoma State Fair. On October 14, 2007, the Centennial Parade in Oklahoma City was the largest parade in state history with helium-filled balloons, floats, marching bands, performance groups, and the greatest assemblage ever of Oklahoma celebrities. An Oklahoma float also appeared for the second year in a row in the Macy's Thanksgiving Parade in New York City.

Statehood Day, November 16, 2007, began with historical reenactments in the state's first capital, Guthrie, including the presidential proclamation of statehood; the inauguration of Charles Haskell, the first governor; the ceremonial wedding of the twin territories; and an inaugural parade. In dozens of other cities and towns, special programs and events marked the moment 100 years earlier when President Theodore Roosevelt signed the proclamation making Oklahoma the 46th state of the Union.

THE OKLAHOMA CENTENNIAL COMMISSION

The grand party to celebrate Oklahoma's centennial was planned and implemented by the Oklahoma Capitol Complex and Centennial Commemoration Commission, a state agency. A forty-two-member board made up of legislators, state agency directors, and mayors guided the shaping of the commemoration.

Lou Kerr was commission president and Lee Allan Smith was chairman of projects and events. J. Blake Wade, former director of the Oklahoma Historical Society, was director of the Centennial Commission.

A CENTENNIAL SONG AND POEM

As part of the Centennial celebration, Oklahoma songwriter Jimmy Webb and singer Vince Gill collaborated to write a special song, "Oklahoma Rising," and Oklahoma native M. Scott Momaday penned a special poem.

OKLAHOMA RISING

By Jimmy Webb and Vince Gill

Vince Gill

Jimmy Web

Chorus
We're Oklahoma Risin,' brighter than a star
Stand up and sing about her, let the world know
who we are

Verse 1
From a rugged territory to the Oklahoma Run
We've made our dreams come true,
just look at what we've done
We're the Heartland of America,
our heart is in the race
We've sailed our prairie schooners
right into outer space
We are young and we are strong,
we are comin' with a roar
Sooner than later we'll be knockin' on your door
Say hello to the future,
gonna shake the future's hand
and build a better world
upon this sacred land

Chorus 2
We're Oklahoma Risin,' brighter than a star. Stand up and sing about her
let the world know who we are
We're the sons and the daughters, children of the West
We're Oklahoma Risin,' risin' up to be the best

Verse 2
Guts and grace and mercy, we have shown them in our turn
When the fields had turned to dust and the skies began to burn
When the storm shook our souls and the mighty buildings fell
Through fires and desperation our faith has served us well I choke back the
emotion, I'm an Okie and I'm proud
So when you call me Okie, man, you better say it loud
Now we look into the heavens at the eagles climbing free
It's the spirit of our people on the wing, can you see?

THE OKLAHOMA CENTENNIAL POEM

By M. Scott Momaday

The Land
The first people to enter upon it
Must have given it a name, wind-borne and elemental,
Like summer rain.
The name must have given spirit to the land,
For so it is with names.
Before the first people there must have been
The profound isolation of night and day,
The blazing shield of the sun,
The darkness winnowed from the stars—
The holy havoc of myth and origin,
True and prophetic and inexorable,
Like summer rain.
What was to become of the land?
What was the land to become?
What was there in the land to define
The falling of the rain and the turning of the seasons,
The far and forever silence of the universe?
A voice, a name,
Words echoing the whir of wings
Swelled among the clouds
And sounded on the red earth in the wake of creation,
A voice. A name.
Oklahoma.

Author's Personal Journey

"You gain strength, courage and confidence by every experience in which you really stop to look fear in the face. You must do the things you cannot do."

—Eleanor Roosevelt

I'm one of the lucky ones! I consider myself one of God's miracles! In November 1999, I was diagnosed with breast cancer. The lump, which I had detected four years prior to my diagnosis and chose to ignore, measured approximately three to four centimeters. Doctors told me I had between stage three and stage four cancer, four being the most detrimental. Suddenly your world stops and fear takes hold when you hear the big "C" word. You close your eyes for a moment and you somehow realize your life is changed forever, but at this point you cannot imagine how much. I remember telling God that I didn't have time for the inconvenience of cancer. I was just too busy. Can you imagine having the audacity to tell that to God? I even tried to convince my surgeon by taking my personal calendar and saying, "You know it will be tough to schedule surgery at this time." My surgeon immediately took the calendar away, laid it on her desk, and told me, *"You have no time to wait!"*

You reach a point where you go beyond tears; it was time to put fear and denial aside. Yes, you can always expect the unexpected, but it's how you handle the unexpected that tells your character. Life's journey is not always fair, but you learn to accept the cards you've been given and you do what you have to do. Simply, that means you stop to look fear in the face and do the things you cannot do. It helped to remind myself of that old philosophical comparison "Probability vs. Outcome." There is a plan for everything. I kept telling myself don't be afraid, there is a plan in God's world. Destiny: you must abide by what is written; it's His time and His destiny. A friend of mine kept reminding me we are all God's children and are carried in the palm of His hand through the best and the worst of times.

My partial mastectomy and removal of seventeen lymph nodes was performed on December 16, 1999, by Dr. Beverly Talbert at Mercy Hospital in Oklahoma City, recommended by my cousin, Dr. Jon Reese. I was scheduled to receive chemotherapy for six months and radiation for three months; however, at that point I did not realize the worst was yet to come.

The incisions from my surgery were not healing, and I was experiencing a great deal of pain. We learned I had staphylococcus, also known as a staph infection, which I contracted during surgery. Dr. Scott Stewart was paramount in keeping me alive during my battle with staph.

Also, my doctor discovered through blood test that I was diabetic, which meant I could not receive antibiotics intravenously, because of the risk of liver damage. Antibiotics through an IV work more quickly. Instead, I was placed on oral antibiotics and my incisions were re-opened to clean out the infection. That's not all. Through several MRIs doctors discovered I needed gall bladder surgery. They found gall bladder stones the size of bird's eggs, but we would have to deal with that diagnosis later. Pain began to be my constant companion. Staph infection is not like most infections, with staph you have and feel intense physical pain.

I began to learn just how delicate the balance of life really is. I began to understand what God was trying to tell me, that what was once important in my life no longer mattered. Once again I surrendered everything to God because my destination, whether I lived or died, was not in my hands. You reach a defining moment. Little did I realize the medical and spiritual journey I was about to travel. And yes, I kept telling myself God has a plan for all of us. There is a reason for everything in life. We are all instruments of God. Also, I kept remembering the words of another favorite poet of mine, Robert Browning, his poem "Rabbi Ben Ezra:" "Grow Old Along With Me! /The best is yet to be, / The last of life, for which the first was made: / Our times are in His hand / who saith "A whole I planned. / Youth shows but half: trust God: see all nor be afraid!" This poem gave me faith, but also made me think in terms of planning the rest of my life, if God chose for me to live. As long as you have a plan and a positive mental attitude, you're never defeated.

At this point, I was no longer concerned about cancer; my focus now was to stay alive with the staph infection. I did not fear death, but I still had too many things to see, do, and accomplish on this earthly plain. Don't get me wrong, I truly believe the hairs on our heads are numbered, but we can do something about the quality of our life, while those hairs are being counted. (Do what your doctor advises—do things that are good for your body, learn to enjoy the moment.)

The doctors had home health care professionals in twice a day to clean my open wounds and pack them. It was a lot like stuffing and basting a turkey, as I laugh to myself, but oh so painful! Probably the most painful physical experience in my life.

I could not begin chemotherapy or radiation until the staph infection was healed and the window of opportunity for me to have these treatments was nearly over. I was told when diagnosed with stage three and stage four cancer, it's imperative you have treatment for survival.

It took, nine months for my body to heal from the infection, and during those nine months my incisions had to be re-opened three times, each time creating a larger open wound to heal. The incision under my arm pit was about 2½ inches deep and 3½ inches wide. The breast incision was 3½ inches across and 1½ inches in depth. There were days the nurses had to keep my attitude balanced. I certainly knew getting well depended on my attitude. The longer I live, the more I realize the impact of attitude on one's life. Quoting Charles Swindoll, "Attitude to me, is more important than facts. It is more important than the past, than education, than money, than circumstances, than failures, than successes, than what other people think or say or do. It is more important than appearance, giftedness or skill. It will make or break a company—church—home."

During those days of healing there was another poem I read many times written by William Earnest Henley, "The Invictus," which means "unconquerable" in Latin. The last couple of lines I have on a plaque, "I am the master of my fate; I am the captain of my soul." Dr. Robert Schuller writes in his book, *If It's Going To Be, It's Up To Me,* "Whatever people make of themselves is really up to them. God can help, but He can't do it for us. Most of the time true wealth is a matter of spirit. The remarkable thing is we have a choice every day regarding the attitude we will embrace for that day. We cannot change our past . . . we cannot change the fact that people will act in a certain way. We cannot change the inevitable. The only thing we can do is play on the one string we have, and that is our attitude." These became the words I lived by every day along with the famous poem "If" by Rudyard Kipling; this poem is all about balance, one of my most favorite words in the vocabulary. *"If* you can dream—and not make dreams your master; / If you can think— and not make thoughts your aim, / If you can meet with Triumph and Disaster, / And treat those two imposters just the same." That's all about balance. "If you can talk with crowds and keep your virtue, / Or walk with kings—nor lose the common touch." Once again balance, holding on to your equanimity.

What sustained me was my faith in knowing there was a reason for all of this and God knew why I was going through this growth. You realize life is a journey, not necessarily a destination. I learned to realize my only control factor was prayer and a positive outlook. Although your life can be laced with tragedy or unusual circumstances, hopefully in time, from these circumstances you gain a greater spiritual strength, purpose, meaning, and eventually something positive comes from these experiences.

The deadline came and went for chemotherapy and radiation treatments. To this day, I have had neither. My checkups show that I remain cancer free and the year is 2007! I'm a *seven year survivor!* I have defied all odds in medical/cancer research studies. Usually I want to absorb all the knowledge I can, but there came a time and point I closed all cancer books and especially books quoting statistics on survival rates.

I'm very fortunate I had many people who traveled this journey with me through breast cancer; they gave me strength, prayers, food, and love. I call them my "earth angels" and of course Abercrombie, my golden retriever, and Nicholas, my Persian cat. I know one thing: we must treasure what we have, while we have it. Thank God in your prayers tonight for those you love.

It's been a humbling experience in my life, and it has not left me the same person. It devastated my soul but redefined my priorities. You realize how very precious life is. I've learned to understand, as many people have, life is a series of new beginnings. Life can be so unkind in so many ways. Fear can dictate your whole existence, even your choices. Faith in God is the only thing that can give us the moments until love gives us the way. At times in your life you have to slow down a little, try and put things into focus, figure out what you need. Not all the things I am today are necessarily good, I try. Not all the changes I have made are improvements, but I deal with the world out of a core of authenticity. I no longer need approval to the point of compromising the basic me. I can risk operating out of my own integrity and depth after these last seven years, which I believe is a plus for me. I don't want to give a moment away. I want to experience it all! I've realized we are here for something bigger than ourselves! And another favorite quote of mine, *"Endings are just beginnings backwards."*

My personal journey is leading up to a point, the point being—why did I want to do this book? *It's all about giving back!* I wanted to give back to a state that has given me so much. I believe this is a unique opportunity to combine the love of Oklahoma through the presentation of history, culture, and food, while capturing the essence of Oklahomans. Why give to charity? After surviving cancer among other personal tragedies, I have a sense of responsibility to give back. Being able to contribute financially to the research and cure of two diseases that touch so many lives is most rewarding. I rely on the biblical phrase, "To those to whom much is given, from them much is expected." My mother always taught me you earn your way through life to earn your place in heaven. And you do the best you can, for as many people as you can, for as long as you can. I believe these thoughts. I have a duty to God, myself, and to the lives taken by cancer and muscular dystrophy. Conveying the message, their lives mattered, their lives had value. And equally important what their deaths were about. Living out the legacy of their lives.

To paraphrase the poet Robert Browning, "One's reach should exceed one's grasp or what's life for?" That measure of reaching out by each of us without fear or awe of all the unknowns that surround us is the difference between growing or vegetating emotionally, intellectually, spiritually and in the blessings that good work done and good friends made can bring to us. If it brings recognition, that's one of life's fringe benefits. But with or without recognition, it is the seed from which any personal achievement must spring. Striving to become a person of value.

Ronnye Perry Sharp

Index

Catfish 24

Chalupas 293

Cheese

    Baked Cheese Grits 248

    Cheese Olives 122

    Cheese Spread with Strawberry Preserves 115

    Cheese Wafers 122

    Holiday Cheese Ball 134

Cheesecake

    Amaretto Cheesecake 451

    Choconut-Almond Cheesecake 450

Cherry

    Cherry Mold with Lemon Cream 229

    Heavenly Cherries 482

Chicken

    Amaretto Chicken Salad 235

    Anna's Brazilian Chicken Stroganoff 281

    Apricot-Glazed Chicken 270

    Baked Chicken with Apples 270

    Cheddar Chicken Lasagna 284

    Chicken and Andouille Gumbo 188

    Chicke n Huntington 284

    Chicken Salad 233

    Chicken Sophia 269

    Chicken Tetrazini 280

    Chicken with Peach Salsa 274

    Chicken with Sour Cream 280

    Firehouse Roasted Mesquite Chicken 278

    Fried Pecan Crusted Chicken with Plum Sauce 285

    Fruity Chicken Salad 238

    Granny's Chicken Fried Steak 548

    Honey Hot Chicken Wings 128

    Jan Ross Chicken Cacciatore 277

    Lizzie's Healthy Chicken 342

    Margarita Chicken 273

    Parmesan Crusted Chicken 275

    Ritzy Chicken 276

    Smoked Chicken and Shrimp with Pasta Alfredo 286

    Southwest Chicken Quesadillas 273

    Walt's Champagne Chicken Salad 220

Pie

Almost Sugar-Free Millionaire Pie 449

Apricot Coconut Cream Pie 486

Banana Pie 466

Banana Cream Cheese Pie 463

Caviar Pie Romanoff 132

Chess Pie 462

Chocolate Pie 557

Cream Cheese Pie 369

Eggnog Banana Cream Pie 176

French Strawberry Pie 458

Fresh Rhubarb Pie 462

Fresh Strawberry Pie 569

Hershey Pie 457

Lemon Meringue Pie 459

Lemon Party Pie 458

Lou's Sugar-Free Banana Cream Pie 426

Lou's Sugar-Free Coconut Pie 425

Mama's Oatmeal Pie 476

Millionaire Pie 449

Nonna's Butterscotch Pie 455

Nonna's Coconut Cream Pie 553

Oklahoma's Best Pecan Pie 570

Out of this World Pie 319

Red Rock Canyon's Famous Key Lime Pie 452

Strawberry Pie 463

Sugar-free Apple Pie 108

Sugar-Free Chocolate Cream Pie with Almonds 426

Polenta with Wild Mushroom Sauce 516

Pork

Grilled Oriental Pork Tenderloin 294

Posole (Pork Stew) 195

Pork Chops

Cinnamon Pork Chops 298

Mongolian Pork Chops 296

Piledriver Pork Chops 340

Pork Chops and Rice 295

Pork Chops in Gravy 295

Quick Baked Pork Chops 297